EU DIPLOMACY AND
THE ISRAELI–ARAB
CONFLICT, 1967–2019

EU DIPLOMACY AND THE ISRAELI–ARAB CONFLICT, 1967–2019

Anders Persson

EDINBURGH
University Press

Edinburgh University Press is one of the leading university presses in the UK. We publish academic books and journals in our selected subject areas across the humanities and social sciences, combining cutting-edge scholarship with high editorial and production values to produce academic works of lasting importance. For more information visit our website: edinburghuniversitypress.com

First published in hardback by Edinburgh University Press 2020

Edinburgh University Press Ltd
The Tun – Holyrood Road
12(2f) Jackson's Entry
Edinburgh EH8 8PJ

Typeset in 11/15 Adobe Garamond by
Servis Filmsetting Ltd, Stockport, Cheshire

A CIP record for this book is available from the British Library

ISBN 978 1 4744 7472 6 (hardback)
ISBN 978 1 4744 7473 3 (paperback)
ISBN 978 1 4744 7475 7 (webready PDF)
ISBN 978 1 4744 7474 0 (epub)

CONTENTS

TABLES

FOREWORD

The Israeli–Palestinian conflict lies at the heart of European foreign policy. Back in 1980, European Community Member States jointly signed the Venice Declaration, delineating their shared position on the Israeli–Palestinian conflict. Doing so at that time was remarkable in at least two respects. First, because back then – thirteen years before the establishment of the Common Foreign and Security Policy – there was no EU foreign policy worthy of the name. Loosely connected by foreign policy information-sharing and a coordination system known as the European Political Cooperation, Member States achieved in 1980 what they often struggle to accomplish today: a commonly agreed and incisive position that swims against the international and local tide of conflict dynamics. Europeans recognized both Israel's right to live in peace and security, and the Palestinians' right to self-determination. They did so at a time in which the international community was a long way away from recognizing collective Palestinian rights, less still the right to self-determination and thus possibly to statehood. In retrospect, this European position was as far-sighted as it was revolutionary.

Over the decades and particularly after the Oslo accords, whereas mediation remained firmly in the hands of the United States, the European Union maintained its standard-setting primacy in determining the accepted contours of Israeli–Palestinian peace. Through its diplomatic initiatives and above all its financial support for the then nascent Palestinian Authority, Europeans sought to shape both in rhetoric and in practice the parameters of what became known as the two-state solution to the conflict. Notwithstanding differences and at times divisions between Member States, the Union as a whole should be given credit for its ability to formulate, stick to and advocate its preferred solution to the conflict over the years. With the international system being in a state of profound structural transformation and disruption, the EU's position on the Israeli–Palestinian conflict must be hailed for its predictability and responsibility.

Alas, this is of little solace. Europeans notwithstanding, the Israeli–Palestinian conflict has been rapidly degenerating, particularly since the turn of the century. Eighteen years have passed since there have been meaningful negotiations between the parties with a reasonable chance of success. There is no Middle East Peace Process anymore. There is, occasionally, a process in the Middle East, but certainly not one that has even the slimmest chance of yielding a sustainable peace. In fact, quite the opposite is true. Whereas one may speculate that the 'process' has at least prevented an outbreak of sustained mass violence, it is certainly true that the same process has entrenched the conditions of structural violence on the ground. The process, to which the EU has greatly contributed, has alleviated the costs and has contributed precious time for the deepening of the Israeli occupation of Palestinian territory, as such reducing over the time the chances for a genuine two-state solution on the ground. In other words, as the years have gone by, the EU's steadfast position towards the conflict has gradually, almost imperceptibly, tilted, from being a ground-breaking move towards peace, into becoming part of the conflict's own dynamic, endurance and resilience.

The EU thus finds itself today in a Catch-22. On the one hand, if it adjusts its policy – for instance by discarding the two-state solution and embracing a one-state alternative – it would implicitly accept the degenerative local, regional and international dynamics which have conspired to erode the ground (literally) of a two-state solution. If the EU sticks to its two-state hymn sheet and the policies based thereon, it would continue to play into the very same conflict dynamics that have led to the deterioration of the situation.

Travelling between this Scylla and Charybdis is an intellectually, politically and practically complex task. It entails living up to principle, while pragmatically keeping eyes wide open to reality. It means removing rose-tinted lenses when analysing the conflict, but remaining steadfast in the promotion of those basic rights whose protection is a *sine qua non* for any form of sustainable peace. Treading this path is certainly not easy for the EU, but neither is it impossible. The EU's own history towards the conflict is testament to the fact that Europeans can be far-sighted, brave and stubbornly principled when they want. In order to be so, understanding the evolution of EU policy towards the conflict as much as the EU's current predicament in the current regional and broader global context is crucial. Anders Persson's book provides a meticulously researched and superbly argued work to this effect. An enticing read for all those with an interest and a passion for the Middle East as much as for the European project.

Enjoy the read!

Rome, September 2019

Nathalie Tocci
Director of the Istituto Affari Internazionali, Honorary Professor at the University of Tübingen, and Special Adviser to EU HRVP Federica Mogherini, on behalf of whom she wrote the European Global Strategy and is now working on its implementation, notably in the field of security and defence.

ACKNOWLEDGEMENTS

Funding for the research behind this book has been provided by the Swedish Research Council (no. 2015-00295). The author would like to thank Professor Ian Manners for all his help and support with this book.

1

MORE IMPORTANT THAN OTHER CONFLICTS

The Member States of the European Community have particularly important political, historical, geographical, economic, religious, cultural and human links with the countries and peoples of the Middle East. They cannot therefore adopt a passive attitude towards a region which is so close to them nor remain indifferent to the grave problems besetting it. The repercussions of these problems affect the Twelve in many ways. (EC Foreign Ministers' declaration on the Middle East, *Bulletin of the EC* 2-1987: 90)

The past years have seen many commemorations in the Israeli–Arab conflict: 100 years since the Balfour Declaration (2017), seventy years since Israel was created (2018), fifty years since the 1967 war (2017), thirty years since the first intifada (2017), and twenty-five years since the Declaration of Principles (2018). In 2021, it will be fifty years since the EU's Foreign Ministers issued their first declaration on the Israeli–Arab conflict and also fifty years since it started to fund the United Nations Relief and Works Agency for Palestine Refugees in the Near East (UNRWA). If not before, this should be an opportune moment for European policy-makers to reflect on the past half-century's involvement of the European Community/European Union in the conflict – and the next fifty years. At present, there is little suggesting that the conflict is about to end in a negotiated agreement any time soon. On the contrary, it may even escalate if a two-state solution is out of reach for the Palestinians. Many Europeans, Israelis, Palestinians and others – from policy-makers and practitioners to students and engaged citizens – have a deep interest in the relations between the EU, including its Member States, and the Israeli–Arab conflict, but few have any knowledge about when, how and why the EC got involved in the conflict. This book aims to be the first historic overview of the EU's almost fifty-year involvement in the conflict, based exclusively on primary sources. It tries to identify and analyse all the big policy departures – when, how and why they happened.

Why has this Conflict been so Important for the EU?

Both the European Community (EC) and Israel emerged from the ashes of World War II. Both drew the same, yet very different conclusion from the war. It consisted of two words: never again. For Israel, it was never again victim; never again would the Jewish people suffer as they had done during World War II. For the EC it was never again victimizer and never again war in Europe. The former victim and victimizer both grew and prospered, yet they developed very different views on the use of force, the primacy of international law, the role of the United Nations (UN) system, and on many other issues of international relations. The EC became involved in Israel's conflicts with her neighbours after the June 1967 war and even more so after the October 1973 war with the subsequent oil crisis. Different paradigms or theories of international relations can account for different phases of the EC/EU's involvement in the Israeli–Arab conflict, but it is impossible for one paradigm or theory to accurately account for the EU's almost five-decade-long involvement in the conflict. There are certainly several aspects of political realism involved, such as security, interests, power rivalry and concerns over resources. The same is true with regards to liberalism: the UN system, international law, trade, democracy promotion, interdependence, regional cooperation and support for non-governmental organizations (NGOs) have all been important features of the EU's involvement in the conflict over the past decades. Constructivism and more critical perspectives contribute to the analysis with their focus on ideas, identity formation, agency, discourse analysis and normative power. This book departs from all these three perspectives of international relations: there is a real political base to the analysis, but many aspects of liberalism and constructivism are also important points of departure. Four broad arguments underlie the book's overarching thesis that the Israeli–Arab conflict has been more important for the EU than other conflicts. It has been more important because the conflict has been central to the formation of the EU's foreign policy, because the conflict has had a persistent unique place in the EU's foreign policy, because the EU's involvement in the conflict has been based on major strategic factors, and finally, because the EU has for a long time been part of the conflict.

The conflict has been central to the formation of the EU's foreign policy

The 1967 war presented what was widely seen in the European Parliament to be a golden opportunity for the EC to unite its foreign policy in the late 1960s and early 1970s. But as important was that many European politicians – from left to right with liberals in between – simultaneously saw an equally golden opportunity for the EC to contribute to help resolving the conflict. The EU's self-perceived 'special', 'moral', 'unique' and 'distinctive' roles have been one of the defining features of its involvement in the conflict. These roles were based on Europe's historical ties to the Middle East, its geographical proximity and past history of overcoming conflicts. What emerged from the two golden opportunities was a widely shared twin belief that the Community could help the conflict to reach peace and that the conflict could help the Community to reach unity. Thus, the conflict became a test case for the EC's emerging foreign policy during the 1970s, especially after the 1973 war. It was a test that the Community passed. The EC managed to speak with a common voice on the Israeli–Arab conflict and started progressively to develop its vision of a just peace in the conflict. Hundreds of declarations followed over the decades. Many of them were visionary and ahead of their time. Other actors involved in the conflict, most notably the United States, often followed later on and adopted policies that the Community had earlier outlined. This development early on pointed to an important normative role for the EU in the conflict. As the decades went by, the conflict continued to be central to the formation of the EU's foreign policy, especially its vision of peace through regional cooperation in its southern neighbourhood during the 1990s. But strategies like the Euro-Mediterranean partnership (EMP) had difficulties moving forward, in large part because the Israeli–Arab conflict remained unsolved.

The conflict has had a persistent unique place in the EU's foreign policy

The coding schedule in the back of this book clearly attests to the conflict's persistent unique role for the EU's foreign policy. The EC/EU's many hundred declarations, other statements and mentions related to the Israeli–Arab conflict are simply remarkable. Without having coded other conflicts, it is obvious through my quantitative and qualitative context analyses of the *Bulletin* that the Israeli–Arab conflict has received far more attention from the EC/EU than other conflicts. There simply is no other conflict which has occupied such a central place in the EC/EU's foreign policy over these past five decades; no other conflict comes even close. The Israeli–Arab conflict was often mentioned first in the *Bulletin*'s sections on the European Political Cooperation (EPC); it had a central place when the Community spoke at the UN; the same is true for the conflict's role in the Euro–Arab dialogue, and in the various presidencies (the rotating leadership of the Council) as well. Moreover, the conflict has also had a very central place in the works of the EU's three High Representatives: Javier Solana, Catherine Ashton and Federica Mogherini. In addition, the very close bilateral relations between the EC/EU and Israel, and later with the Palestinian Authority (PA), also contributed to generating many matches in the coding schedule.

The EU's involvement in the conflict has been based on major strategic factors

The Middle East is geographically much closer to Europe than to the US or Russia. The EC was also much more dependent on oil from the Middle East than both of the superpowers during the Cold War. The *Bulletin* gives different figures as to exactly how dependent the Member States were on Middle Eastern oil in the late 1960s and during the 1970s, but there can be no doubts that oil was a major strategic factor for the EC's original involvement in the conflict after the June 1967 war. It became an acute matter after the October 1973 war and the subsequent oil crisis, which had a shocking effect on the then nine Member States. The high oil prices led to massive transfers of wealth from the industrialized world to the oil producers in the Middle East, which in turn led to massive increases in trade, thereby creating another strategic objective. During the 1970s, exports from the EC to the Arab members of OPEC (the Organization of the Petroleum Exporting Countries) increased almost tenfold.

The security threat that the conflict posed to Europe – from instability in the region, to tensions between the superpowers, to terrorism – were constant factors in the EC/EU's declarations over the decades, but peaked during the 2000s after the 9/11 attacks and the invasion of Iraq. The EU's 2003 security strategy (ESS) outlined what had long been the EU's twin narrative regarding the Middle East: (1) that the Israeli–Arab conflict was the key to deal with other problems in the Middle East; and (2) that resolution of the Israeli–Arab conflict would lead to positive developments elsewhere in the Middle East. The fact that the EU's involvement in the conflict had a strong real political basis meant that the importance of the conflict for the EU could go up and down depending on the real political circumstances. This was obvious during the past decade, the 2010s, when major geopolitical events – such as the Arab Spring, the rise and fall of Islamic State, the signing and exit of the nuclear agreement with Iran, the refugee crisis – all contributed to make the Israeli–Arab conflict less of a burning priority for the EU, which was clearly visible in its global strategy from 2016.

The EU is part of the conflict

The EU's long involvement in the conflict, its close political and economic ties with Israel, its massive economic support to the Palestinians, and its peace-building missions on the ground in the conflict have all contributed to make the EU part of the conflict. During the 1990s, third party involvement in the conflict was widely seen as necessary and beneficial to the Oslo peace process, which was meant to be a temporary, interim period, before a final peace agreement was to be reached. But the longer this process has lasted, the more it has been questioned. The EU's support for the Palestinian Authority and the peace process is now more and more seen, even by mainstream analysts, as helping Israel to uphold its illegal occupation rather than helping the Palestinians to achieve statehood. Even if top EU officials routinely argue that the EU's support to the PA has saved it, and thereby the whole peace process, from collapsing during the most troublesome moments of the second intifada, it is unclear to what extent, if any, this really has helped the peace process – which has not really been a peace process during the 2010s. In the present era, there is a big risk that the EU will be an even bigger part of the conflict as the US scales back its support to the Palestinians, and the EU, including its Member States, steps up to help fill the holes left behind by the US.

Material and Methodology

This book has a different research design compared to other similar books on the EU's foreign policy and role in the conflict in that it uses an innovative methodology on a previously little-studied material. The material consists of all EC/EU declarations, other statements and mentions related to the Israeli–Arab conflict published in the *Bulletin of the European Communities* for the period between 1967 and 1993 and in the *Bulletin of the European Union* for the period between 1994 and 2009, after which the *Bulletin* ceased to exist. The last empirical chapter, which covers the period from 2009 to 2019 consists of material from Council Conclusions on the conflict, statements from the EU's High Representatives, reports from the European Commission, press interviews with EU officials, and other similar material. Typically, the *Bulletin* came out with 10–11 issues each year, with 1–2 double issues, each issue consisting of between 100 and 250 pages. The double issues were coded for the first month; for example, a January/February double issue was coded only for January and coded zero for February. Altogether, the material for the 1967–2009 period consists of around 70,000 pages of EU texts and around 2,500 different statements related to the Israeli–Arab conflict. For many years, the *Bulletin* existed only in libraries, which made quantitative content analysis an overwhelming task for a single researcher. But in 2003, the University of Pittsburgh's Archive of European Integration (AEI) began (and then stopped) uploading research materials on the topic of European integration and unification, among them many original EC/EU documents, including the *Bulletin of the European Communities* for the period 1967–93 and the *Bulletin of the European Union* for the period 1994–5. For the other issues of the *Bulletin* between 1996 and 2009, I turned to the online portal *EU bookshop*.[1] In each issue, five keywords were coded: 'Israel' (which includes

---

[1] For more information about the University of Pittsburgh's Archive of European Integration (AEI), visit <http://aei.pitt.edu/information.html>. For more information about the EU bookshop, visit <https://bookshop.europa.eu/en/home/>.

Israeli, Israelis), 'Palest' (which includes Palestine, Palestinian, Palestinians), 'Arab' (which was the term used before Palestinian became accepted EC/EU language and even after that sometimes), 'Occupied' (referring to the occupied territories, a phrase often used by the EC/EU before Palestinian became accepted EC/EU language). The final key word is 'Middle East' (which includes the Middle East Peace Process, the conflict in the Middle East and so on). It would certainly be possible to code more keywords; for example, Jewish, Muslim/Islamic, West Bank, Gaza and so on, but each keyword means many hours of extra work. There is also an elegancy in keeping things simple in academic research, which makes replications easier.

All mentions of 'Israel' and 'Palest' in the *Bulletin* have been included in the coding schedule, while all mentions of 'Arab', 'Occupied' and 'Middle East' have been included if they somehow were related to the Israeli–Arab conflict. A statement was coded as '1' no matter if it was five sentences or five pages long, no matter if it included one or several of the five keywords. The next such statement was coded as '2' and so on. Consequently, if the coding schedule has listed, for example, three matches in the *Bulletin* for a specific month it means that there were three different EC/EU declarations/ statements that month on the Israeli–Arab conflict corresponding to the keywords.

The method used can best be described as a form of quantitative and qualitative content analysis. Basic quantitative content analysis enables the researcher to discover the broad pattern in a large volume of source material, which is where the analysis starts. The method is very useful for finding the manifest meaning in a text, which, at the same time, means that it has a much harder time finding the latent meaning (Bryman 2016: 284). It can count the occurrence of the keywords, but the method cannot, at least not without extra coding, say whether one occurrence of a keyword is more important or less important than another. In order to find the more latent meaning of a text, the researcher must go from quantitative to qualitative content analysis. David Altheide and Christopher Schneider (2013: 26) have described qualitative context analysis as being

> systematic and analytic but not rigid. Categories and variables initially guide the study, but others are allowed and expected to emerge during the study,

including an orientation to constant discovery and constant comparison of relevant situations, settings, styles, images, meanings, and nuances.

After having coded the material, I went back into each coded statement to see if there is a latent meaning in it. It could, for example, be a new policy departure or the introduction of new terminology, which are not captured by a quantitative content analysis. Through a qualitative content analysis, it is further possible to see how much space and what kind of space the EC/EU has devoted to declarations on this conflict. For example, it is possible through this method to see how central the conflict was when the EC spoke at the UN, and so on.

Locating the Study in Existing Research

A quite solid body of research exists on the relations between the EU and the Israeli–Arab conflict. Israeli scholars Sharon Pardo and Guy Harpaz, with their respective colleagues, have for over a decade led the research on the EU's bilateral relations with Israel, often focusing on the EU's normative power vis-à-vis Israel (see, for example, Pardo and Peters 2010, 2012; Pardo 2015; Gordon and Pardo 2015a, 2015b; Harpaz 2007; Harpaz and Shamis 2010). In addition, Stefan Ahlswede's (2009) *Israel's European policy after the Cold War* is also a major contribution to the research on EU–Israel relations. There is considerably less research done on the EU's wider bilateral relations with the Palestinians. Major studies have been done by Rouba al-Fattal (2010) and Amjad Fouad Abu El Ezz Banishamsa (2012). Adeeb Ziadeh (2017) has done a major study on the EU's policies vis-à-vis Hamas. Simona Santoro and Rami Nasrallah (2007) and Patrick Müller and Yazid Zahda (2017) have done smaller studies on Palestinian perceptions of the EU. A number of European scholars have also written on EU–Palestinian relations, often focusing on the EU's assistance to the PA, democracy promotion, EU–Hamas relations, and state-building (see, for example, Stetter 2003; Pace 2010; Huber 2011; Bouris 2014; Persson 2015; Charrett 2018).

A number of good overview studies exist on the EU's role in the conflict, each focusing on different aspects of the conflict: Costanza Musu (2010) has analysed why the EU has failed to develop an autonomous and effective policy towards the conflict; Rory Miller (2011) has analysed the historical disarray in Europe's policies vis-à-vis Israel and the Palestinians; Patrick Müller (2012) has analysed the 'big-three' Member States' roles in the EU's policies vis-à-vis the conflict; Taylan Özgur Kaya (2013) has analysed the EU's foreign and security policies vis-à-vis the conflict after 9/11; Amr Nasr El-Din (2016) has focused on the EU's security missions in the conflict and, finally, Raffaella Del Sarto (editor, 2015) has used a 'borderlands approach' in her analysis of the EU's role in the conflict. This book is different from all the previous in that it is the first systematic study of the *Bulletin*'s reporting on the conflict. As such, it is a study based exclusively on primary sources. It also focuses exclusively on the EC/EU's policies, whereas several of the previous studies were more European in nature and focused on the deliberations before EU policy was made and the reactions afterwards. Finally, the book covers a longer time span than the previous books.

Much of the foundations of this body of research were laid by Ilan Greilsammer and Joseph Weiler in successive works after the first international conference on the relations between the EC and Israel took place at Bar-Ilan University in 1984. Greilsammer and Weiler's (1984, 1987, 1988) work offers in many ways a broader analysis than this book of the EC's policy vis-à-vis the conflict and bilaterally vis-à-vis Israel between the early 1970s to the mid-1980s. Two of this book's key arguments – that the conflict has been central to the formation of the EU's foreign policy and that the conflict has had a unique place in the EU's foreign policy – are to a large extent based on their work. As Alain Dieckhoff concluded in Greilsammer and Weiler's edited volume,

> It is above all through the Arab-Israeli conflict that the EEC has become a political unit which articulates a common European interest and maintains its own political voice. It is through this conflict that the European States have perfected the EPC framework and that they have introduced Europe on the international scene as an actor which has an effective capacity to behave continuously and deliberately. Nevertheless, even if the European Community is now an actor, she remains an imperfect one . . . She remains 'some sort of half-developed international actor'. (Dieckhoff 1988: 281)

However, while their work overall is very solid, factors such as oil, settlements, and the EU's normative power are not given prominence in their analysis. To a certain degree, this is because an issue like settlements was a smaller issue during their time than it is today. The same can be argued about the EU's normative power, but it has a prominent place in Rory Miller's (2011) *Inglorious Disarray: Europe, Israel and the Palestinians since 1967*. Miller has many quotes in his book on how important Israeli and Palestinian leaders regarded the EU's normative power. The most illustrative is perhaps a 1980 quote from Israel's Prime Minister Menachem Begin, who believed that there was 'nothing graver' than Europe's attempt to legitimize the Palestine Liberation Organization (PLO) (quoted in Miller 2011: 84–5). In contrast to Miller, who focused on the disarray in the EC/EU vis-à-vis the Israeli–Arab conflict, this book is based on the EU's declarations and other statements on the conflict, which means much less disarray as compared to books like Miller's focusing on the deliberations before the EU issues declarations and the reactions afterwards.

The EC's dependence on energy supplies from the Middle East, both when it came to stabilizing the price of oil and to ensuring its supply, and how oil acted as a catalyser for the EC's involvement in the conflict, have been analysed by, among others, Panayiotis Ifestos (1987), Alain Dieckhoff (1988), Soren Dosenrode and Anders Stubkjaer (2002), and Miller (2011). According to Ifestos, the 1973 war and the subsequent oil embargo

> made Europeans brutally aware of their vulnerability in both economic and political terms; it changed the pattern of relationships with both Israel and the Arab world, and brought about a dramatic shift towards more pro-Arab attitudes; it revealed the extent of European external disunity and generated calls for more integration as a result of this experience; it had economic effects not imaginable before the crisis; and last but not least, it brought to the surface the uneasy nature of Euro-American relations. (Ifestos 1987: 421)

The oil crisis led to a massive increase in trade between the EC and the Arab world. In 1972, before the crisis, EC exports to the Arab members of OPEC were valued at $2.97 billion. In 1979, they were valued at $27.7 billion, an almost tenfold increase. Imports also rose dramatically, from $13.2 billion in 1972 to $40.5 billion in 1975 to $65.5 billion in 1979 (Garfinkle 1983: 7–8). Oil, together with security and trade, formed the real political basis of the EC's involvement in the conflict, which is the third key argument of this book, that the EU's involvement in the conflict has been based on major strategic factors.

After Greilsammer and Weiler's pioneering work in the 1980s, another generation of scholars followed in the 1990s and 2000s. Their focus was mainly threefolded: the EU's role in the peace process, including in building up Palestinian institutions; the EU's regional cooperation with Israel and the Palestinian Authority as case studies; and other types of bilateral relations between the EU and the two sides (see, for example, Hollis 1997; Behrendt and Hanelt 2000; Ginsberg 2001). Since this was overall an optimistic time, the research was overall more positive than in the decades before and after, even if it was clear that the EU was nowhere near either enforcing its declarations or of being a mediator in parity with the US in the peace process. That being said, the EU was very active in the peace process. Ahlswede (2009: 248) has argued that Israel's central tactic to cope with the EU's unwelcome quest for political relevance during the peace process has been to provide the EU with only token roles in order to keep the Europeans more predictable and less dissatisfied.

During the 2000s, the research on the role of the EU in the conflict became much more critical. Many questions were raised about the effectiveness, or lack thereof, of the EU's assistance to the peace process (see, for example, Le More 2005, 2008; Asseburg 2003; Brynen 2008). With neither peace nor a Palestinian state in sight, the gap between the EU's rhetoric and the reality on the ground also grew much larger than it had been in the past decade (Tocci 2005, 2009; see also Aoun 2003). This gap is clearly visible in this book as well, in particular concerning the EU's repeatedly stated willingness to use all of its power to reach a solution in the conflict and the reality of never doing so. By the end of the 2000s and the beginning of the 2010s, much of the research was focused on the EU's role in Palestinian state-building (see, for example, Bouris 2014; Persson 2015). If not before, it was by now clear that the EU was part of the conflict, which is also the fourth key argument of this book. A very clear example of how the EU was part of the conflict was the reports around the time by leading human rights organizations of European complicity in both Israeli and Palestinian human rights abuses (see, for example, Amnesty International 2009; Human Rights Watch 2012).

The difficulty of achieving a two-state solution to the conflict in the latter half of the 2010s shifted much of the academic attention away from EU state-building in the Palestinian territories to instead focusing more and more on the EU's normative power, differentiation, and other legal instruments for the EU vis-à-vis the Israeli–Arab conflict (see, for example, Pace 2007; Gordon and Pardo 2015a, 2015b; Bicchi and Voltolini 2017; Persson 2017a, 2018; Lovatt and Toaldo 2015; Lovatt 2016; Müller and Slominski 2017; Nikolov 2017; Azarova 2017; Beck 2017; Isleyen 2018). These measures have had some success so far, but have changed very little on the ground. Critics like Gordon and Pardo (2015b: 417) have, for example, argued that the EU's 2013 guidelines against the Israeli settlements allowed 'Israel to continue the occupation as if business was usual'. Others, like International Crisis Group's senior analyst Nathan Thrall (2017: 72–3), have gone even further, arguing that differentiation measures that only focus on settlements, and not the Israeli state behind them, are a distraction and a substitute for real pressure that actually prolong the occupation by assuring that only the settlements and not the government that created them will suffer consequences for their repeated violations of international law. Even if no EU official yet officially acknowledges it, the differentiation strategy could actually be a strategy for dealing with Israel in a post-two-state solution reality. If the occupation continues and no Palestinian state materializes over the foreseeable future, the differentiation strategy will actually make it possible for the EU to deal with the internationally recognized Israel within the 1967 borders in such eventualities, even if this was not the original purpose behind the strategy.

The Book's Outline

This book is organized into seven chapters. Chapter 2, the following chapter, is about how the EC got involved in the Israeli–Arab conflict after the 1967 war and even more so after the next war in 1973. The chapter outlines the EC's diplomacy vis-à-vis the conflict during the 1970s, ending with the 1979 Israeli–Egypt peace treaty. Chapter 3 opens with the 1980 Venice Declaration, which is the most important EC/EU declaration on the Israeli–Arab conflict. The chapter analyses the EC's diplomacy vis-à-vis the 1982 Lebanon war and the first intifada. A big part of the chapter is the EC's forward-thinking on the long diplomatic road that eventually led to the Oslo peace process, which is analysed in Chapter 4. The focus of Chapter 4 is the EC/EU's vision of peace through regional cooperation. It also analyses the ups and downs of the peace process during the 1990s. The following chapter, 5, opens with the outbreak of the second intifada and continues with the impact of the 9/11 attacks on the EU's role in the conflict during the 2000s, ending with the first Gaza war of 2008–9. Chapter 6 covers the period 2009–19 and focuses on the process leading up to the two Palestinian bids for statehood at the UN, the EU's differentiation strategy, and resilience in the wake of Donald Trump's diplomacy vis-à-vis the Israeli–Arab conflict. Finally, Chapter 7 presents the conclusions of the book and their ramifications.

2

1967–79:

A 'MARVELLOUS OPPORTUNITY' OPENS UP FOR THE EC'S EMERGING FOREIGN POLICY

Europe is too small and disunited and therefore weak. It has no hand in shaping the world of today and tomorrow; it is in danger of slipping into a state of dependence and technical and economic underdevelopment. If Europe wants to regain the lead it must show the world a new image, demonstrate fresh vitality, make use of her moral, intellectual and material resources and really become Europe. (*Bulletin of the EEC* 8-1967: 68)

On 22 June 1967, less than two weeks after the June 1967 war had ended, the European Parliament (EP) held a debate on what was called 'the situation in the Middle East'. The rapporteur, Fernand Dehousse, opened the debate by particularly deploring the 'lack of a politically united Europe at this juncture', which 'was a marvellous opportunity for the Six to work out the first elements of a common foreign policy', according to Dehousse (*Bulletin of the EEC* 8-1967: 82). Members of the Parliament from all party groups unanimously supported Israel, with René Pleven, the representative of the Liberal and Allied Group stating:

The Europe of the Six was alone in its moral right to preach reconciliation: it had known wars, untold suffering, massacres, and humiliations more appalling than anything the presence of Israeli soldiers in El Kantara [an Egyptian city on the western side of the Suez Canal] could represent. Yet the peoples of Europe had made their peace with one another and were now an example to the world. (*Bulletin of the EEC* 8-1967: 83)

The representative of the Christian Democrat Group, Henri Moreau de Melen, stated that it would be more profitable to discuss the consequences of the war than its cause, and that it was of no great consequence who had fired the first shot. He went on to deplore the fact that Europe had not yet made sufficient progress to be able to present a concerted policy (*Bulletin of the EEC* 8-1967: 82). The representative of the Socialist Group, Ludwig Metzger, stated that the Middle East crisis did not permit neutrality, and that Israel, whose survival was at stake according to the representative, must be supported (*Bulletin of the EEC* 8-1967: 82). Echoing the words of the representative of the Christian Democrat Group, Metzger stated:

> Israel was threatened with destruction; faced with a threat of this kind, the question of who was the aggressor was no longer important. The quantity of arms captured in the Sinai desert showed that the threat of annihilation made against Israel was not an empty one and that Israel had been justified in its attitude. But the State of Israel would not be able to exist for ever if Europe did not help. Israel had applied for associate membership of the EEC. As early as 1965 the Parliament had adopted a resolution stressing the need for an association agreement between Israel and the EEC. Association should be agreed as soon as possible. (*Bulletin of the EEC* 8-1967: 83)

Walter Hallstein, President of the EEC Commission, summed up the debate by stating that a new European policy must be worked out without delay: it was unthinkable he said that European power should not assert itself in the Middle East (*Bulletin of the EEC* 8-1967: 81). Hans Furler, speaking on behalf of the Christian Democrat Group, stated that the impotence of Europe to deal with the June 1967 crisis should give fresh impetus to the unification of the continent (*Bulletin of the EEC* 8-1967: 80).

In the resolution adopted by the European Parliament, there was not one hint of criticism of Israel's acquisition of territory and no demand for Israeli withdrawal. Instead, the declaration expressed grave concern at the situation 'where the existence of a State [Israel] is being threatened' (*Bulletin of the EEC* 8-1967: 96). The EP resolution also regarded the 1967 war as being 'of immediate import to the security and development of Europe' and 'that world peace is being seriously threatened by the absence of a peace treaty between Israel and the Arab States' (*Bulletin of the EEC* 8-1967: 96). The resolution also noted that the 'countries of Europe are not individually in a satisfactory position to defend the interests of their continent' (*Bulletin of the EEC* 8-1967: 96). The resolution, moreover, called for a comprehensive peace based on five points:

- recognition of the State of Israel;
- demarcation and safeguarding of the frontiers of all the countries concerned;
- free access to the holy places for persons of all religious denominations;
- the guarantee of freedom of navigation in the Gulf of Aqaba and through the Suez Canal;
- the question of refugees. (*Bulletin of the EEC* 8-1967: 96)

The *Bulletin* also reported in this issue that the Heads of State or government had decided to strengthen the political links between the Six, which was to be welcomed, according to the *Bulletin*, because 'the Middle East crisis had proved once again that Member States acting alone cannot achieve much' (*Bulletin of the EEC* 8-1967: 79).

In the following two years, there was not much discussion about the conflict in the *Bulletin*. When the Middle East was discussed, the focus was instead on reaching a new trade agreement with Israel, but the *Bulletin* reported in late 1969 that the President of the Commission, Jean Rey, had noted that while the time was not yet ripe for the establishment of new institutions, Europe should undertake a number of practical projects that would, little by little, yield results in the future. Focusing on the Middle East was most important, as it should not simply be left to the USSR or the United States to find solutions in this area, according to Rey (*Bulletin of the EC* 12-1969: 12). The year after, in 1970, Rey said that 'Europe had an obvious duty to help the search for a solution to the Middle East conflict.' It was an unacceptable paradox in his view that the common market was unable to intervene to damp down an armed conflict taking place on its own doorstep (*Bulletin of the EC* 7-1970: 119). The new trade agreement with

Israel, referred to as a preferential commercial agreement, 'the culmination of a fairly long procedure' (*Bulletin of the EC* 8-1970: 54), was concluded in mid-1970. One of the main points of discussion had been tariffs on Israeli citruses. Mid-1970 was also the first time when the conflict was referred to as the 'Israel–Arab conflict' in the *Bulletin* (*Bulletin of the EC* 6-1970: 88).

The First Steps Towards a United Position

In November 1970, the Foreign Ministers of the then six Member States of the EC met in Munich for what was called the 'Foreign Ministers Conference on Political Union'. This was within the framework of the newly established European Political Cooperation (EPC). The *Bulletin* reported that

> the chairman of the conference indicated that the most detailed exchanges of views had been on the Middle East situation. On some points difference of opinion had probably been narrowed, and on these a common attitude of the Six was not an impossibility. (*Bulletin of the EC* 1-1971: 15)

In May 1971, the second Foreign Ministers' conference on political cooperation was held for the purpose of consultation on various problems of common interest, of which the situation in the Middle East was one (*Bulletin of the EC* 6-1971: 31). The communiqué that was issued after the meeting is the first statement by the EC's Foreign Ministers on the conflict. Its main points were:

- It was of great importance to Europe that a just peace should be established in the Middle East.
- The declaration expressed approval of United Nations Security Council (UNSC) resolution 242, which constituted the basis of a settlement, and stressed the need to put it into effect in all its parts.
- The six governments declared their willingness, as far as lies in their power, to contribute, at the appropriate time, to the social and economic stabilization of the Middle East. (*Bulletin of the EC* 6-1971: 31)

It is important to note that the term 'Palestinian' was not used in the declaration, which was also the case with the UNSC resolution 242, issued after the 1967 war. The *Bulletin* reported after the communiqué was issued that it appeared that a fairly wide agreement was reached on the Middle East situation among the Six (*Bulletin of the EC* 6-1971: 33). But there has been much academic debate on how united the six members actually were. In a later issue in 1971, the *Bulletin* referred to an interview that Walter Scheel, the West German Foreign Minister, had given to *The Jerusalem Post* where he said that there were differences between the French and West German positions on the Middle East, and that the so-called 'Schuman document' was only a working document, which was far from having received approval. However, in what seems to have been a political U-turn, the *Bulletin* noted in the same report that Foreign Minister Scheel now had explained to the Bundestag that the 'Schuman document' 'was not a reflection of the views of one country, it recorded the joint political view of the Six' (*Bulletin of the EC* 11-1971: 123).[1]

A report in the *Bulletin* in early 1971 argued that the EC had lived isolated from major world issues until the 'Middle Eastern conflict' broke out in 1967 (*Bulletin of the EC* 4-1971: 30). Another issue of the *Bulletin* reported in August 1971 that the argument was made by the Liberal and allied group in the European Parliament that it was the pragmatic approach towards political unification in Europe that had enabled the Six to adopt a common position on the Middle East problem (*Bulletin of the EC* 8-1971: 100). In December 1971, the European Parliament adopted a resolution that sought to provide an early description of the concrete role that an independent and democratic Europe can and must play in the world. Adopting a common position regarding the problems of the Middle East was the first priority (*Bulletin of the EC* 12-1971: 101).

This issue of the *Bulletin* also included for the first time since the 1967 war an appeal from Israel for a balanced European approach towards the conflict. It included a reference to a speech that Abba Eban, Israel's Foreign

---

[1] Within the framework of the EPC, the Member States in 1971 agreed on a secret report, known as the 'Schuman document' that called for Israeli withdrawal from occupied territories in return for recognition of Israel by the Arab states. The status of the 'Schuman document' has been the subject of much academic debate. The most common argument has been that France considered it an official policy, whereas Germany was more hesitant and described it only as an informal working paper (Dosenrode and Stubkjaer 2002: 81). For an analysis of the Schuman document, see Pardo and Peters (2012: 74).

Minister, had just given to Consultative Assembly of the Council of Europe, where he urged 'Europe to apply the principle of a peace balanced by the dialogue between the countries of the Middle East and not by pressure from foreign powers' (*Bulletin of the EC* 12-1971: 97). There would be many more similar appeals from Israel in the years ahead. Also, for the first time in the material I have studied, there is a reference to EC payment to help Palestinian refugees through UNRWA in this issue of the *Bulletin* (*Bulletin of the EC* 12-1971: 162). Many more similar references would follow.

Enter Oil and the Palestinians

When the Parliament debated the situation in the Middle East right after the June 1967 war, the argument was made that

> it was a paradox that while Europe depended for 80% of its oil consump-
> tion (48% of its supply of power) on the countries of the Middle East,
> the USSR and the United States (on whose mutual agreement Europe's
> supplies from these countries actually depended) could manage without
> oil from the Middle East and rarely if ever needed to use the Suez Canal.
> (*Bulletin of the EEC* 8-1967: 83)

A couple of years later, in 1972, the *Bulletin* reported that 60 per cent of the Community's oil imports came from the Middle East (*Bulletin of the EC* 5-1972: 74). In early 1973, around half a year before the October 1973 war broke out, the European Parliament again discussed the situation in the Middle East. As was the case after the previous war of 1967, there was strong support for a more assertive role for the Community, with members seeing 'a unique opportunity for the Community to make its debut in the field of European foreign policy' (*Bulletin of the EC* 3-1973: 92). Member of the European Parliament (MEP) Christian de la Malène (DE/F)[2] argued that the Community could play a special role in the Middle East, because unlike some of the Member States, 'its past is untrammeled' (*Bulletin of the EC* 3-1973: 92). MEP John Brewis (C/UK) argued that Europe had just as important interests in this part of the world as the US and the USSR had (*Bulletin of the*

---

[2] The abbreviation (DE/F) means that this MEP was a member of the European Democratic Union Group in the Parliament from France.

EC 3-1973: 92). The resolution adopted by the Parliament called on Member States to lay down a Community policy to help bring about a peaceful settlement in the Middle East, focusing specifically on peaceful reconstruction in the social and economic spheres of the countries concerned (*Bulletin of the EC* 3-1973: 93).

During a session in the European Parliament in May 1973 on the Community's relations with the oil-producing countries, Sir Christopher Soames, Vice-President of the Commission, stated that the Commission had recognized the importance of developing appropriate relations with the oil-producing countries. The Vice-President further stated that the Commission believed that establishing a climate of confidence between the Community and its suppliers was the best guarantee for stability of supply (*Bulletin of the EC* 5-1973: 87). In the same issue of the *Bulletin*, another Vice-President of the Commission, Henri Simonet, lamented the fact that the Community had no independent oil policy towards the Middle East (*Bulletin of the EC* 5-1973: 123).

The European dependence on oil from the Middle East became an acute matter after the October 1973 war, and the shift in the EC's conception of what it perceived to be a just peace in the conflict became apparent in its first declaration after the war. On 13 October 1973, the Foreign Ministers issued a long declaration which stated that a peace agreement should be based on four points:

1. The inadmissibility of the acquisition of territory by force.
2. The need for Israel to end the territorial occupation which it has maintained since the conflict of 1967.
3. Respect for the sovereignty, territorial integrity, and independence of every state in the area and their right to live in peace within secure and recognized boundaries.
4. Recognition that in the establishment of a just and lasting peace account must be taken of the legitimate rights of the Palestinians. (*Bulletin of the EC* 10-1973: 106)

It is important to note that all of these points, except for point (iii), represented new policy departures for the EC. Even if points (i) and (ii) can be found in UNSC resolution 242, this was the first time they were spelled out by the EC. They were, again except for point (iii), also anathema to Israel. Most important of all, for the first time in an EC declaration, the term 'Palestinians' was used not just implicitly in terms of refugees, but 'the Palestinians' were explicitly recognized as a party to the conflict. At a sitting a month after the war in November 1973, the Council reaffirmed 'the resolve of the EEC Member States to contribute individually and collectively to an equitable solution of the Middle East problem' (*Bulletin of the EC* 10-1973: 54). Emphasizing the early importance of path-dependency in the EC's declarations, it is clear from the moment when terms like 'just peace' or 'Palestinians' are introduced into the discourse, they tended to be mainstreamed very fast.

After the October 1973 war, there were many references in the *Bulletin* as to how important oil imports from the Middle East were for the EC, how important it was for the EC to form a common foreign policy and how important the conflict in the Middle East was, both when it came to oil imports and to forming a common foreign policy. As UK Prime Minister Edward Heath told the December 1973 Copenhagen Summit Conference:

> The Community was, in my judgment, entirely correct in concentrating its efforts on a statement of foreign policy, made in the Declaration of 6 November. We can build on that substantial beginning, so that Europe can make the maximum possible contribution to the restoration of peace in the Middle East. It is only by using all the resources of foreign policy that we can hope to give Europe secure access to the oil it needs. (*Bulletin of the EC* 12-1973: 24)

West German Chancellor Willy Brandt and French President George Pompidou made more or less exactly the same comments in various EC settings around the same time. Brandt stated that the energy crisis showed that the Member States were all in the same boat and urgently appealed to the competent institutions of the Community to do everything within their means to mobilize cooperation (*Bulletin of the EC* 11-1973: 10), whereas Pompidou added that European involvement in the Middle East would ease the tensions between the superpowers (*Bulletin of the EC* 11-1973: 25).

The European Parliament adopted a resolution the same month calling on Member States to recognize that the Community must assert its position as a separate entity in the international context (*Bulletin of the EC* 11-1973: 82). The December 1973 issue of the *Bulletin* included an extract from a declaration adopted by the Arab League at their 26–8 November 1973 meeting in Algiers. It stated that

> by adopting clear and equitable positions, especially by undertaking all available means to work for the evacuation by Israel of all the occupied Arab territories, particularly Jerusalem, and for the restoration of the Palestinian people to its national rights, Europe would strengthen both her resolve to be independent and her role in world affairs. (*Bulletin of the EC* 12-1973: 127)

The Arab League's resolution went on to state that 'the Kings and Heads of State have noted carefully and with interest the first signs of a better understanding by the western European countries of the Arab cause' (*Bulletin of the EC* 12-1973: 127). While this is one of the earliest manifestations in the *Bulletin* that there had indeed been a change in EC policy which may have repercussions, the same issue of the *Bulletin* published an interview with Mahmoud Riad, General Secretary of the Arab League, who said that 'We have read the Declaration of the Nine. We liked it, but it is a piece of paper. I said in Algiers that action must match fine words' (*Bulletin of the EC* 12-1973: 127). He went on to say that the Arab League was not asking Europe to sever her relations with Israel, as it had done with the African States and Japan, but only to halt European arms export to Israel (*Bulletin of the EC* 12-1973: 127).

Dependence and Independence from the US

The EC's declarations on the Middle East after the 1973 war took place against an unprecedented backdrop of West European estrangement from the United States over the war in Vietnam, monetary and trade policies, and strategic defence issues in the light of the period of *détente* (1969–79). In a major speech in early 1974 titled 'Relations between the United States and the Community', the President of the Commission, Francois-Xavier Ortoli, said that it was 'imperative to dedramatize Euro-American relations' (*Bulletin of the EC* 3-1974: 6).[3] The President of the Commission went on to note that the US must realize that Europe had 'obligations and interests of her own which may sometimes differ from American interests', and that 'she is duty bound, without running against her overall policy, to negotiate on her own' (*Bulletin of the EC* 3-1974: 8). In directly addressing the US, the President of the Commission said:

> I would like to be quite clear on this point, that the renewal and strengthening of our relations with the United States cannot affect the determination of the Nine to assert themselves as a distinct and original entity. You cannot applaud the sight of Europe taking wing and at the same time insist that she clips her wings, meaning that she denies herself her concepts and her policy. Europe wants to be adult and mature. This must be understood and acknowledged . . . It is pointless to cover one's eyes to refuse to see the realities. Europe's dependence on Arab oil (90% of Europe's supply as against only 10% for the United States) is a case in point which, highlighted by its immediacy, shows the measure of the differences. (*Bulletin of the EC* 3-1974: 7–8)

With considerable resentment in the US, the EC had launched the Euro–Arab dialogue in December 1973, which sought to establish a special relationship between the EC and the Arab states. The aid from the Community to UNRWA had been increased from about 7 million u.a. for the 1972–3 campaign to about 10 million u.a. for the 1973–4 campaign (*Bulletin of the EC* 4-1974: 61).[4] It was reported in the *Bulletin* in May 1974 that as

---

[3] A week before this speech, US President Richard Nixon had himself delivered a major speech on US–Europe relations. Among other things, Nixon said 'the Europeans cannot have it both ways. They cannot have the United States participation and cooperation on the security front and then proceed to have confrontation and even hostility on the economic and political front . . . It does not mean that we are not going to have competition, but it does mean that we are not going to be faced with a situation where the nine countries of Europe gang up against the United States – the United States which is their guarantee for their security. That we cannot have' (Nixon 1974).

[4] u.a. stood for 'unit of account', which was a composite (or basket) currency unit using a number of the currencies of Member States of the European Community, later to be superseded by the European Currency Unit (ECU). In 1974, 1 million u.a. was equivalent to 1.2 million USD (Ungerer 1997: 138).

UNRWA was 'facing financial difficulties owing to increased operational costs for its services', the EC would contribute 11.5 million u.a. to UNRWA for 1974 and bear 'all the 1974 running expenses of UNRWA for the secondary education of Palestinian refugees', estimated at 6.5 million u.a. (*Bulletin of the EC* 5-1974: 61). There was already at this time a debate in the Parliament about the effectiveness of the aid to the Palestinians. MEP Erik Blumenfeld (C-D/G) asked the Commission whether UNRWA could not be better financed by a donation from oil-producing Arab countries. MEP Blumenfeld also wanted to make sure 'to train the children of Palestinian refugees to become productive members of society instead of terrorists'. The Commission responded that the aid to UNRWA was yielding the most effective possible result (*Bulletin of the EC* 4-1974: 61). Two months later, in June 1974, MEP Blumenfeld asked again, this time without getting a proper response, what precautions the Commission has taken, or what precautions it intended to take, to ensure that Community funds which were to be paid to UNRWA for the training of Palestinian refugees were in fact used for the intended purpose and not to finance other Palestinian activities (*Bulletin of the EC* 6-1974: 97).

The Euro–Arab Dialogue

The years following the October 1973 war witnessed a sharp turn in the EC's rhetoric as it drew closer to the Arab/Palestinian narrative of the conflict. Some of these statements took place within the framework of the Euro–Arab dialogue, which was given extensive coverage in the *Bulletin* (see, for example, *Bulletin of the EC* 6-1974: 123–4, 5-1976: 6–12, 2-1977: 64–8). The *Bulletin* reported that the Arab side sometimes demanded that EC statements on the conflict should be included in the political part of the final communiqués of the Euro–Arab dialogue's meetings, which the EC sometimes agreed to (see, for example *Bulletin of the EC* 10-1977: 83). This should be viewed as a way for the Arab side to politicize the dialogue. The June 1975 Euro–Arab dialogue meeting was described by the *Bulletin* as 'a major development in relations between the Nine and the Arab World' (*Bulletin of the EC* 6-1975: 109). The two sides set out the following areas of cooperation:

- agriculture and rural development;
- industrialization;
- basic infrastructure;
- financial cooperation;
- trade;
- scientific and technological cooperation, cultural, labour, and social questions. (*Bulletin of the EC* 6-1975: 109)

The Euro–Arab dialogue was portrayed at the time by top EC Member States leaders, such as West Germany's Foreign Minister Hans-Dietrich Genscher, as being a 'well balanced' and 'very long-term venture' (*Bulletin of the EC* 6-1974: 123–4), while the French Foreign Minister Jean Sauvagnargues described it as focusing on developing 'fruitful economic and technical cooperation between the two groups'. Sauvagnargues went on to say that the dialogue 'neither bore on oil nor was concerned with the question of a peaceful settlement in the Middle East' (*Bulletin of the EC* 10-1974: 92). But questions such as whether the Palestinians, and especially the PLO, should participate immediately exposed the politicized nature of the Euro–Arab dialogue. The *Bulletin* reported in December 1974 that the Member States were not in agreement on the question of Palestinian representatives taking part in a planned meeting of the Euro–Arab dialogue, which in turn led the Arab states to cancel the upcoming meeting (*Bulletin of the EC* 12-1974: 92). The *Bulletin* reported in April 1975 that all groups in the European Parliament objected to the participation of the PLO in the Euro–Arab dialogue (*Bulletin of the EC* 4-1975: 74). There were several other reports in the *Bulletin* that indicated the politicized nature of the dialogue. The European Parliament, for example, adopted a resolution on what it called the present state of the Euro–Arab dialogue. The resolution affirmed

> that the success of the dialogue depends on a solution being found to the political problems which will permit an effective contribution to peace, allowing all the States of the Middle East – including the State of Israel – to live within secure frontiers recognized by all parties. (*Bulletin of the EC* 4-1976: 84)

The same resolution also expressed hope that in the context of the Euro–Arab dialogue particular attention will be paid to the principle of non-discrimination and that actual or threatened boycott measures will not be tolerated (*Bulletin of the EC* 4-1976: 84).

The May 1976 issue of the *Bulletin* devoted no less than six pages to covering the first General Committee meeting of the Euro–Arab dialogue, describing the ties between Europe and the Arab World as an interchange between civilizations (*Bulletin of the EC* 5-1976: 9). The *Bulletin* reported that with this meeting the dialogue had entered into a new phase of practical cooperation; it had now become a permanent reality, adding a new global dimension to the bilateral relations of the EC and its Member States (*Bulletin of the EC* 5-1976: 6). The report in the *Bulletin*

> confirmed the importance of entering into negotiations with oil-producing countries on comprehensive arrangements comprising cooperation on a wide scale for the economic and industrial development of these countries industrial investments, and stable energy supplies to the Member countries at reasonable prices (*Bulletin of the EC* 5-1976: 6).

In the final communiqué of this meeting, both sides outlined their principles for a just peace in the conflict. For the EC, it was the same four points from its October 1973 declaration. For the Arab side, all of their three demands were explicitly related to the situation for the Palestinians (see Table 2.1) (*Bulletin of the EC* 5-1976: 10). Both sides 'recognized that a solution to the question of Palestine based on the recognition of the legitimate rights of the Palestinian people is a crucial factor in the achievement of a just and lasting peace' (*Bulletin of the EC* 5-1976: 10).[5] At the same time, the *Bulletin* reported that for the nine EC Member States, the Euro–Arab dialogue was clearly not the appropriate framework for embarking upon any negotiations for a peace settlement in the Middle East. This should fall within the framework of the UNSC. The EC further believed that a peace agreement should be accompanied by sound international guarantees. Without specifying what these international guarantees might consist of, the *Bulletin* reported that the nine Member States were ready to envisage the possibility of contributing to such a system of guarantees (*Bulletin of the EC* 5-1976: 7).

---

[5] This is one of very few instances where the term 'Palestine' was used by the EC during the 1970s.

Table 2.1 The European and Arab sides' 1976 conceptions of a just peace

The European side recalled the four points of their Declaration of 6 November 1973 (first formulated on 13 October 1973) and their statement during the last session of the United Nations General Assembly (UNGA). They expressed the firm hope that early progress could be made towards this objective and affirmed their determination to do all in their power to contribute to its achievement.	The Arab side shares the European view that force and *fait accompli* are not elements upon which stable international relations can be based. They affirmed that a just and lasting peace in the Middle East requires the fulfilment of the following elements:
1. The inadmissibility of the acquisition of territory by force.	1. Withdrawal by Israel from the occupied territories.
2. The need for Israel to end the territorial occupation which it has maintained since the conflict of 1967.	2. Recognition of the national rights of the Palestinian people.
3. Respect for the sovereignty, territorial integrity, and independence of every state in the area, and their right to live in peace within secure and recognized boundaries.	3. Participation of the Palestine Liberation Organisation, the representative of the Palestinian people, in all international peace efforts.
4. Recognition that in the establishment of a just and lasting peace account must be taken of the legitimate rights of the Palestinians.	

Source: *Bulletin of the EC* 5-1976: 10.

The Euro–Arab dialogue continued to get wide coverage in the *Bulletin*. In early 1977, the *Bulletin* reported that of the two parts of the dialogue, the economic part was increasingly becoming more important than the political part as successive meetings were held (*Bulletin of the EC* 2-1977: 64). In October 1977, the *Bulletin* reported that there 'were no really great political difficulties' between the two sides (*Bulletin of the EC* 10-1977: 82).

Trade without Political Demands

A new EEC–Israel agreement was signed in May 1975 and went into effect on 1 July 1976. It superseded the previous agreement from 1970. On the industrial side, the agreement stipulated gradual, but in the end complete elimination of tariff and quota barriers for all industrial products, according to the *Bulletin*. By 1 January 1980, 60 per cent of Israel's industrial imports from the Community would be free of restrictions and the remainder by 1 January 1985. In agriculture, the Community was granting substantial tariff reductions over some 85 per cent of Israel's exports (*Bulletin of the EC*

5-1975: 63). The *Bulletin* noted some complaints from Arab states over the agreement, but noted simultaneously that similar agreements were about to be signed with Egypt, Jordan and Syria (*Bulletin of the EC* 5-1975: 76).[6] During the mid-1970s, there were several reports in the *Bulletin* stating that the Community aimed for balanced economic relations vis-à-vis all the countries of the Middle East (see, for example, *Bulletin of the EC* 1-1975: 63).

Nowhere in the *Bulletin* is there any criticism from any EC institution or official against this agreement and neither is there any discussion of linking the agreement to peace negotiations or to political demands on Israel. On the contrary, the agreement was widely praised within the EC. The European Parliament welcomed the new agreement and unanimously adopted a resolution approving it (*Bulletin of the EC* 5-1975: 76). The rapporteur to the European Parliament, Schelto Patijn (S/NL), reminded the House that as far back as 1965 the Parliament had called for a more active relationship between the Community and Israel, in fact even for Israel's association with the EEC (*Bulletin of the EC* 5-1975: 76). Later in 1975, the rapporteur reported back to the Parliament that the 1975 EEC–Israel agreement 'should be viewed as a contribution to peace in the Middle East' (*Bulletin of the EC* 12-1975: 85). Claude Cheysson, Commissioner with special responsibility for Mediterranean policy, told the Parliament that the agreement would have a corrective effect on trade relations. The EC's exports to Israel at the time were three times larger than Israel's exports to the EC (*Bulletin of the EC* 5-1975: 77).

The 1975 EEC–Israel agreement was followed up in 1977 by the signing of an additional and a financial protocol between the Community and Israel. The *Bulletin* described this upgrade as 'a unique contribution' by the EC 'to the economic and social development of Israel' (*Bulletin of the EC* 1-1977: 21). Among other things, these new protocols were to promote:

- the development of production and economic infrastructure in Israel, in order to foster the complementarity of the economies and the industrialization of Israel;

[6] Similar agreements were signed between the EEC and Egypt, Syria and Jordan in January 1977 (*Bulletin of the EC* 1-1977: 18).

- sales promotion for products exported by Israel;
- industrial cooperation, to be encouraged by the organisation of contacts and meetings between industrial policy-makers or business operators, by easier access to technological know-how and facilities for the acquisition of patents or other forms of industrial property, by the elimination of non-tariff barriers to trade in industrial products;
- the encouragement of private investment;
- joint projects in the fields of science, technology, and the protection of the environment. (*Bulletin of the EC* 1-1977: 21)

The January 1977 issue of the *Bulletin* had a long text about the trade relations between EC and Israel that noted that the ties which united the Community and Israel were as old as the EEC itself. As far back as 1958, the Israeli government had sought to open a dialogue with the common market, and the setting up of contractual ties with Israel was one of the Community's first foreign policy measures. Negotiations that had begun in 1962 resulted in the conclusion of a non-preferential trade agreement for a period of three years, signed in June 1964 (*Bulletin of the EC* 1-1977: 20). Later in 1977, another rapporteur from the European Parliament, Mario Martinelli (C-D/I), reported that 'the House unequivocally opposed any boycott against firms having business contacts with Israel and welcomed Israel's request that the Commission establish a permanent delegation there' (*Bulletin of the EC* 5-1977: 85).

Also noteworthy is the fact that the worst and largest terror attacks in Israel, the 1974 Ma'alot school massacre and the 1978 Coastal Road massacre, were not mentioned by the *Bulletin*.[7] Other terror attacks around this time, for example the kidnapping of former Italian Prime Minister Aldo Moro, which happened at the same time as the Coastal Road massacre, were harshly condemned by the EC (see, for example *Bulletin of the EC* 3-1978: 92). Throughout the 1970s and 1980s, with the exception of the 1972 Munich Massacre (*Bulletin of the EC* 10-1972: 202), which happened on

---

[7] The 1974 Ma'alot school massacre killed twenty-six Israelis, including twenty-two children. The 1978 Coastal Road massacre killed thirty-seven Israelis, the largest terror attack in Israel's history, excluding attacks on Israeli military facilities in Lebanon.

European soil, there was a very soft treatment by the EC of Arab/Palestinian terrorism. The only other exceptions from the 1970s are two condemnations by the European Parliament of a terror attack by the PLO on 4 July 1975 at Jerusalem's Zion Square, where a bomb killed thirteen Israelis and wounded seventy-two (*Bulletin of the EC* 7/8-1975: 86), and a November 1979 condemnation of an attack on the Israeli Ambassador in Portugal (*Bulletin of the EC* 11-1979: 82).

Legal Rights of the Palestinians, Illegal Israeli Settlements

The latter half of the 1970s witnessed great diplomatic activity on behalf of the Community vis-à-vis the situation in the Middle East. In December 1975, the *Bulletin* reported that the EC was completely against equating Zionism with racism as a United Nations General Assembly (UNGA) resolution had done in November 1975. All, then nine, EC members had voted against the resolution (*Bulletin of the EC* 12-1975: 73). The European Parliament termed the resolution 'incomprehensible and absurd', and all party groups in the Parliament were against it (*Bulletin of the EC* 11-1975: 61). There was another resolution in the UNGA around the same time requesting the PLO be invited to take part in the efforts to achieve peace in the Middle East. On this the nine EC members were split (*Bulletin of the EC* 12-1975: 73).

In 1976, a top EC official – Max van der Stoel, the Netherlands' Foreign Minister, President of the Council and Chairman of political cooperation among the Nine – talked for the first time about the Palestinians as a 'people' with 'legal rights' to 'express its national identity in concrete terms'. This happened in an EPC report to the European Parliament (*Bulletin of the EC* 11-1976: 96). He also said that it would only be possible to solve the conflict in the Middle East if these rights, which would be the EC's guiding principles at an upcoming meeting in the UN, were respected (*Bulletin of the EC* 11-1976: 96). In February 1977, the EC opposed Israeli settlements for the first time. In the final communiqué of the February 1977 Euro–Arab dialogue meeting of the General Committee, the EC stated:

> The European side restated its view that a solution of the conflict in the Middle East will be possible only if the legitimate right of the Palestinian people to give effective expression to its national identity is translated into

fact. The European side reiterated the concern of the Nine over the continued Israeli occupation of Arab territories since 1967. They maintained that the Fourth Geneva Convention was applicable to the occupied territories and opposed the policy of establishing settlements there, which could only prejudice the prospects for peace. They were also opposed to any moves to alter unilaterally the status of Jerusalem. The Arab side expressed its appreciation of this attitude. (*Bulletin of the EC* 2-1977: 65)

This communiqué marked significant changes when compared to all previous EC statements on the conflict. Not only was this the first time the EC opposed Israeli settlements, the communiqué also stated that the Fourth Geneva Convention was applicable to the occupied territories. It went on to say that the Palestinians were a people with a national identity that needed to be translated into fact, unclear at this point how and what kind of fact the EC was thinking of. Finally, this was the first time the EC explicitly raised the status of Jerusalem as part of the conflict. It was not surprising that the Arab side expressed its appreciation of this attitude (*Bulletin of the EC* 2-1977: 65).

The fact that this happened in a Euro–Arab dialogue meeting and that settlements were not mentioned in the 1977 London European Council is an indication that the Euro–Arab dialogue was used to push EC policy in a more pro-Arab/Palestinian and anti-Israeli direction, whether knowingly or unknowingly by the EC. It is also important to note that this first EC declaration opposing the settlements came in February 1977, three months before Menachem Begin's Likud party won an upheaval election victory, which ended three decades of Labour dominance in Israeli politics. The EC's declaration was therefore not a response to the rise of Likud, but the Begin government's increased settlement building led the EC to stiffen its positions even further, which in turn resulted in Israeli counter-reactions, accelerating the downward spiral in EC–Israel relations.

The June 1977 London European Council was another landmark EC statement on the Israeli–Arab conflict. It reiterated the four points from October 1973 that the EC believed a peace settlement should be based on. But even more importantly, this declaration stated that the Community believed that a solution to the conflict in the Middle East will be possible only if the legitimate right of the Palestinian people to give effective expression to its national identity is translated into fact, which would take into account the need for a homeland for the Palestinian people. They [the Member States] consider that the representatives of the parties to the conflict including the Palestinian people, must participate in the negotiations in an appropriate manner to be worked out in consultation between all the parties concerned. (*Bulletin of the EC* 6-1977: 62)

This declaration represented another milestone in legitimizing the Palestinians and their rights. It was the first time that the Community outlined that a translation of the Palestinian people's national identity into a fact meant a homeland for the Palestinians. It was also the first time that the EC explicitly called for representatives of the Palestinian people to be part of the negotiations. The June 1977 London European Council also stated that,

in the context of an overall settlement, Israel must be ready to recognize the legitimate rights of the Palestinian people: equally, the Arab side must be ready to recognize the right of Israel to live in peace within secure and recognized boundaries. It is not through the acquisition of territory by force that the security of the States of the region can be assured; but it must be based on commitments to peace exchanged between· all the parties concerned with a view to establishing truly peaceful relations. (*Bulletin of the EC* 6-1977: 62)

This call for a kind of mutual recognition between Israel and the Arab/ Palestinian side was the first of its kind by the EC and was followed by many similar calls by the Community and its members over the next decade leading up to the signing of the 1993 Declaration of Principles (DoP; together with other agreements, also called the Oslo Accords).

Later in 1977, the EC issued several very critical statements of the Israeli settlements. In September 1977, Henri Simonet, Belgian Foreign Minister and President of the Council of the European Communities and of the European Political Cooperation, spoke on behalf of the Community at the UNGA. He referred to the settlements as 'illegal measures taken recently by the Government of Israel in the occupied territories', which 'constitute an additional obstacle in the process of negotiation which should lead to a peaceful solution'. He went on to call on all parties involved in the conflict to 'refrain from making any declarations and adopting any measures, administrative, legal, military or other, which would constitute an obstacle to the process of peace' (*Bulletin of the EC* 9-1977: 86). In a report to the European Parliament in November 1977, Simonet described Israel's settlements as a 'policy of colonizing the occupied territories', terminology the EU would not use today (*Bulletin of the EC* 11-1977: 111).

The Camp David Process

The Camp David process consisted of two framework agreements. The first agreement from 1978, called *A Framework for Peace in the Middle East*, provided the principles for establishing peace in the Middle East, including through the establishment of an autonomous regime in the West Bank and Gaza, and withdrawal and redeployment of Israeli forces. The second agreement from 1979, called *A Framework for the Conclusion of a Peace Treaty between Egypt and Israel*, provided the framework for the peace between Israel and Egypt, including resolution of the Sinai issue. The nine Member States very much welcomed the Camp David process. They had previously welcomed the second interim agreement from September 1975 between Israel and Egypt as 'an important contribution to *détente* and towards the eventual negotiation of a peaceful, just and lasting settlement' (*Bulletin of the EC* 9-1975: 95). In this statement, the Member States also declared that the 'Middle East situation' and 'the interest of the Nine in this area' was of 'the utmost importance to Europe and to the whole world' (*Bulletin of the EC* 9-1975: 95). Egyptian President Anwar Sadat's visit to Israel on 19 November 1977 was hailed by the EC as a 'bold initiative' and as a 'historic meeting' (*Bulletin of the EC* 11-1977: 52). The Foreign Ministers of the EC were convinced that mistrust was 'one of the chief obstacles to a peaceful settlement of the Israeli–Arab conflict' (*Bulletin of the EC* 11-1977: 52). They issued a statement where they expressed their hope

> that the unprecedented dialogue begun in Jerusalem will open the way to comprehensive negotiations leading to a just and lasting overall settlement taking account of the rights and concerns of all parties involved. It is a

matter of urgency that genuine peace at last be achieved for all the peoples of the area, including the Palestinian people, on the basis of principles recognized by the international community and embodied in particular in the declaration of the European Council of 29 June 1977. (*Bulletin of the EC* 11-1977: 52)

There can be little doubt as to how important the EC regarded the Camp David process. When West German Foreign Minister and President of the Council of the European Communities and of the EPC, Hans-Dietrich Genscher, spoke on behalf of the Community at the UNGA in September 1978, he said that 'the bitter Middle East conflict' had 'threatened the security of the world for the past thirty years' (*Bulletin of the EC* 9-1978: 103). Achieving a peace settlement in the region was a 'vital interest to us', which was 'reflected in our determination to support all efforts to bring about such a settlement' (*Bulletin of the EC* 9-1978: 103). Genscher indicated an opening towards the PLO when he said that

> if such a peace settlement is to be achieved it is imperative that all parties concerned participate in its negotiation and completion. Meanwhile no obstacle should be placed in the way of this process, which should be kept open and should, through further development and wider participation, lead to a comprehensive settlement. (*Bulletin of the EC* 9-1978: 103)

From Genscher's speech and from several similar statements in the *Bulletin*, it was also clear that the EC envisaged the rapprochement between Israel and Egypt to lead to a comprehensive, meaning regional, peace treaty, which would include the Palestinians. Genscher further noted that 'the situation in the Middle East is inseparably linked with the situation in Lebanon' (*Bulletin of the EC* 9-1978: 103).

When the European Parliament discussed the Camp David process around the same time, there were for the first time in the *Bulletin* calls by MEPs for the PLO to recognize Israel (*Bulletin of the EC* 10-1978: 85). Even top EC leaders speaking on behalf on the Community began more and more to call on the PLO to accept the principles of a peace agreement in the late 1970s (see, for example, *Bulletin of the EC* 9-1979: 110). The Arab states, on their part, called on the EC 'to recognize the PLO as the sole representative of the Palestinian people' (*Bulletin of the EC* 12-1978: 18). In the final communiqué of the Euro–Arab dialogue's fourth meeting of the General Committee in 1978, the EC reaffirmed its four points from October 1973 while the Arab side reaffirmed that the continued occupation by Israel constituted a threat to peace and security in the Middle East, and to international peace and security (*Bulletin of the EC* 12-1978: 19). The Arab side further set forth the Arab position as regards the solution to the Palestine question, which was based on three main points, plus a long section on the growing importance of halting the expansion of Israeli settlements:

- A solution must enable the people of Palestine to establish their independent state on their territory and exercise the right to return to their homeland.
- The Arab side noted the necessity of not putting any constraints on the rights of the representatives of the Palestinian people to speak in their name.
- In order to achieve a comprehensive settlement, the Arab side felt that it was time for the European Community to recognize the PLO as the legitimate representative of the Palestinian people, which was already recognized by all the Arab states, most of the other nations of the world, and indeed by the United Nations.
- In addition, the Arab side referred to and condemned measures and actions taken by Israel in the occupied territories since 1967, such as the establishment of settlements in addition to changing their legal status and demographic structure, including in Jerusalem.
- A final point by the Arab side was their refusal to settle Palestinians in Lebanon. (*Bulletin of the EC* 12-1978: 19–20)

The 1979 Israel–Egypt Peace Treaty

The Camp David process culminated with the signing of the March 1979 peace treaty between Israel and Egypt. It was met with the 'greatest attention' by the EC (*Bulletin of the EC* 3-1979: 86). The nine Member States were 'fully appreciative of the will for peace which has led President Carter to engage himself personally in these negotiations, as well as of the efforts made by President Sadat and Prime Minister Begin' (*Bulletin of the EC* 3-1979:

86). At the same time, the Member States recognized that 'a difficult road remains to be trodden before Security Council Resolution 242 is implemented in all its aspects and on all fronts' (*Bulletin of the EC* 3-1979: 86). The Member States nevertheless regarded the peace treaty as 'a correct application of the principles of that Resolution' (*Bulletin of the EC* 3-1979: 86), but envisaged the peace treaty 'not as a separate peace but as a first step in the direction of a comprehensive settlement designed to bring to an end thirty years of hostility and mistrust', with 'representatives of the Palestinian people' included (*Bulletin of the EC* 3-1979: 86). The European Parliament adopted a resolution which warmly welcomed the peace treaty and congratulated the protagonists (*Bulletin of the EC* 4-1979: 82). The resolution also urged the Council, the Commission and the Member States to intensify the existing links between the Community and Egypt and Israel, particularly on the basis of industrial cooperation. Lastly, the resolution emphasized the Parliament's desire to seek to make an effective contribution to the Community's efforts to assist in the achievement of a comprehensive settlement (*Bulletin of the EC* 4-1979: 82).

In the aftermath of the peace treaty, the EC welcomed the withdrawals of Israeli forces from Sinai and progress towards improved relations between Egypt and Israel (*Bulletin of the EC* 10-1979: 131). But the optimism of the Camp David process and the Israel–Egypt peace treaty went hand in hand with a rapidly growing awareness of the problems constituted by the Israeli settlements. When Israel stepped up attempts to establish settlements in the occupied territories, the Foreign Ministers of the EC felt compelled, on 18 June 1979, to issue a long and strong statement, particularly singling out the issue of the Israeli settlements as impeding the pursuit of a comprehensive settlement. According to the Foreign Ministers, the settlements were problematic for two reasons:

1. Israel's claim to eventual sovereignty over the occupied territories, which is incompatible with Resolution 242 establishing the principle of the inadmissibility of the acquisition of territory by force.
2. The Israeli government's policy of establishing settlements in the occupied territories is in violation of international law. (*Bulletin of the EC* 6-1979: 93)

Another consequence of the Israel–Egypt peace treaty was a stalemate in the Euro–Arab dialogue, as 'Egypt came under heavy criticism from the other Arab States', as the *Bulletin* put it (*Bulletin of the EC* 10-1979: 131).[8] While technical cooperation continued, a major meeting of the Euro–Arab dialogue's General Committee was cancelled in February 1978. In November 1978, the *Bulletin* reported that the hopes for the impetus needed to revive the dialogue had come to nothing (*Bulletin of the EC* 11-1978: 119), but the scheduled February 1978 meeting was nevertheless held the next month in December 1978 (*Bulletin of the EC* 12-1978: 18). A year later, the *Bulletin* reported that the division among the Member States of the Arab League had put a brake on the momentum gained at earlier Euro–Arab dialogue meetings (*Bulletin of the EC* 10-1979: 136). In November 1979, the nine EC Member States expressed their hope that conditions would soon be such as to allow all the countries concerned to take part in the Euro–Arab dialogue (*Bulletin of the EC* 11-1979: 82).

The last major thing that happened in the Community during the 1970s with a bearing on the Middle East was a long speech by Ireland's Foreign Minister Michael O'Kennedy, speaking on behalf of the Community at the yearly UNGA meeting in his capacity as President of the Council and of the EPC. O'Kennedy welcomed the Israel–Egypt peace treaty and recalled that 'one of the basic requirements of a comprehensive settlement is an end to the territorial occupation which Israel has maintained since the conflict of 1967' (*Bulletin of the EC* 9-1979: 111). He went on to state that the nine Member States 'are opposed to the Israeli Government's policy of establishing settlements in occupied territories in contravention of international law and they cannot accept claims by Israel to sovereignty over occupied territories, since this would be incompatible with Resolution 242' (*Bulletin of the EC* 9-1979: 111). In his speech, O'Kennedy also began equalizing Israeli and Palestinian rights and claims:

> The Nine emphasize that it is essential that all parties to the negotiations accept the right of all States in the area to live within secure and recognized

[8] Egypt not only came under heavy criticism from the other Arab states but was in fact suspended from the Arab League in 1979 after signing the peace treaty with Israel. The Arab League's headquarters were moved from Cairo to Tunis. Egypt was readmitted in 1989.

boundaries with adequate guarantees. Equally, of course, it is essential that there be respect for the legitimate rights of the Palestinian people. These include the right to a homeland and the right, through its representatives, to play its full part in the negotiation of a comprehensive settlement . . . Such a settlement would win the endorsement and support of the international community and would meet the legitimate rights and interests of all parties. This includes Israel, which is entitled to exist at peace within secure boundaries that are accepted and adequately guaranteed; and the Palestinian people, who are entitled, within the framework set by a peace settlement, to exercise their right to determine their own future as a people. (*Bulletin of the EC* 9-1979: 110)

This was the first sign of a trend that would be prevalent over the next decade in the lead-up to the Oslo peace process.

Conclusions

As the 1970s ended, the EC had come a long way in formulating a distinct policy vis-à-vis the Israeli–Arab conflict. This policy was anchored in the four major points first outlined after the October 1973 war: the inadmissibility of the acquisition of territory by force; the need for Israel to end the territorial occupation which it had maintained since the conflict of 1967; the respect for the sovereignty, territorial integrity and independence of every state in the area; and the recognition of the legitimate rights of the Palestinians. These four points were then repeated in EC statements throughout the decade. The question of the Israeli settlements was added in 1977 and the legitimate rights of the Palestinians were progressively expanded after the term was first used in 1973, from the EC acknowledging the Palestinians as being a people to their need for a homeland, to them having legal rights, to including their representatives in negotiations, to them determining their own future. This remarkable development took place during the Cold War period of *détente*, which allowed the EC room for manoeuvre between the two superpowers. This consisted of the EC issuing many statements on the conflict and financially supporting UNRWA during the 1970s, but there was no attempt whatsoever during the 1970s by the EC of actually trying to enforce its rhetorical positions on the conflict. There were, for example, no discussions in the

Bulletin during this period of linking trade agreements with Israel to peace negotiations or political demands. Although playing no role in it, the EC was supportive of the Camp David process, which the EC had hoped would lead to a comprehensive regional peace treaty with the Palestinians included.

3

1980–91:
FORWARD-THINKING ON
THE LONG ROAD TO OSLO

Too much passion, suffering and hate has accumulated in a land which had seemed promised a future of concord and fraternity between its peoples. It is time for an end to the language of violence and for all the parties to start talking to one another as equals. And it is time to move from rhetoric to the negotiation of terms and arrangements for restoring peace. It is in this context that the declaration issued at Venice is to be regarded. (Gaston Thorn, President of the Council and of European Political Cooperation, quoted in *Bulletin of the EC* 7/8-1980: 86)

It is certainly possible to view the 1980s as a lost decade for the Israeli–Arab conflict, as it provoked a major war in Lebanon in the first half of the decade and an intifada in the occupied territories in the second half. Adding to that, it was also clear early on in the decade that the much-celebrated Israel–Egypt peace treaty would not solve the Palestinian part of the Israeli–Arab conflict. In the wider region, the Soviet invasion of Afghanistan was vigorously condemned by the EC and regarded as a threat to peace, security and stability in the Middle East (*Bulletin of the EC* 1-1980: 7). This meant that the Cold War period of *détente*, which had characterized the 1970s, was replaced by the 'New Cold War' (1979–86). While the tightening of the bipolar structure that followed is widely interpreted to have made it harder for the EC to have an active, alternative policy to that of the United States, the 1980s was also a decade when the EC's diplomacy was very successful in legitimizing the two ideas that came to underpin the Oslo peace process: mutual recognition and the 'land for peace' principle. The EC's most important declaration ever on the Israeli–Arab conflict, the 1980 Venice Declaration, established the EC as a fairly independent international actor in the shadow of the Cold War rivalry. Four decades after it was issued, it still constitutes the basic principles of the EU's policy towards the conflict. When the Declaration of Principles (DoP) was finally signed in 1993, thirteen years after the Venice Declaration was issued, it looked much closer to the Venice Declaration than anything the US, the Israelis or the Arab side, including the Palestinians, had previously outlined.

The Venice Declaration

In April 1980, a month before the Venice Declaration was issued, the then nine Member States 'reiterated their belief that only a comprehensive, just, and lasting settlement can bring true peace to the Middle East' (*Bulletin of the EC* 4-1980: 13). The Council also stated 'that Europe may in due course have a role to play', and instructed the Foreign Ministers 'to submit a report on this problem on the occasion of its next session in Venice' (*Bulletin of the EC* 4-1980: 13). Two months later, in June 1980, the Venice Declaration was issued. Its part on the Israeli–Arab conflict consisted of eleven articles, plus two short paragraphs on the Euro–Arab dialogue and the situation in Lebanon, which together took up little less than a page and a half in the *Bulletin* (*Bulletin of the EC* 6-1980: 10–11). Of the eleven articles, two represented new and controversial policy departures: article six, which called for Palestinian self-determination, and article seven, which called for the PLO to be associated with the negotiations. While being very controversial at the time, it is easy to see that both articles were a logical continuation of the EC's diplomacy from the 1970s.

Both internal and external factors had contributed to the issuing of the Venice Declaration. The President of the Commission, Roy Jenkins, explicitly mentioned that the United Kingdom's contribution to the EC's budget had been settled, and the challenges of successive international crises (i.e. the Soviet invasion of Afghanistan, the revolution and hostage crisis in Iran, the new oil crisis, and the negotiations on Palestinian autonomy within the

Table 3.1 The 1980 Venice Declaration's eleven articles on the Israeli–Arab conflict in shortened form

Art. 1	The growing tensions in the region render a comprehensive solution to the conflict more necessary and pressing than ever.
Art. 2	The nine Member States consider that their traditional ties to the Middle East oblige them to play a special role and now work in a more concrete way towards peace.
Art. 3	The nine Member States base themselves on UNSC resolutions 242 and 338.
Art. 4	The time has come to promote the recognition and implementation of the right to existence/security of all the states in the region, including Israel, and justice for all the peoples, including the Palestinian people.
Art. 5	The necessary guarantees for a peace settlement should be provided by the UNSC. The nine Member States declare that they are prepared to participate.
Art. 6	A just solution must finally be found to the Palestinian problem, which is not simply one of refugees. The Palestinian people must be placed in a position to exercise fully their right to self-determination.
Art. 7	The peace settlement which the nine Member States are endeavouring requires the involvement and support of all the parties concerned. The PLO will have to be associated with the negotiations.
Art. 8	The nine Member States stress that they will not accept any unilateral initiative designed to change the status of Jerusalem and that any agreement on the city's status should guarantee freedom of access for everyone to the Holy Places.
Art. 9	The nine Member States stress the need for Israel to put an end to the territorial occupation which it has maintained since the conflict of 1967, as it has done for part of Sinai. They are deeply convinced that the Israeli settlements constitute a serious obstacle to the peace process in the Middle East. The nine Member States consider that these settlements, as well as modifications in population and property in the occupied Arab territories, are illegal under international law.
Art. 10	The nine Member States consider that only the renunciation of force can create a climate of confidence in the area, and constitute a basic element for a comprehensive settlement of the conflict in the Middle East.
Art. 11	The nine Member States have decided to make the necessary contacts with all the parties concerned and in the light of the results of this consultation process determine the form which an initiative on their part could take.
Euro–Arab dialogue	The nine Member States note the importance which they attach to the Euro–Arab dialogue at all levels and the need to develop the advisability of holding a meeting of the two sides at the political level.
Lebanon	The nine Member States reiterate once again their total solidarity with Lebanon, a friendly country whose equilibrium is seriously jeopardized by the clashes in the region.

Camp David process, which had reached an impasse) (*Bulletin of the EC* 6-1980: 12). Jenkins went on to state that the Council had 'again achieved a considerable success in the field of political cooperation in a significant statement on the Middle East' (*Bulletin of the EC* 6-1980: 12). The Council's

President, Italy's Foreign Minister Emilio Colombo, stated that the Venice Declaration 'had come at the right moment to relaunch the dialogue' and 'in no way intended to obstruct the process set off by the Camp David agreements' (*Bulletin of the EC* 6-1980: 105). The *Bulletin* reported that the Venice Declaration was inspired by the principle of justice for all, which meant recognition both of Israel's right to existence and of the legitimate rights of the Palestinian people, which in turn implied the need for a process of self-determination and negotiation in which the PLO would have a part (*Bulletin of the EC* 6-1980: 103).

In the European Parliament, the spokespersons for the various groups took different views on the Venice Declaration. Sir James Scott-Hopkins (ED/UK) welcomed the 'Community's restatement, concerning the Middle East problem, of the principles universally accepted by the international community: the declaration of the Nine on the Middle East betrayed no one' (*Bulletin of the EC* 6-1980: 104). Jacques Denis of the Communist and Allies Group argued that France was backpedalling on the Middle East issue and was hiding behind the other Member States. 'If Europe spoke with one voice, then it was the voice of America', argued Denis (*Bulletin of the EC* 6-1980: 105). Martin Bangemann (Lib/D) contested the remarks of the spokesperson from the Communist and Allies Group and 'declared that the Community was under no allegiance' (*Bulletin of the EC* 6-1980: 105).

'The Thorn Mission'

The Venice Declaration became a platform to which the EC/EU often referred back, even decades later. In accordance with articles two and eleven, Gaston Thorn, President of the Council and of the EPC, was appointed to lead the EC's mission to consult with all the parties involved in the conflict, including the PLO. This became known as 'the Thorn mission' (*Bulletin of the EC* 11-1980: 13). A month after the Venice Declaration was issued, in July 1980, Gaston Thorn gave a long speech at the UNGA, where he said that the need to end the language of violence, the need for all parties to start talking to one another as equals, and the need to move from rhetoric to negotiations was the background context of the Venice Declaration (*Bulletin of the EC* 7/8-1980: 86). Thorn went on to state that there must be an end to ambiguities and a coming to terms with the realities, which were that both the State of Israel and the Palestinian people existed. The solution to the Middle Eastern problem, according to Thorn, lay 'in reconciling these two essential realities and enabling them to coexist' (*Bulletin of the EC* 7/8-1980: 86). Consequently, the two fundamental principles that ruled the nine Member States' search for a comprehensive peace settlement were, according to Thorn:

- the right to existence and security of all States in the region, including Israel;
- justice for all the peoples, which implies recognition of the legitimate rights of the Palestinian people. (*Bulletin of the EC* 7/8-1980: 86)

This was another development in the process of equalizing Israeli and Palestinian rights and claims: Israel's right to exist and live in security was now equal to the Palestinians' legitimate demands. In this speech, Thorn also stated that the Member States recognized that UNSC resolution 242 had 'shortcomings, particularly with regard to the Palestinian people, and they have made their attitude on that point known several times' (*Bulletin of the EC* 7/8-1980: 87). However, this was the first and only time that the *Bulletin* reported that the EC had reservations with UNSC resolution 242. Despite this, Thorn was clear that 'the basic principles set out in resolution 242 remain fundamentally relevant to any settlement of the conflict' (*Bulletin of the EC* 7/8-1980: 87). The nine Member States were, according to Thorn, 'convinced that no comprehensive and lasting peace settlement is possible in the Middle East if the occupation of territories by force continues' (*Bulletin of the EC* 7/8-1980: 86). But if a settlement was to be reached, it will be 'possible to define frontiers for the State of Israel which will be internationally recognized and guaranteed' (*Bulletin of the EC* 7/8-1980: 86). He finished his speech by saying that without explicit references to UNSC resolution 242 Israel would simply be 'exhorted and invited to negotiate without being offered the necessary guarantees for its existence' (*Bulletin of the EC* 7/8-1980: 86).

Thorn was back at the UNGA in September 1980 and gave another long speech on the Israeli–Arab conflict. He praised Israel's withdrawal from parts of Sinai in accordance with UNSC resolution 242, but noted, at the same time, that the Camp David process had 'so far not yielded the desired results, particularly with regard to the promotion of a fair, lasting and comprehensive peace settlement for all parties concerned, which is still our ultimate objective' (*Bulletin of the EC* 9-1980: 94). Referring to article eleven of the Venice Declaration, Thorn said that he had started making the necessary contacts with all the parties concerned, including meeting with PLO chairman Yasser Arafat in Tunis (*Bulletin of the EC* 9-1980: 95). This is the first mention in the *Bulletin* of an EC official meeting Arafat within an EC context. He also expressed hope that he would be able to meet with local Palestinian representatives in the occupied territories in a few days, but there are no reports in the *Bulletin* about whether these meetings actually took place. Thorn said that the aim of the consultations was 'to determine the form which a European initiative could take' (*Bulletin of the EC* 9-1980: 95). In the same speech, Thorn called on Israel to clearly demonstrate its intention to put an end to the territorial occupation it had maintained since the 1967 war. In the meantime, Thorn called on Israel to refrain from making any fait accompli in the form 'of installing further settlements, which can only raise new barriers in the search for an agreement' (*Bulletin of the EC* 9-1980: 96). He went on to call on the Arab countries and the Palestinians to explicitly recognize Israel's right to exist. Referring again to the Venice Declaration, Thorn said that the nine Member States sought to play their 'role to the full and make more material efforts to secure peace' (*Bulletin of the EC* 9-1980: 94). The aim was to 'work out guidelines and firm proposals which will mark the role of Europe in the search for and implementation of a peace settlement in the Middle East' (*Bulletin of the EC* 9-1980: 97). It was a bit vague what these guidelines, firm proposals and more material efforts might consist of, but Thorn declared the EC's 'readiness to participate within the context of an overall settlement in a system of concrete and binding international guarantees, including guarantees in the area itself' (*Bulletin of the EC* 9-1980: 94).

In December 1980, the *Bulletin* reported that Thorn's mission 'had made clear the great interest aroused by the position taken up by Europe and that in this respect it had been a success' (*Bulletin of the EC* 12-1980: 10). It further noted that in order to give substance to the Venice Declaration, Thorn had drafted a report on the principal problems related to a comprehensive settlement under the following headings: withdrawal, self-determination, security in the Middle East, and Jerusalem. According to this report, different formulas were possible to give substance to some of the Venice Declaration's articles, in particular on the duration of the transitional period leading up to the electoral procedure for self-determination, the definition of the provisional authority for the vacated territories, the conditions and modalities for self-determination, the guarantees of security, and Jerusalem (*Bulletin of the EC* 12-1980: 11). A year after the Venice Declaration was issued, in June 1981, the European Council concluded that the efforts undertaken by the now ten Member States 'to promote the conclusion of a peaceful settlement should be continued energetically and without respite' (*Bulletin of the EC* 6-1981: 9) The Council instructed the Foreign Ministers 'to elaborate further the practical possibilities available to Europe to make an effective contribution towards a comprehensive peace settlement in the Middle East' (*Bulletin of the EC* 6-1981: 10).

In early 1981, Egypt's President Anwar Sadat was invited to the European Parliament. The President of the Parliament, Simone Veil, said in her welcome speech that it 'was thanks to President Sadat that something which nobody thought possible had been achieved in the Middle East – the signing of a peace treaty between Israel and Egypt' (*Bulletin of the EC* 2-1981: 47). In his speech to the Parliament, Sadat said

> Egypt urges you to support their [the Palestinians] right to self-determination and national dignity . . . The establishment of a Palestinian entity, after a transitional period, would be a positive development to all countries in the region. It poses no threat to the security of Israel. In fact, it is the best guarantee for it . . . We should like you to participate with us in persuading both Israelis and Palestinians to accept a formula of mutual and simultaneous recognition . . . We invite you also to take part in additional security guarantees as a European contribution to peace in the Middle East. (*Bulletin of the EC* 2-1981: 48)

The *Bulletin* reported that Sadat's speech was met with a standing ovation in the Parliament (*Bulletin of the EC* 2-1981: 48).

When the President of the Council, the UK's Foreign Secretary Lord Carrington, spoke on behalf of the Community and its Member States at the UNGA on 22 September 1981, he said that 'the conflict which perhaps poses most dangers is the Arab/Israel dispute' (*Bulletin of the EC* 9-1981: 75). In line with the Venice Declaration, he also said that the Community 'believes that it has a distinctive role to play' in the conflict, and that it will 'energetically' promote a peace settlement (*Bulletin of the EC* 9-1981: 75). One of Europe's main aims, according to Lord Carrington, was to facilitate negotiations between the parties, complementing the efforts of others towards the same objective (*Bulletin of the EC* 9-1981: 75). Later in 1981, four Member States (France, Italy, The Netherlands and the United Kingdom) made public that they intended to participate in the multinational force in Sinai that would be deployed there following Israel's withdrawal. The *Bulletin* reported that the European participation met 'the wish frequently expressed by the members of the Community to facilitate any progress in the direction of a comprehensive peace settlement in the Middle East' (*Bulletin of the EC* 11-1981: 59). When the withdrawal took place in April 1982, it was welcomed by the EC, which considered it as 'an important step forward – not only for the development of peaceful relations between Israel and Egypt but also for efforts to achieve a peaceful settlement in the Middle East in accordance with Security Council Resolution 242' (*Bulletin of the EC* 4-1982: 48). Finally in 1981, following the Israeli government's annexation of the Golan Heights in December that year, the Foreign Ministers of the EC issued a harsh response:

> The Foreign Ministers of the Member States of the European Community strongly deplore the decision of the Government and Knesset of Israel to extend Israeli law, jurisdiction and administration to occupied Syrian territory in the Golan Heights. Such an extension, which is tantamount to annexation, is contrary to international law, and therefore invalid in our eyes. This step prejudices the possibility of the implementation of Security Council Resolution 242 and is bound to complicate further the search for a comprehensive peace settlement in the Middle East to which we remain committed. (*Bulletin of the EC* 12-1981: 69–70)

The *Bulletin* reported in March 1982 that the European Council had discussed developments in the Middle East and was 'deeply concerned by the grave events taking place in the West Bank' (*Bulletin of the EC* 3-1982: 20). The European Council 'appealed urgently for an end to the dangerous cycle of violence and repression' (*Bulletin of the EC* 3-1982: 20). It particularly denounced measures imposed on the Palestinian population such as the dismissal of democratically elected mayors by the Israeli authorities, as well as the violations of the liberties and rights of the inhabitants of these territories which followed the measures taken by Israel with regard to the Golan Heights, and which could only damage the prospects for peace, according to the Council (*Bulletin of the EC* 3-1982: 20). This was the first EC statement in the *Bulletin* that highlighted the situation for the Palestinian population living under Israeli rule in the occupied territories. Many similar statements would follow during the rest of the 1980s.

Resumption of the Euro–Arab Dialogue

The Euro–Arab dialogue, which had been in abeyance since April 1979, was resumed at a political-level meeting in Luxembourg in November 1980. The *Bulletin* reported that the last meeting of such importance was that held in Paris in July 1974 at the beginning of the dialogue (*Bulletin of the EC* 11-1980: 13). The aim of the Luxembourg meeting was to formulate general guidelines and ways of resuming the dialogue at all levels: political, economic, technical, financial, social and cultural. The *Bulletin* reported that the Arab side wanted the dialogue to be resumed on a more political basis, and the adoption by the EC of the Venice Declaration responded to that wish (*Bulletin of the EC* 11-1980: 14). The Arab delegation was led by Ahmad Sedki al Dajani, Member of the Executive Committee of the PLO and representing the current presidency of the Arab League. This was the first report in the *Bulletin* of PLO participation in the Euro–Arab dialogue. It was further proof that the PLO was being legitimized by the EC to participate in different types of negotiations, not just those concerned with the Israeli–Arab conflict. The *Bulletin* reported that the two sides took note of each other's explanatory statements concerning the conflict. The European side referred to the Venice Declaration and to Gaston Thorn's ongoing consultation mission. The nine Member States stressed the importance that the Venice Declaration 'attached to the Euro–Arab dialogue at all levels and the need to develop the political dimension thereof' (*Bulletin of the EC* 11-1980: 14). They also stressed 'Europe's desire to play a special role and to make a more positive contribution to the attainment of peace' (*Bulletin of the EC* 11-1980: 14).

The Arab side stressed that it wanted to develop the mutual interests of the two communities, with the objective of creating a close link between the economic relations and the political positions of the Community with regard to Arab problems and especially with regard to the central element, 'the Palestinian question' (*Bulletin of the EC* 11-1980: 14). In further emphasizing the centrality of the Palestinian question, the Arab side stressed three major issues it wanted addressing by the EC:

- The need for the EC to do whatever was necessary to implement the UN resolutions on the surrender by Israel of all the occupied Arab territories and on the national rights of the Palestinian people, including their right of return, self-determination, and the establishment of an independent state of their own.
- The need for the EC to persevere with its efforts to put an end to Israeli practices in the occupied Arab territories, including the annexation of Jerusalem, the establishment of settlements, the annexation of the Golan Heights, and the acts of aggression perpetrated against the Palestinian and Lebanese peoples.
- The recognition of the PLO by the EC as the sole legitimate representative of the Palestinian people will be an essential step in the efforts made to bring about a just and lasting peace in the Middle East. (*Bulletin of the EC* 11-1980: 15)

The *Bulletin* reported that the European side took note of these issues without responding to them (*Bulletin of the EC* 11-1980: 15).

Very little else happened with the Euro–Arab dialogue for the rest of the 1980s, despite the repeated willingness by the EC to see it relaunched. Slowly but steadily, it seemed that the EC–Gulf Cooperation Council (GCC) meetings took over parts of the roles the dialogue previously had had (see, for example *Bulletin of the EC* 10-1985: 63). After many years of inaction, the Euro–Arab dialogue was finally relaunched in 1990 with a new structure where the political part was separated from the other parts (*Bulletin of the EC* 6-1990: 97).

The 1982 Lebanon War

A civil war had raged in Lebanon since 1975 and there had been repeated clashes between Israel and Palestinian guerrilla/terror groups in Lebanon in the years leading up to the June 1982 Israeli invasion of Lebanon. The fighting in Lebanon had received a lot of attention in the *Bulletin* even before the 1982 Israeli invasion. For example, the nine Member States had in the Venice Declaration expressed 'their total solidarity with Lebanon, a friendly country whose equilibrium is seriously jeopardized by the clashes in the region' (*Bulletin of the EC* 6-1980: 11). It is widely recognized in the academic literature that the 1982 Lebanon war marked a negative turning point in Israel's international relations, primarily with the West.[1] This is clearly visible in the *Bulletin*, which had never before published declarations and other statements that were harshly critical of Israel's behaviour, in addition to the first small but concrete punishments by the EC against Israel.

The Israeli invasion of Lebanon was met with 'vigorous condemnation' by the European Council held on 28 and 29 June 1982, which further demanded 'an immediate withdrawal of Israeli forces from their positions around the Lebanese capital as a first step towards their complete withdrawal', and 'a simultaneous withdrawal of the Palestinian forces in West Beirut' (*Bulletin of the EC* 6-1982: 16). At a special meeting in Bonn on 9 June, which was held in direct response to the Israeli invasion three days earlier, the ten Member States stated that the Israeli invasion constituted 'a flagrant violation of international law and of the most basic humanitarian principles' (*Bulletin of the EC* 6-1982: 79). The Member States further called on Israel to withdraw its forces from Lebanon in accordance with UNSC resolution 508 and 509. Should Israel continue to refuse compliance with the two resolutions, the Member States would examine the possibilities for future action (*Bulletin of the EC* 6-1982: 79).

The European Council of 28–9 June 1982 further made a clear connection between Israel's invasion of Lebanon and the situation for the Palestinians by conveying to Israel that it would not obtain the security to which it has a right by using force and creating fait accomplis, but that it could only find this security by satisfying the legitimate aspirations of the Palestinian people (*Bulletin of the EC* 6-1982: 16). In further legitimizing the Palestinians, the European Council stated that the Palestinian people 'should have the opportunity to exercise their right to self-determination with all that this implies',

---

[1] See, for example Schiff and Ya'ari (1984: 218).

and that the Member States 'believe that for negotiations to be possible the Palestinian people must be able to commit themselves to them and thus to be represented at them' (*Bulletin of the EC* 6-1982: 16). It is also important to note that instead of condemning the Palestinian terrorism which had preceded the 1982 invasion and highlighting the PLO's involvement in it, the European Council called on the Palestinian people 'to pursue their demands by political means' (*Bulletin of the EC* 6-1982: 16).

In realizing its threats against Israel, the *Bulletin* reported in its June 1982 issue that the Heads of State or government had had a detailed discussion of the situation in Lebanon and agreed that the signing of the second Financial Protocol between the Community and Israel would be deferred, as would the next ministerial-level meeting of the EEC–Israel Cooperation Council. The President of the Council, Belgian Prime Minister Wilfred Martens, also stated that no Member States were to sell any military equipment to Israel at present (*Bulletin of the EC* 6-1982: 17). According to Martens, these were appropriate measures to take against Israel under the present circumstances (*Bulletin of the EC* 6-1982: 80). This was the first mention in the *Bulletin* of any kind of concrete punishment against Israel. Finally, the *Bulletin* reported that the ten Member States had 'made public the representations they had made to the Israeli government the previous week in an attempt to obtain assurances regarding Israel's immediate intentions in the region; these had failed to elicit a satisfactory reply' (*Bulletin of the EC* 6-1982: 80).

The European Parliament held what the *Bulletin* called 'a very lively debate' on Israel's invasion of Lebanon on 17 June 1982. It passed 'a resolution condemning both the armed action by Israeli troops and all the acts of terrorism against Israel which preceded it' (*Bulletin of the EC* 6-1982: 85). The *Bulletin* reported that the debate in the Parliament

> disclosed subtle differences, not to say contradictions, within one and the same Group . . . Speeches ranged from total condemnation of Israel's action to support for what was regarded as a riposte to terrorist harassment, other judgments being less emphatic. (*Bulletin of the EC* 6-1982: 85)

MEP Jean-Thomas Nordmann (Lib/F) remarked during the debate in the Parliament that the Israelis had not gone into an idyllic Lebanon but a country already wracked by Syrian occupation and Palestinian terrorists. The Israelis had invaded in self-defence, according to Nordmann. MEP Gerard Israel (EPD/F) reminded the House that the aim of the Palestinian organizations was to wipe Israel off the map. In language completely unacceptable by today's standards, the *Bulletin* published a statement by Raymonde Dury (Soc/B) who said that Israel could not solve the Palestinian problem by a 'final solution' (*Bulletin of the EC* 6-1982: 86).

In September 1982, the ten Member States expressed through the European Council 'their profound shock and revulsion at the massacre of Palestinian civilians in Beirut', which became known as the Sabra and Shatila massacre (*Bulletin of the EC* 9-1982: 53). Speaking on behalf of the Community at the UNGA in late September 1982, the President of the Council, Danish Foreign Minister Uffe Ellemann-Jensen, strongly condemned what he called 'this criminal act', and called for an 'authoritative inquiry into the circumstances of this incident' (*Bulletin of the EC* 9-1982: 74). He further stated that the Member States were 'horrified by the terrible suffering and damage which were inflicted upon Lebanon and its civil population' (*Bulletin of the EC* 9-1982: 73), but there was no mention in the *Bulletin* of any EC officials blaming Israel for involvement in the massacre or for being responsible for it. Underlining the centrality of the Palestinian issue for wider peace in the region, Ellemann-Jensen said that the events in Lebanon confirm that the need for a negotiated, comprehensive settlement of the Israeli–Arab conflict is more pressing than ever (*Bulletin of the EC* 9-1982: 74). These events furthermore confirmed, according to Ellemann-Jensen, 'that there can be no real peace or stability in the region unless also the legitimate rights of the Palestinian people are recognized' (*Bulletin of the EC* 9-1982: 74). He went on to say that the ten Member States 'do not believe it is either wise or just for Israel to seek to deny another people the right it claims for itself' (*Bulletin of the EC* 9-1982: 74).

The Equalizing and Legitimization Process Continues

The process of equalizing Israeli and Palestinian rights and demands continued and even expanded after the 1982 Lebanon war. In a long declaration published in September 1982, right after the Sabra and Shatila massacre, the EC stated:

The Ten remain convinced that two essential principles must be accepted and reconciled: the right to existence and security of all the States and justice for all the peoples. Our commitment to the right of Israel to live in security and peace is absolute and unwavering. So also is our commitment to the right of the Palestinian people to self-determination with all that this implies. (*Bulletin of the EC* 9-1982: 74)

The most basic Israeli demand for security was now equal to the most basic Palestinian demand for justice, while Israel's right to exist was now equal to the Palestinians' right to self-determination. Another such equalizing statement came in 1984, when the European Council stated that 'all the problems which exist between Israel and its neighbours must be resolved in accordance with the principles recognized by the international community, including non-recourse to the use of force and non-acquisition of territory by force' (*Bulletin of the EC* 3-1984: 79). These two principles: 'the principle of the non-use of force' (clearly meant for the Palestinians) and 'the non-acquisition of territory by the use of force' (clearly meant for Israel) were often mentioned by the EC during the 1980s (see, for example, *Bulletin of the EC* 9-1985: 109).

Speaking on behalf of the EC at the yearly UNGA meeting in 1985, Jacques Poos, Luxembourg's Foreign Minister and current President of the Council, bluntly addressed the parties of the Israeli–Arab conflict in stating that 'denial of the opponent's existence is an act of blindness and is an admission of a lack of strong desire for peace. Recognition by the parties of their mutual existence and rights is a matter of priority' (*Bulletin of the EC* 9-1985: 109). In the same speech, Poos told the Assembly that measures taken by Israel in the occupied territories, which were 'aimed at altering the legal, geographical and demographic structure of the territory, are contrary to international law' (*Bulletin of the EC* 9-1985: 109).

The Reagan and Fez Plans

Two new diplomatic initiatives were presented in the wake of the 1982 Lebanon war: the Reagan plan of 1 September 1982 and the Fez plan of 9 September.[2] The Reagan plan was a continuation of the Camp David

---

[2] The Reagan plan's official name was 'Address to the Nation on United States Policy for Peace in the Middle East'. It can be found at the Ronald Reagan Presidential Library, <https://

process and advocated self-government by the Palestinians in the West Bank and Gaza in association with Jordan, while the Fez plan was a Saudi-authored plan for peace which was adopted after the twelfth Arab Summit at Fez. The Fez plan advocated a PLO-led Palestinian state in the same territories, including Jerusalem, but excluding explicit recognition of Israel. The EC welcomed both these initiatives, especially the Fez plan, which was regarded by the EC 'as an expression of the unanimous will of the participants, including the PLO, to work for the achievement of a just peace in the Middle East encompassing all States in the area, including Israel' (*Bulletin of the EC* 9-1982: 53). The ten Member States called 'for a similar expression of a will to peace on the part of Israel' (*Bulletin of the EC* 9-1982: 53). Later in 1982, the European Council 'expressed its disappointment at the delay in grasping the political opportunity' provided by these two initiatives (*Bulletin of the EC* 12-1982: 12). It called upon each of the parties to cease to ignore UNSC resolutions and assume their international responsibilities (*Bulletin of the EC* 12-1982: 12). On behalf of the Community, the Danish Foreign Minister had travelled to Israel in late 1982 in order to inform the Israeli government of the damaging effects of its policy in the occupied territories, in particular regarding the establishment of settlements. The Foreign Minister also informed the Israeli government that the political impetus provided by the Reagan plan and the Arab Summit in Fez could be weakened if Israel showed no sign of flexibility (*Bulletin of the EC* 11-1982: 60).

In January 1983, the Council stated that it had started to notice 'a more realistic assessment by the parties concerned of the possibilities for settling the Arab–Israeli conflict' in the wake of the two initiatives (*Bulletin of the EC* 1-1983: 91). The Council noted that the Arab states had approved the principles of a negotiated peace at the Fez summit, and now 'a serious discussion has begun on how this principle is to be translated into specific action' (*Bulletin of the EC* 1-1983: 91).

The Brussels European Council of March 1983 stated that the Reagan

www.reaganlibrary.gov/research/speeches/90182d>. The Fez plan (also called King Fahd's plan) was originally an eight-point 1981 plan of King Fahd of Saudi Arabia. It can be found on the UNGA's website, <https://unispal.un.org/DPA/DPR/unispal.nsf/0/A65756251B75 F6AD852562810074E5F4>.

plan 'indicated a way to peace', and the Fez plan 'demonstrated a readiness for it'. The Council also welcomed the recent discussions between Jordan and the PLO, as well as the conclusions of the recent meeting of the Palestine National Council (the PLO's legislative body), which the Council stated 'can and should contribute to the peace process' (*Bulletin of the EC* 3-1983: 20). The ten Member States urged the Palestinian people and the PLO to 'seize the present opportunity by declaring themselves in favour of peace negotiations. This would be a major step forward, to which the Ten would expect all concerned to respond constructively' (*Bulletin of the EC* 3-1983: 21). The Council further stated that the Member States 'look to the Arab States to play their part by supporting those who seek a solution to the demands of the Palestinian people by political means' (*Bulletin of the EC* 3-1983: 21). It also stated that the efforts of the United States 'will continue to be indispensable to create the conditions in which negotiations can begin' (*Bulletin of the EC* 3-1983: 21). Perhaps most importantly, the Council stated:

> Above all the time has come for Israel to show that it stands ready for genuine negotiations on the basis of Security Council Resolutions 242 and 338, in the first place by refraining from enlarging existing settlements or creating new ones. These settlements are contrary to international law and a major and growing obstacle to peace efforts. (*Bulletin of the EC* 3-1983: 21)

There could be little doubt that the EC held Israel as primary responsible for the lack of will to negotiate around this time. Equally important to note is that it was the Reagan and Fez plans, not the Venice Declaration, that dominated the efforts towards peace negotiations in the years after Israel's invasion of Lebanon. But these plans were short-lived. In 1984, the Foreign Ministers of the ten Member States expressed

> their concern at the collapse of the hopes engendered in September 1982 by certain converging and promising peace initiatives [i.e. the Reagan and Fez plans] and they declare that the absence of all progress towards a negotiated solution since then exacerbates antagonisms and entrenches the positions of those who favour confrontation. (*Bulletin of the EC* 3-1984: 79)

The Aftermath of the 1982 Lebanon War

It is often forgotten today that the 1982 Lebanon war took place during a very intense phase of the Cold War with both superpowers backing their respective allies, mainly the United States backing Israel and the Soviet Union backing Syria. In light of this, it is not surprising that several strong EC statements in the wake of the Lebanon war emphasized the centrality of the Israeli–Arab conflict for peace in Europe and even for the whole world. In January 1983, the programme of the German Presidency stated that 'the Ten are aware of the fact that there is an indissoluble connection between peace in this region and their own security' (*Bulletin of the EC* 1-1983: 91). Six months later, the Greek Presidency of Council issued an even stronger statement, which stated that 'the Middle East situation could spark off a world conflagration, and should for that reason have our undivided attention'.

Economically, the punitive measures taken by the EC against Israel seemed not to have been too hard for Israel. A year after the Lebanon war began, in June 1983, the second EEC–Israel Financial Protocol was finally signed (*Bulletin of the EC* 6-1983: 95). At the same time, the European Parliament adopted a resolution on the unfreezing of financial relations with Israel (*Bulletin of the EC* 6-1983: 95). The key to this was 'the May 17 Agreement'[3] between Israel and Lebanon, which was welcomed by the European Council (*Bulletin of the EC* 6-1983: 23). The European Parliament referred to the May 17 Agreement as 'a key element of the Lebanese and Middle-East peace process' (*Bulletin of the EC* 6-1983: 112).

Politically, however, the ten Member States argued that 'a direct consequence of the stalemate in Lebanon' was that 'no progress has been made towards the solution of the broader Arab–Israeli conflict' (*Bulletin of the EC* 9-1983: 110). There were also several very strong statements against the Israeli settlements in the wake of the Lebanon war. The programme of the Greek Presidency of the Council bluntly stated that it did not believe 'that a viable peace is possible in this region, which is so sensitive and geographically

---

[3] The May 17 Agreement of 1983 was a US-brokered peace agreement between Israel and Lebanon, which included the terms of Israeli withdrawal from Lebanon. It collapsed because of several factors, including opposition from Syria and from within Lebanon.

so close to us . . . unless Israel evacuates all the Arab territories which it has occupied since 1967' (*Bulletin of the EC* 7/8-1983: 115). In a very strong statement against the Israeli settlements, Ioannis Kharalabopoulos, President of the Council and speaking on behalf of the Community at the UNGA in September 1983, said that

> in the interest of the search for peace, the Ten ask Israel to abandon its policy of gradual annexation and of unilaterally creating new facts in the occupied territories, in particular its settlement policy which is contrary to international law and a major and growing obstacle to peace efforts. (*Bulletin of the EC* 9-1983: 110)

Again, this is an example of terminology that the EU would not use today, even if the settlements are much more entrenched now than they were in the early 1980s. The language in the European Parliament against Israel's settlements was also very harsh during this time. A January 1983 report by MEP Jean Penders (EPP/NL) stated that 'the use of force and annexation was unacceptable as a means of gaining control of territory, which meant "No" to Israel's settlement policy in Gaza and on the West Bank' (*Bulletin of the EC* 1-1983: 55). By 135 votes to 25 with 32 abstentions, the Parliament adopted the Penders report with some slight amendments. Most notable was the one by MEP Joachim Seeler (Sod/D), which 'stipulated that Israel must immediately stop putting colonies of settlers into the occupied territories' (*Bulletin of the EC* 1-1983: 55).

In December 1983, the *Bulletin* reported that the General Committee of the Euro–Arab Dialogue held its fifth meeting in Athens on 14 December. The proceedings ended differently from the previous four meetings, since this time the two sides were unable to reach agreement on the text of the usual final communiqué with a political, technical and economic section (*Bulletin of the EC* 12-1983: 72). It is unclear to what extent, if any, the war in Lebanon impacted on this. The same issue of the *Bulletin* also reported that senior Israeli, PLO and Jordanian officials spoke at the European Parliament in December 1983. According to the *Bulletin*, 'the succession of distinguished visitors' from the Middle East 'came to remind Europe – represented by its Parliament – that it has a role to play independent of that of the superpowers' (*Bulletin of the EC* 12-1983: 91). This was also the first mention in the

Bulletin of a PLO official (Ibrahim Souss, the PLO representative in France) addressing the Parliament (*Bulletin of the EC* 12-1983: 91).

In December 1984, the European Council noted 'with satisfaction expressions of interest of both sides in a process of movement towards negotiations' and hoped 'that this declared interest will be further built on' (*Bulletin of the EC* 12-1984: 19). 'In order to find a lasting solution', declared the European Council, 'no amount of effort by third parties can be a substitute for direct negotiations among the parties themselves – the Arab States, Israel and the Palestinian people – which must recognize mutually each other's existence and rights' (*Bulletin of the EC* 12-1984: 19).

The 1985 Jordan–PLO Agreement

Hopeful and pessimistic statements regarding the Israeli–Arab conflict overlapped each other in the mid-1980s. In early 1985, a statement in the *Bulletin* said that the conflict was in 'total stagnation' (*Bulletin of the EC* 1-1985: 92). Yet despite this, the EC constantly reiterated how important it was for the EC to solve the conflict (see, for example, *Bulletin of the EC* 4-1985: 59). In June 1985, the *Bulletin* reported that the European Parliament had passed resolutions on recent events in the Middle East, which 'stressed the need for swift settlement of the Palestinian question, the essential prerequisite for restoring peace in the Middle East' (*Bulletin of the EC* 6-1985: 112). A possible chance to break the deadlock came in February 1985 when Jordan and the PLO reached an agreement on a five-point bid for joint action, which included advocating a complete Israeli withdrawal from the occupied territories, Palestinian self-determination within a confederation between Jordan and Palestine, but no recognition of Israel. The Foreign Ministers of the ten Member States welcomed the Jordan–PLO initiative as a 'step forward' (*Bulletin of the EC* 4-1985: 59). Later that year, in September 1985, the Member States stated that the Jordan–PLO agreement represented 'a ray of hope' (*Bulletin of the EC* 9-1985: 109) and was 'an important step towards a peaceful and comprehensive solution to the Israeli–Arab conflict' (*Bulletin of the EC* 9-1985: 78). The ten Member States, moreover, believed that any movement in favour of a peaceful settlement of the conflict should be encouraged (*Bulletin of the EC* 9-1985: 109). In two resolutions in October 1985, the European Parliament called on the Council to launch an appropriate EC initiative for peace in conflict, based on the Jordanian–Palestinian proposal. Peace was the only way to halt the tragic spiral of terrorism and reprisals, according to the resolutions (*Bulletin of the EC* 10-1985: 85–6). A rare condemnation of Arab/Palestinian terrorism against Israel also appeared in the *Bulletin* after the December 1985 attacks (presumably by the Abu Nidal organization) on the airports in Rome and Vienna, which killed eighteen plus four terrorists. In the condemnation, the ten Member States noted that

> only a fair, lasting and global solution to the Middle East question, for which the Ten, Spain and Portugal have repeatedly stressed the need, can end the climate of tension in the region, which is giving rise to the acts of terrorism and violence. Efforts to find such a solution must be pursued unremittingly. (*Bulletin of the EC* 12-1985: 110)

An 'International Peace Conference' on the Conflict

Another idea that saw the light in the mid-1980s was that an international conference on the conflict could make a major contribution towards peace. It was first mentioned in the *Bulletin* in September 1986 and became mainstreamed from 1987 onwards (*Bulletin of the EC* 9-1986: 115). In February 1987, the twelve Foreign Ministers issued a declaration where they stated that they were in favour of an international peace conference to be held under the auspices of the UN with the participation of the parties concerned and of any party able to make a direct and positive contribution to the restoration and maintenance of peace in the region. The Foreign Ministers, moreover, stated that they believed that this conference should provide a suitable framework for the necessary negotiations between the parties directly concerned (*Bulletin of the EC* 2-1987: 91). In July 1987, the Foreign Ministers stated that 'such a conference seemed to them at present the only formula which would allow the peace process in the region to move forward' (*Bulletin of the EC* 7/8-1987: 102). At the yearly UNGA speech in September 1987, the EC's representative, Danish Foreign Minister Ellemann-Jensen, said that the Israeli–Arab conflict lay 'at the heart of continuing tension in the Near East' (*Bulletin of the EC* 9-1987: 110). He called 'upon the parties involved in the Arab/Israeli conflict to open the doors to peace by recognizing each other's rights' (*Bulletin of the EC* 9-1987: 110). He also said that the Foreign Ministers would 'do all in our power' to bring the parties closer in order to allow for such an international conference to be held (*Bulletin of the EC* 9-1987: 110). In December 1987, the Member States welcomed 'the endorsement given to such a conference by the Arab League Summit in Amman under the chairmanship of King Hussein of Jordan' (*Bulletin of the EC* 12-1987: 105). The EC's calls for an international conference to negotiate peace in the Israeli–Arab conflict continued all the way up until 1991, when such a conference was finally held in Madrid.

Increased EC Attention to the Situation in the Occupied Territories

Throughout the 1980s, the *Bulletin* routinely reported on EC support for UNRWA, but this support almost never got a prominent place in the European Council's statements, in the Foreign Ministers' statements, or when top Member States officials spoke on behalf of EC at the UNGA. A new trend emerged in the mid-1980s whereby the local situation for the Palestinians living under Israeli military rule in the occupied territories was given much more attention by the EC. At the beginning of 1984, the Foreign Ministers had stressed 'their wish to develop the activity of the European Community on behalf of the populations of the occupied territories' (*Bulletin of the EC* 3-1984: 80). From 1986 onwards, this new trend became very apparent in the *Bulletin*. In March 1986, the *Bulletin* condemned the murder of the Israel-appointed Mayor of Nablus (*Bulletin of the EC* 3-1986: 74). In September 1986, speaking on behalf of the Community at the UNGA, Sir Geoffrey Howe, the UK's Foreign Secretary and President of the Council, directly addressed the situation in the occupied territories:

> The Twelve are working individually and collectively to help development in the Occupied Territories. We call on Israel, pending its withdrawal in accordance with SCR 242, to fulfil scrupulously its obligations as the occupying power and to ease restrictions on political activity and economic development. But such measures must be a prelude to, not a substitute for, true peace negotiations. (*Bulletin of the EC* 9-1986: 115)

The following month, the *Bulletin* reported that the Council had adopted a proposal from the Commission to help the Palestinians living in the West Bank and Gaza Strip. These measures involved financial assistance and trade arrangements. The financial assistance, which totalled some ECU 3 million,[4] was intended primarily for small job-creating projects, training projects, and for improving the operation of local Palestinian institutions. Regarding trade with the occupied territories, the Community was to extend preferential arrangements to products from these territories similar to those granted for products from certain Mediterranean non-member countries, meaning duty-free access to the Community's market for industrial products and preferential treatment for certain agricultural products (*Bulletin of the EC* 10-1986: 70).

In February 1987, the Foreign Ministers of the twelve Member States issued a declaration where they stated that they wished 'to see an improvement in the living conditions of the inhabitants of the occupied territories, particularly regarding their economic, social, cultural, and administrative affairs' (*Bulletin of the EC* 2-1987: 91). The Foreign Ministers recalled again in the July/August 1987 issue of the *Bulletin*

> their commitment to the respect of human rights in the occupied territories. They agreed that the deterioration of the economic and social situation in these territories, as well as in the region as a whole, threatens to complicate the search for peace. For this reason, the Twelve will continue to contribute to economic and social development, although this cannot be a substitute for a political solution. (*Bulletin of the EC* 7/8-1987: 102)

Three million more ECU to the occupied territories, including to UNRWA, was approved by the EC in July 1987 (*Bulletin of the EC* 7/8-1987: 97). At the yearly UNGA speech in September 1987, Danish Foreign Minister Ellemann-Jensen said that the twelve Member States were 'increasingly concerned about the situation of human rights in the Occupied Territories' (*Bulletin of the EC* 9-1987: 110). The aid from the EC was designed to allow the Palestinians 'to enjoy the fruits of normal economic development', according to Ellemann-Jensen (*Bulletin of the EC* 9-1987: 110). The September 1987 issue of the *Bulletin* also included the first protest by the

---

[4] Replacing the previous European Unit of Account, the European Currency Unit (ECU) was a basket of currencies of some EC Member States that was itself replaced by the euro on 1 January 1999. In 1987, 1 ECU was roughly equivalent to 1 USD.

twelve Foreign Ministers against the establishment of a particular settlement (Avnei Hefetz) in the West Bank (*Bulletin of the EC* 9-1987: 74). The Foreign Ministers stated that

> the opening of new settlements as well as the disturbing increase of the number of settlers in existing settlements pose a serious risk of jeopard-izing the prospects for peace. They consider that every new and every existing settlement is in violation of international law and call upon the Israeli Government to put an end to the illegal policy of settlements in the Occupied Territories. (*Bulletin of the EC* 9-1987: 74)

In November 1987, the European Parliament called for the immediate release of Faisal Husseini, President of the Society of Arab Studies (and later Arafat's 'unofficial Foreign Minister'), together with 'all other prisoners of conscience' held by Israel (*Bulletin of the EC* 10-1987: 86). The same issue of the *Bulletin* also reported that progress was made in talks with Israel on the possibility of Palestinian producers exporting to the Community under the preferential arrangements established (*Bulletin of the EC* 10-1987: 62).

The First Intifada

After the outbreak of the first intifada in December 1987, the Member States 'called upon the Israeli authorities to assure the immediate protection of the inhabitants of the occupied territories, in compliance with interna-tional law and human rights standards' (*Bulletin of the EC* 12-1987: 106). At first, the EC referred to the uprising as 'a dangerous new situation in the Arab—Israeli conflict' (*Bulletin of the EC* 1-1988: 92). Almost every month in the following three years, the *Bulletin* included statements by the EC on the developments in the occupied territories. There was massive and persistent criticism in the *Bulletin* against Israeli human rights abuses of Palestinians in the occupied territories, more so than in any period before or after. The criticism included:

- concerns regarding Israel's 'policy of deportation in the occupied territo-ries' (*Bulletin of the EC* 1-1988: 49);
- deeply deploring 'the repressive measures taken by Israel' (*Bulletin of the EC* 2-1988: 79);

- 'the destruction of houses which is in clear contradiction of international law' (*Bulletin of the EC* 4-1988: 73);
- the closure 'of the Palestinian press service, which has been an important source of information for those concerned with developments in the occupied territories. The Twelve believe that suppression of facts and restrictions on the freedom of the media will endanger the search for a negotiated solution in the region' (*Bulletin of the EC* 4-1988: 73);
- mistreatment in prison – where more than 10,000 Palestinians were being detained for political reasons, according to the European Parliament (*Bulletin of the EC* 10-1988: 81);
- 'serious concern about the persistence of the Israeli authorities in their decision to keep the schools closed in the West Bank, including the UNRWA schools' (*Bulletin of the EC* 5-1989: 76). This was further referred to by the *Bulletin* as 'Israel's education ban in the West Bank' (*Bulletin of the EC* 5-1989: 78);
- calling on Israel to implement UNSC resolution 605, 607 and 608 and to respect the provisions of the Geneva Convention on the protection of civilian populations in times of war (*Bulletin of the EC* 6-1989: 16);
- 'the consequent loss of life, impoverishment and violation of the most elementary rights of the [Palestinian] population' (*Bulletin of the EC* 1/2-1990: 149);
- that Israel had failed to adhere to the Fourth Geneva Convention (*Bulletin of the EC* 6-1990: 23), and calls on Israel to 'fulfil scrupulously its obligations as an occupying power, in accordance with the Geneva Convention of 12 August 1949' (*Bulletin of the EC* 9-1988: 108);
- a resolve from the Member States to step up their already significant support for the protection of the human rights of the population living in the occupied territories (*Bulletin of the EC* 6-1990: 22–3);
- 'use of excessive force by the Israeli occupying forces in repressing Palestinian demonstrations' (*Bulletin of the EC* 10-1990: 98);
- 'repeated violations of international law' (*Bulletin of the EC* 10-1990: 98);
- deploring 'the recent decision to place moderate Palestinians under administrative arrest' (*Bulletin of the EC* 12-1990: 15).

A consequence of Israel's behaviour during the first intifada was that the European Parliament initially refused to give its assent to three pending EC–Israel protocols: one on financial cooperation, one on agricultural products, and one on EC–Israel relations after accession of Spain and Portugal to the Community. The *Bulletin* reported that the debate in the Parliament was very heated with accusations of double standards against Israel, over-politization of the debate, and failure to keep technical problems and political issues apart (*Bulletin of the EC* 3-1988: 109–12). The European Parliament finally gave its consent to the three protocols later in 1988 (*Bulletin of the EC* 10-1988: 66), but the *Bulletin* continued to express 'concern that Israel was not correctly applying the provisions agreed with the Community for the direct export to the Community and the marketing of Palestinian products' (*Bulletin of the EC* 12-1989: 89). According to the *Bulletin*, the European Parliament did not exclude suspension of economic cooperation between the Community and Israel because of these problems (*Bulletin of the EC* 12-1989: 89).

Besides the condemnations of Israeli human rights abuses, the first intifada also led the EC to become much more involved on the ground in the occupied territories, primarily through substantially increasing its aid to the Palestinians. In several statements during the intifada, the EC declared its willingness to improve the living conditions for the population of the occupied territories through direct imports and the encouragement of development projects (see, for example, *Bulletin of the EC* 6-1988: 180). This set in motion a long and complicated discussion that is still ongoing today on Palestinian exports and 'originating products' from the West Bank and Gaza. This discussion had begun before the intifada (*Bulletin of the EC* 9-1986: 75, 10-1986: 70, 12-1986: 51) and is the root of the differentiation strategy. The question of originating products was one of the reasons why the European Parliament had initially rejected the three EC–Israel protocols, one of which directly concerned this question (*Bulletin of the EC* 3-1988: 109–12).

The Strasbourg European Council of December 1989 pledged to increase EC aid to UNRWA and double direct aid to the Palestinians during the coming years, 1990–2 (*Bulletin of the EC* 12-1989: 15). The *Bulletin* reported that the Community had contributed more than ECU 388 million to UNRWA since 1971 and ECU 23 million in direct aid to the Palestinians since 1981 (*Bulletin of the EC* 12-1989: 15). With the aid, the EC intended to 'preserve the common future of the Palestinian people' by contributing to the economic and social development of the occupied territories, mainly in the areas of health and education, as well as by support for local Palestinian institutions (*Bulletin of the EC* 12-1989: 15). In early 1990, the *Bulletin* reported that the programme of direct access for Palestinian produce to the Community market appeared to be working satisfactorily, although there had been some incidents of administrative hurdles being placed in its way by the Israeli authorities (*Bulletin of the EC* 1/2-1990: 149). No statistics are available in the *Bulletin* as to how much the Palestinians really exported to the EC during this period.

'Land for Peace' and Mutual Recognition

The PLO's acceptance of UNSC resolutions 242 and 338 in November 1988, which implied acceptance of the right of existence and security for Israel, was warmly welcomed by the EC, as were the PLO's explicit condemnation of terrorism and the United States government's decision to open up a dialogue with the PLO (*Bulletin of the EC* 11-1988: 88, 12-1988: 139). In the Madrid Declaration of June 1989, considered by the EC to be its 'most important advance since the Venice Declaration' (*Bulletin of the EC* 7/8-1989: 139), the EC stated for the first time that the peace negotiations should be based on a 'land for peace' principle (*Bulletin of the EC* 6-1989: 17). For the first time in a couple of years, a European Council declaration spoke of 'favourable circumstances' for negotiations and peace between the parties (*Bulletin of the EC* 6-1989: 16). Together with the 'land for peace' principle, the Madrid Declaration also included mutual recognition, the other keystone of the Oslo peace process:

> The European Council launches a solemn appeal to the parties concerned to seize the opportunity to achieve peace. Respect by each of the parties for the legitimate rights of the other should facilitate the normalizing of relations between all the countries of the region. The European Council calls upon the Arab countries to establish normal relations of peace and cooperation with Israel and asks that country in turn to recognize the right of the Palestinian people to exercise self-determination. (*Bulletin of the EC* 6-1989: 17)

The Israeli–Arab Conflict in the New World Order

The last two years of the 1980s, as well as 1990 and 1991, saw a lot of diplomatic activity from the EC vis-à-vis the Israeli–Arab conflict, which the coding schedule at the end of this book clearly attests to. These were indeed tumultuous years, from the fall of the Berlin wall in November 1989, to Iraq's invasion of Kuwait in 1990, to the Gulf war in 1991. The first consequence of this new world order for the conflict was the liberation of Soviet Jewry, many of whom emigrated to Israel. While the Community warmly welcomed the liberalization of Soviet emigration controls, alarm bells were immediately set off in the EC that new immigrants may be housed in settlements in the occupied territories, which the EC was strongly against (*Bulletin of the EC* 1/2-1990: 98). The next month, March 1990, the *Bulletin* referred to the settlements as 'Israel's colonization policy in the occupied territories' (*Bulletin of the EC* 3-1990: 58). A second consequence of the new world order was that Iraq's invasion of Kuwait, according to a statement from the Foreign Ministers, 'delayed the search for progress towards a solution to other problems of the region, such as the Arab–Israeli conflict, the Palestinian problem and the situation in Lebanon' (*Bulletin of the EC* 9-1990: 79). As it often had done in crisis situations in the Middle East, the EC responded to Iraq's invasion of Kuwait by stating that it was determined to multiply its efforts aimed at resolving the other conflicts of the region, most notably the Israeli–Arab conflict (*Bulletin of the EC* 9-1990: 83). After Saddam Hussein launched Scud missiles at Israel in January 1991, the Member States responded by calling the attacks 'non-provoked and entirely unjustified' (*Bulletin of the EC* 1/2-1991: 105). They went on to state that 'Israel's right to security constitutes one of the fundamental principles of the policy of the Community and its Member States in the Middle East' (*Bulletin of the EC* 1/2-1991: 105). The day after the missile attack against Israel, the Member States issued another declaration where they stated that 'the Community and its Member States believe that the Arab–Israeli conflict and the Palestinian question are fundamental sources of instability in the region' (*Bulletin of the EC* 1/2-1991: 107). In April 1991, the Council presented what it believed were the three conditions needed for peace and stability in the region:

1. A solution to the Israeli–Arab conflict and the Palestinian question.
2. Greater democratic legitimacy of governments.
3. Economic development with reduced disparities in income levels. (*Bulletin of the EC* 4-1991: 46)

In May 1991, when things were set in motion for a diplomatic breakthrough, the EC was fully supportive of the initiative of US Secretary of State James Baker to launch substantive negotiations between the parties (*Bulletin of the EC* 5-1991: 83). Baker's initiative coincided with the establishment of new Israeli settlements, which led the EC to issue several strong statements against them, stating in May 1991 that 'Jewish settlements in the territories occupied by Israel since 1967, including East Jerusalem, are illegal under international law and under the fourth Geneva Convention in particular' (*Bulletin of the EC* 5-1991: 83). The Member States added that they also considered 'that any establishment of new settlements in the Occupied Territories, which is in any case illegal, is especially harmful' (*Bulletin of the EC* 5-1991: 83). In June 1991, the European Council singled out the issue of the settlements when it stated:

> It believes specifically that the policy of establishing settlements in the territories occupied by Israel, which is in any case illegal, is incompatible with the will expressed to make progress with the peace process. (*Bulletin of the EC* 6-1991: 16)

At the yearly meeting of the UNGA in September 1991, the representative for the EC, Dutch Foreign Minister Hans van den Broek, said that

> in a number of regional conflicts we can discern there are rays of hope. Bringing about peace in the Middle East is now an urgent task. In particular this is true of the Arab–Israeli conflict and the Palestinian question. (*Bulletin of the EC* 9-1991: 90)

Van den Broek went on to state that the Community had from the outset supported the initiative of the US to set in motion a process of parallel negotiations between Israel and its Arab neighbours and between Israel and the Palestinians. He urged all parties not to miss this historical opportunity to have a peace conference convened and added that the Community and its

Member States would actively contribute to make a success of the upcoming peace conference, which was held the next month in Madrid (*Bulletin of the EC* 9-1991: 90). It was more than five years after the EC had started advocating for it.

Conclusions

The 1980s certainly witnessed many ups and downs regarding the Israeli–Arab conflict and the EC's involvement in it. The decade began with the optimism of the Camp David process, the Israel–Egypt peace treaty, and the Venice Declaration. However, the optimism soon faded with the Israeli invasion of Lebanon, which led to massive criticism from the EC. The conflict continued to be stalemated during the mid-1980s until the outbreak of the first intifada in 1987, which again led to massive criticism from the EC against Israel. But amid all the criticism of Israel, it is important to also highlight that Israel's right to exist and to exist in peace and security were mentioned in basically all EC declarations, even the ones most critical of Israel's behaviour. In the late 1980s, there was a remarkable shift in tone in the EC's declarations from hopelessness to rays of hope. The 'new world order' brought about by the end of the Cold War opened up new possibilities for the Israeli–Arab conflict. Many of the ideas that the EC had long advocated for, such as negotiations with the PLO, having the PLO recognizing Israel, an international conference on the conflict, a peace process based on a land for peace formula, suddenly materialized at the end of the 1980s and the beginning of the 1990s. In the 1980 Venice Declaration, the EC had sought a 'special role' for itself in the Israeli–Arab conflict, which required the Member States 'to work in a more concrete way towards peace' (*Bulletin of the EC* 6-1980: 10). By the end of the 1980s and early 1990s, it was clear that the EC had five distinct roles to play in the conflict:

- it was a major normative power in the conflict;
- it was a major financer to the Palestinians;
- it was a major trading partner to Israel;
- it was probably the most enthusiastic supporter of the peace process;
- it was becoming more and more involved on the ground in the occupied territories.

At the same time, it is also important to emphasize what the EC was not: it was not an actor that led the high-level negotiations between the parties, it had no military power in the conflict, and it used mostly carrots and almost never any sticks in its diplomacy towards the parties.

4

1991–2000:
PEACE THROUGH REGIONAL
COOPERATION

The future will show that he was right . . . May his example remain the inspiration for those who will persist on the path to lasting peace in the Middle East. By doing so, they will pay the strongest tribute to Prime Minister Rabin's achievement. They can count on the strong and continuing support of the European Union. (Jacques Santer, President of the European Commission, quoted in *Bulletin of the EU* 11-1995: 81)

The Oslo peace process was a period of great hope and perhaps even bigger frustrations for all parties involved in the Israeli–Arab conflict, including for the EC/EU. Six major and several minor agreements were signed between Israel and the PLO during the Oslo peace process of the 1990s: the 1993 Declaration of Principles (DoP), the 1994 Gaza–Jericho Agreement, the 1995 Oslo II Agreement, the 1997 Hebron Protocol, the 1998 Wye River Agreement and the 1999 Sharm el-Sheikh Memorandum. In retrospect, it is clear that these were not real peace agreements: rather, they were agreements of intent, interim agreements or agreements on implementing previous agreements, on the way to a full-scale agreement. This however, did not stop the EC and later the EU from describing some of them, at the time when they were signed, as more than they were, or at least came to be. While the Israeli–Palestinian conflict was always at the heart of the Oslo peace process, it is almost forgotten today that the peace process of the

1990s also had a Jordanian, a Syrian, a Lebanese, and a multilateral track, of which only the Jordanian was successful. From the beginning of the peace process, the EC emphasized 'the need for interregional cooperation to help make the peace process irreversible' (*Bulletin of the EC* 9-1993: 57). The Commission also underlined the need for outside third parties to support the peace process, 'particularly the Community, which could have a major role to play because of its geopolitical situation, its close links with all the parties concerned and its own experience of regional cooperation' (*Bulletin of the EC* 9-1993: 58). The spirit of the time was indeed regional cooperation in what was often at the time referred to as 'the new Middle East'.[1]

The Madrid Peace Conference

The EC regarded the Madrid peace conference, which took place between 30 October and 1 November 1991, as 'an unprecedented opportunity to create peace between Israel and the Arabs' (*Bulletin of the EC* 10-1991: 87). It was a 'historical opportunity' not to be missed, according to the EC (*Bulletin of the EC* 9-1991: 90). The Community and its Member States gave their full support to the conference and sought to play an active role in it alongside the co-sponsors, the US and the USSR (*Bulletin of the EC* 10-1991: 87). The *Bulletin* reported that two subsequent phases were planned for the conference: a series of bilateral negotiations between the direct protagonists, followed by multilateral negotiations in which the Community had been allotted a leading role, according to the *Bulletin* (*Bulletin of the EC* 10-1991: 71). In the Community's view, the multilateral negotiations had a dual purpose: (1) from the economic viewpoint, to make efficient use of the region's assets to provide a basis for new forms of regional solidarity; (2) from a political viewpoint, to back up the bilateral negotiations by creating a climate of confidence, which would facilitate the bilateral process by taking stock of mutual interest and working out common approaches (*Bulletin of the EC* 10-1991: 71).

In a declaration issued a month after the Madrid conference, in December 1991, the European Council stated that the bilateral and multilateral agendas

---

[1] See, for example, Peres (1993). At an EEC–Israel Cooperation Council in January 1993, Peres, in his capacity of being Israel's Foreign Minister, argued for establishing, in due course, a common market in the Middle East region (*Bulletin of the EC* 1/2-1993: 71).

should go hand in hand, each one reinforcing the other. It also noted that regional cooperation cannot progress faster than movement towards a political settlement (*Bulletin of the EC* 12-1991: 11). The same declaration also suggested what was a common EC confidence-building idea around the time: an Israeli settlement freeze in return for a renunciation of the Arab boycott against Israel (*Bulletin of the EC* 12-1991: 10; see also *Bulletin of the EC* 10-1991: 87). With regards to the situation in the occupied territories, the declaration noted that the levels of violence had gone down after the Madrid conference, and that an 'atmosphere of hope' had been created in the occupied territories and elsewhere as a result of the conference (*Bulletin of the EC* 12-1991: 11).

The Madrid conference started a process of bilateral and multilateral meetings between the parties in Washington and Moscow. The EC took part in the inaugural meeting for the multilateral negotiations in Moscow in January 1991, but it is unclear exactly how important the EC's role was in the multilateral negotiations. There are very few reports in the *Bulletin* on how the multilateral negotiations proceeded, which is probably an indication that they did not go very well, and that the EC's role was more aspirational than real. Around this time, there were many declarations in the *Bulletin* emphasizing the importance the EC attached to the peace process. In December 1991, the European Council stated that it was determined 'to undertake all possible efforts' to support the peace process (*Bulletin of the EC* 12-1991: 10). The next month, January 1992, a joint statement said that 'the Community and its Member States will not spare any efforts to provide their good offices if requested by the parties involved themselves' (*Bulletin of the EC* 1/2-1992: 111). This statement went on to say that

> the achievement of lasting peace in the region is of vital importance for Europe. This is why the Community and its Member States are fully committed to playing a consistent role in this process, bearing in mind that the Middle East is a neighbouring region, with which Europe has long-standing political, historical, cultural, economic and commercial ties, and whose stability and security are essential to Europe's own stability and security. (*Bulletin of the EC* 1/2-1992: 111)

The same issue of the *Bulletin* also included a European Parliament resolution which asked the Commission to ensure that funds provided to Israel from the EC were not used to finance new building in the occupied territories (*Bulletin of the EC* 1/2-1992: 87). In June 1992, the European Council reaffirmed its support for the peace process, which it considered to be 'of paramount importance for the world and Europe in particular' (*Bulletin of the EC* 6-1992: 23).

During this time, the EC repeatedly called upon the members of the Arab League to lift the boycott against Israel, which it said was incompatible with the spirit of the peace process (*Bulletin of the EC* 6-1992: 23). There was also relatively little criticism of Israel for human rights violations during 1992–3 with one exception: Israel's deportation to south Lebanon of 415 Palestinian residents of the occupied territories in December 1992, which the EC said was in violation of the Fourth Geneva Convention and an infringement of the sovereignty of Lebanon (*Bulletin of the EC* 12-1992: 148). The European Parliament called on the Commission and the Council to use the implementation of the financial protocol within the EEC–Israel cooperation agreement to put pressure on the Israeli government to allow all the expelled Palestinians to return in accordance with UNSC resolution 799 (*Bulletin of the EC* 1/2-1993: 88). A senior Commission official, Peter Schmidhuber, responded that the 'Commission would do everything possible to influence Israel's position without actually adopting economic sanctions at this stage' (*Bulletin of the EC* 1/2-1993: 102).

The 1993 Declaration of Principles

The DoP was welcomed by a flurry of diplomatic activity from the various EC institutions, all of whom were very supportive of the agreement. The President of the European Commission, Jacques Delors, was the first EC official to comment on the DoP, a few days before the actual signing of the agreement in Washington:

> All of us at the European Commission are delighted to welcome the agreement on mutual recognition between Israel and the PLO. It is a major step towards lasting peace in the Middle East and lays the ground for Palestinian autonomy in the Gaza Strip and Jericho. The European Community has already expressed its admiration for the farsightedness and the courage shown by the leaders of the Israeli and Palestinian peoples who have set this

historic process in motion and I have spoken to Shimon Peres about the aid we can provide to help the peace process. The Commission is already working on practical proposals to demonstrate the Community's political, financial and economic commitment in the short, medium and long term. Everything must be done to create an area of peace, mutual understanding and cooperation in the region. (*Bulletin of the EC* 9-1993: 58)

In a joint statement published on the day of the signing, the EC and its Member States paid 'tribute to the vision and courage of the Israeli and Palestinian leaders who signed this historic agreement', which represented 'a positive breakthrough in the peace process' (*Bulletin of the EC* 9-1993: 78). The quickly expanding peace process and the EU's growing role in it meant, among other things, that the European Commission now became much more involved than before in the EC's diplomacy in the region, something which is clearly visible in the *Bulletin*. One of the first roles for the EC in the peace process was to chair the Regional Economic Development Working Group (REDWG). The Commission immediately started examining the conditions for successful regional cooperation involving Israel, the occupied territories, Egypt, Jordan, Lebanon and Syria. It also started examining the role that the Community and its Member States should play to promote such cooperation and the prospects for triangular relations between the Community, Israel and the Mashreq region. The Commission underlined the importance of developing interdependence between the various parties involved, developing appropriate institutions and a free trade area in the region, as well as strengthening the peace settlement with bilateral and multilateral Israeli–Arab cooperation agreements (*Bulletin of the EC* 9-1993: 57–8).

Financing the Peace Process and Palestinian Self-rule

On the same day as the DoP was signed, 13 September 1993, the Council approved the Commission's decision to grant ECU 20 million to the occupied territories. The sum would be used to help establish the necessary administrative structures in Jericho and the Gaza Strip, particularly in the education and health spheres, to set up small businesses, and to provide food aid (*Bulletin of the EC* 9-1993: 58). Two weeks after the DoP was signed, the Commission had examined how the Community could best contribute to the success of the peace process. It set up two objectives: (1) to help bring about a satisfactory level of economic development in the occupied territories; and (2) to give active support to the economic development of the region as a whole (*Bulletin of the EC* 9-1993: 59). The Commission earmarked ECU 500 million for the occupied territories for the period 1994–8, and as the main financial contributor to the occupied territories, the Commission believed that the Community would have a decisive role to play in donor coordination (*Bulletin of the EC* 9-1993: 59). The European Parliament welcomed this financial commitment to the peace process, but underlined the need to involve Arab states in these plans and the importance of the Euro–Arab dialogue (*Bulletin of the EC* 9-1993: 59). When Yasser Arafat visited the Commission in Brussels in November 1993, it was decided that the Community's sole partner with regard to reconstruction in the occupied territories would be the Palestinian Council for Reconstruction and Development (*Bulletin of the EC* 11-1993: 73). The *Bulletin* reported that Arafat thanked the Community for its aid to the Palestinian people. He also 'said that the Community's early years served as an example and a source of inspiration for the future of regional cooperation in the Middle East' (*Bulletin of the EC* 11-1993: 73).

At the Brussels European Council, held on 29 October 1993, it was decided that the EU should use its political, economic and financial means to support the peace process (*Bulletin of the EC* 10-1993: 8). Two months later, the European Council had identified seven areas as suitable for EU initiatives to be implemented. The most important were:

- Participating in international arrangements in support of a peace settlement in the framework of the process initiated in Madrid.
- Strengthening the democratic process, including through assistance, if requested, with the preparation and monitoring of the elections to be held in the autonomous Palestinian Territories.
- Consolidating peace through building regional cooperation. The Union''s efforts would be channelled in particular through the multilateral working groups on regional economic development, arms control, and regional security.
- Supporting the Palestinian Interim Self-Government Authority to be established under the Israeli–PLO Agreement through the rapid, efficient

and transparent implementation of European Union aid programmes for the development of the occupied territories. As the largest donor of aid to the Palestinians, the EU would play an important role in the Ad Hoc Liaison Committee, coordinating international aid to the occupied territories. (*Bulletin of the EC* 12-1993: 13)

There is no aggregated figure in the *Bulletin* for how much money the EU pumped into the Palestinians during the peace process. A report in the July/ August 1996 issue of the *Bulletin* mentioned that the Union as a whole for 1995 (Community budget, The European Investment Bank (EIB), and Member States) had 'allocated some ECU 183 million to Palestinian development and covered a significant proportion of the start-up costs and day-to-day expenditure of the Palestinian Authority, in particular for the Palestinian police force' (*Bulletin of the EU* 7/8-1996: 187). A 1997 report in the *Bulletin* noted that the EU had provided around half of the aid to the Palestinian territories and around a third of the total aid for the Middle East, according to its own figures (*Bulletin of the EU* 9-1997: 85).

A Special Status for Israel in the EU

In the spirit of regional cooperation as a vehicle for peace in the Middle East, the *Bulletin* reported in late 1993 that the conclusion of a new agreement with Israel was one of the key elements of the development of cooperation between the EU and the Middle East region (*Bulletin of the EC* 12-1993: 13). Similar agreements were negotiated with other states in the region around the same time. It was the hope of the Commission that the new agreement with Israel, which was to be broader in scope than the 1975 agreement, would 'help strengthen the region's political stability and economic development' (*Bulletin of the EC* 12-1993: 104). The 1994 Essen Declaration of the European Council concluded that 'Israel, on account of its high level of economic development, should enjoy special status in its relations with the European Union on the basis of reciprocity and common interests' (*Bulletin of the EU* 12-1994: 14). It took almost another year before the agreement was signed on 20 November 1995, a little more than two weeks after Yitzhak Rabin's assassination (*Bulletin of the EU* 11-1995: 82).

The new agreement, which was called an association agreement, was based on respect for human rights and democracy and was effected for an indefinite period (*Bulletin of the EU* 11-1995: 82). It included a regular political dialogue, the gradual establishment of a free trade area in line with World Trade Organization arrangements, the liberalization of services, free movement of capital and competition rules, the strengthening of economic cooperation on the widest possible basis in all areas of relations between the two parties, cooperation on social matters, and cultural cooperation. An Association Council, which was to meet once a year at ministerial level, was set up, and also an Association Committee with responsibility for implementing the agreement (*Bulletin of the EU* 11-1995: 82). The *Bulletin* reported that the association agreement fitted well into the Euro–Mediterranean partnership (EMP, also called the Barcelona process), which was launched around the same time (*Bulletin of the EU* 9-1995: 58).

The Euro–Mediterranean Partnership

During the peace process of the 1990s, the EU often highlighted that the Euro–Mediterranean partnership (EMP) was the only regional dialogue mechanism that brought together all the regional players in the Mediterranean, including the newly established Palestinian Authority (see, for example, *Bulletin of the EU* 1/2-1998: 103). While this was indeed a source of pride for the EU, it was often emphasized in EU declarations that there was no link between the EMP and the peace process, and that the EMP was not meant to replace other initiatives (see, for example, *Bulletin of the EU* 1/2-1995: 101; see also *Bulletin of the EU* 11-1995: 137). At the same time, somewhat paradoxically, the declaration that established the EMP clearly stated that the initiative would contribute to the success of the peace process (*Bulletin of the EU* 11-1995: 137). In reality, there was a clear link, however, as EMP meetings sometimes were dominated by talks about the peace process (*Bulletin of the EU* 4-1997: 81). When there were problems in the peace process, these tended to negatively affect the EMP (*Bulletin of the EU* 5-1998: 115). In the spirit of the time, the 1997 Amsterdam European Council stated:

> The peoples of Europe and the Middle East are linked by a common des-
> tiny, which was affirmed in 1995 at the Euro-Mediterranean Conference in
> Barcelona. In the knowledge of our common history, we invite the peoples

of the Middle East to join the peoples of Europe in building a future of harmony, founded on shared principles. (*Bulletin of the EU* 6-1997: 21)

A key problem with the EU's 'regional cooperation approach' was that the Arab states had historically feared being economically dominated by a stronger and more technically advanced Israel, while the EU envisioned the association agreement with Israel to 'contribute to the success of the Middle East peace process by enabling Israel to act as a driving force in fostering economic and social development in the region' (*Bulletin of the EU* 11-1995: 82). This was clearly not what the Arabs and Palestinians wanted.

The EMP declaration also talked about pursuing 'a mutually and effectively verifiable Middle East Zone free of weapons of mass destruction, nuclear, chemical and biological, and their delivery systems' (*Bulletin of the EU* 11-1995: 138). The declaration, including the text on the Middle East Zone free of weapons of mass destruction, was adopted by Israel, represented by Foreign Minister Ehud Barak, but there were never any reports in the *Bulletin* of the EU taking any action against Israel's arsenal of nuclear weapons (*Bulletin of the EU* 11-1995: 138).

The Peace Process Runs into Trouble

It did not take long before the peace process was tested by violence. The first big test came when Israeli settler Baruch Goldstein massacred twenty-nine Palestinians in the shrine in Hebron in February 1994. Riots followed across the occupied territories and another twenty-five Palestinians were killed by Israeli forces in the following days. The massacre was strongly condemned by the EU but not referred to as a terror attack (*Bulletin of the EU* 1/2-1994: 67). It led to the establishment of an international presence in Hebron, which later became the civilian observer mission the Temporary International Presence in Hebron (TIPH) (*Bulletin of the EU* 4-1994: 66). The EU has been very supportive of the civilian observer mission in Hebron, which came to consist of three EU members (Denmark, Italy, Sweden) plus Norway, Switzerland and Turkey.[2]

---

[2] In January 2019, nearly twenty-five years after the mission was established, Israeli Prime Minister Benjamin Netanyahu announced that Israel would not extend the mandate of the TIPH.

Nineteen ninety-four was also the year when Palestinian suicide bombings against Israel started to accelerate. The first came in Afula in April 1994 and left eight dead Israelis.[3] Many more would follow. The peace process witnessed a clear change in how the EU responded to terror attacks against Israel. From normally not having mentioned them at all in the 1970s and 1980s, the *Bulletin* started to routinely publish statements condemning terror attacks against Israel during the peace process. At one point in 1996, during a wave of suicide bombings against Israel, the EU condemned 'the barbaric terrorist acts in Israel' (*Bulletin of the EU* 3-1996: 70). At another point in 1995, the European Parliament 'condemned everyone in the Palestinian Territories who supported or protected terrorists', including 'Hamas and Islamic Jihad' (*Bulletin of the EU* 1/2-1995: 101). But it was still quite rare in the 1990s that the EC/EU, including the European Parliament, called out Hamas and Palestinian Islamic Jihad for their involvement in terror attacks against Israel. Instead, the typical response of the EU to the Palestinian terror attacks was to state that 'those who seek to destroy the peace process must not be allowed to succeed', and that 'the best way of ensuring this is through the reinforcement of the collective determination of the regional parties and the international community to make the process a success' (*Bulletin of the EU* 10-1994: 50).

Another blow to the peace process came in November 1995 when Israeli Prime Minister Yitzhak Rabin was assassinated. The President of the European Commission, Jacques Santer, said in his eulogy that the assassination was a 'severe blow to the peace process' and that Israel had lost a great leader who deserved 'our highest admiration' (*Bulletin of the EU* 11-1995: 81). Rabin's contribution to the peace process and his courageous determination to keep it on track against short-sighted resistance had been crucial, said Santer (*Bulletin of the EU* 11-1995: 81). The Madrid European Council of December 1995 deeply regretted the tragic assassination of Prime Minister Rabin and supported the undertaking given by the new Prime Minister, Shimon Peres, to take the peace process forward with the same resolve (*Bulletin of the EU* 12-1995: 21).

[3] The Israeli Ministry of Foreign Affairs has on its website a list of 'Fatal Terrorist Attacks in Israel (Sept 1993–1999)', which includes both terror attacks against civilians and attacks against soldiers: <http://www.mfa.gov.il/mfa/foreignpolicy/terrorism/palestinian/pages/fatal%20terrorist%20attacks%20in%20israel%20since%20the%20dop%20-s.aspx>.

The Palestinian Authority is Set Up

In May 1994, Israel and the PLO signed the agreement on the Gaza Strip and the Jericho Area, also known as the 1994 Cairo Agreement. It was a follow-up agreement to the DoP which provided for an Israeli military withdrawal from parts of the Gaza Strip and the West Bank city of Jericho. The agreement formally established the Palestinian Authority to have limited self-rule in these areas with a newly established Palestinian police force. The European Council warmly welcomed the agreement and regarded it 'as an important step towards the full implementation of the Declaration of Principles' (*Bulletin of the EU* 6-1994: 14). The Council also looked 'forward to the establishment of the Palestinian Authority in the Gaza Strip and Jericho, which should lead to the early extension of its responsibilities to the rest of the Occupied Territories' (*Bulletin of the EU* 6-1994: 14). Yasser Arafat returned to Gaza and Jericho in July 1994, an event that the EU regarded as 'proof of the progress already achieved in the Middle East peace process and, in particular, relations between the Israeli and Palestinian sides' (*Bulletin of the EU* 7/8-1994: 71). The EU expressed hope that the PA would become operational in the near future and become a partner for dialogue with the Union (*Bulletin of the EU* 7/8-1994: 71). Additional optimism was provided by Israel and Jordan signing the Washington Declaration the same month, which led to a full peace treaty being signed in October 1994. The EU warmly welcomed both of these breakthroughs and regarded the peace treaty as being 'of paramount importance for comprehensive peace in the Middle East' (*Bulletin of the EU* 7/8-1994: 69). In the spirit of the time, the EU was convinced that the peace treaty would make an important contribution to political and economic stability in the region, encourage constructive progress in the other bilateral tracks of the peace process and, in due course, benefit regional cooperation as a whole (*Bulletin of the EU* 10-1994: 50–1).

In the beginning of 1995, the European Parliament began calling for elections to be held in the occupied territories, which had been postponed since June 1994 (*Bulletin of the EU* 1/2-1995: 101). In April the same year, the EU again announced its willingness to help preparing and observing the Palestinian elections, as provided for in Article III of the DoP (*Bulletin of the EU* 4-1995: 54). The Parliament stressed the urgent need to implement the DoP 'by means of actual, visible deeds and, in particular, to hold elections in the Gaza Strip and Jericho' (*Bulletin of the EU* 5-1995: 68). Holding elections would confer democratic legitimacy on the PA, the Parliament argued (*Bulletin of the EU* 5-1995: 68). The Cannes European Council of June 1995 confirmed that the Union was 'fully ready, when the time comes, to send observers to the forthcoming Palestinian elections and to coordinate the various international observer missions at those elections' (*Bulletin of the EU* 6-1995: 14). Later in 1995, the EU decided to send a team of 300 observers, of whom thirty would be appointed by the European Parliament, to the Palestinian elections (*Bulletin of the EU* 9-1995: 58).

Palestinian elections were finally held on 20 January 1996. They were widely praised by the EU, which had observed them. In a long declaration, the EU expressed 'its deep satisfaction at the successful conclusion of the first-ever Palestinian general election' (*Bulletin of the EU* 1/2-1996: 79). It conveyed its congratulations to all candidates elected to the Palestinian Legislative Council and to Arafat on his election as President of the Council. It also welcomed 'the fact that the electoral process itself was conducted in a generally peaceful atmosphere' without bigger incidents (*Bulletin of the EU* 1/2-1996: 80). Moreover, the EU declaration drew a line between the successful elections and the peace process:

> Not only have they conferred democratic legitimacy on the Palestinian Authority, they have confirmed the commitment of the Palestinian people and their democratically elected leaders to the Palestinian track of the peace process and the peaceful resolution of the Middle East conflict. They have confounded opponents of the Middle East peace process who seek to undermine it through violence and terror. (*Bulletin of the EU* 1/2-1996: 79)

What the EU declaration did not mention, however, was that Hamas, Palestinian Islamic Jihad, the Popular Front for the Liberation of Palestine and other opposition groups boycotted the 1996 elections, which limited voter choices.

Putting the Peace Process Back on Track

In November 1994, the EU issued a long declaration which stated that the peace process had 'reached a crucial stage in which it is necessary for all sides to do their utmost to bring it to a successful conclusion' (*Bulletin of the EU* 11-1994: 74). The declaration stated that further development of the Palestinian territories was of paramount importance. It went on to call upon other donors, especially those from the region, to carry their share of the international burden (*Bulletin of the EU* 11-1994: 74). It was vital, the declaration stated, particularly during the phase in which autonomy was being created and Palestinian institutions set up, that the inhabitants of the occupied territories saw concrete evidence in their daily lives of the positive effects of the political changes (*Bulletin of the EU* 11-1994: 74). But instead of progress in the peace process, pessimism started to build up. In January 1995, a presidency statement on behalf of the EU expressed concern at the difficulties in implementing the DoP (*Bulletin of the EU* 1/2-1995: 84). Another EU statement from February 1995 took note of the 'critical period through which the peace process is currently passing' (*Bulletin of the EU* 1/2-1995: 84). The *Bulletin* reported that a ministerial EU troika visited the region in February 1995 'to revive the peace process which had broken down' following a double suicide bombing in Netanya on 22 January in which twenty-one Israelis died.[4] In meetings with the two sides, the representatives of the EU underlined the importance which they attached to the continuation of the peace negotiations, despite the pressure of increasingly hostile Israeli and Palestinian public opinion (*Bulletin of the EU* 1/2-1995: 101).

EU critique against the settlements was rather soft during the first years of the peace process, but it intensified in early 1995 when the peace process did not move forward. A strong European Parliament resolution from February 1995 'called on the Israeli authorities to prevent all confiscation of land and any further colonization' (*Bulletin of the EU* 1/2-1995: 101). A strong presidency statement on behalf of the EU concerning the expropriation of land in East Jerusalem was published in May 1995. The EU believed 'that this measure, contrary to the spirit of the Declaration of Principles and the maintenance of the status quo in the city of Jerusalem, could put the peace process at risk' (*Bulletin of the EU* 5-1995: 53).

---

[4] This meant that the EU delegation included ministers from the Member State currently holding the Presidency, from the Member State that held the Presidency in the previous six months and from the Member State who would hold the Presidency in the next six months.

The Oslo II Agreement

The Cannes European Council of June 1995 had expressed a 'fervent hope' that negotiations for completing the interim agreements would be successfully completed by 1 July 1995 (*Bulletin of the EU* 6-1995: 14). That deadline was missed, but a chance to put the peace process back on track came on 24 September 1995 when Israel and the PLO signed the Interim Agreement on the West Bank and the Gaza Strip, commonly known as the Taba Agreement or the Oslo II Agreement. It was, as usual, warmly welcomed by the EU (*Bulletin of the EU* 9-1995: 94). The EU, moreover, expressed 'its deepest satisfaction at the achievement of the Interim Agreement', and applauded the 'clear-sightedness and political courage shown by both parties, which highlight their sincere will to achieve full and long-lasting peace in the Middle East' (*Bulletin of the EU* 9-1995: 47). The EU further noted that the Oslo II Agreement would 'pave the way for the second phase of Palestinian autonomy as envisaged in the Declaration of Principles' (*Bulletin of the EU* 9-1995: 47). Finally, the EU reiterated its 'unreserved support for peace and prosperity among the peoples of the region' (*Bulletin of the EU* 9-1995: 48).

At the time, the Oslo II Agreement was referred to by the EU as an 'agreement on the extension of autonomy to the whole of the West Bank' (*Bulletin of the EU* 9-1995: 58). The most important feature of the agreement was that it divided up the West Bank and Gaza into three areas: Areas A, B and C. The PA would have full civil and security control in Area A, civil but not security control in Area B, whereas Israel remained in full control, meaning both civil and security, in Area C. As Palestinian self-rule was gradually expanded during the subsequent agreements of the peace process, the size of these areas changed accordingly. This Palestinian self-rule was to last for an interim period not exceeding five years from the signing of the Gaza–Jericho Agreement (i.e. no later than 4 May 1999), after which a permanent settlement based on UNSC resolution 242 and 338 was to be concluded, according to the Oslo II Agreement.

The Council further concluded in October 1995 that economic and social development was a key factor for achieving a just and lasting peace, and that the peoples of the region must be the prime beneficiaries of peace. It invited the Commission to begin exploratory talks with the PA to conclude an EU-PA Interim association agreement as soon as circumstances permitted (*Bulletin of the EU* 10-1995: 90).

Continued Ups and Downs in the Peace Process

The year 1996 was a turbulent one for the peace process. It began with the Palestinian elections in January and continued with a very violent spring. Israel had assassinated Hamas' chief bomb-maker Yahya Ayyash on 5 January 1996, which led to a wave of suicide bombings against Israel in the following months, which in turn paved the way for Benjamin Netanyahu's election victory in May that year. During the same period, an outbreak of violence occurred between Israel and Hezbollah in Lebanon (the April war/Operation Grapes of Wrath), which culminated in the killing by Israel of 106 Lebanese civilians in Qana on 18 April. The EU referred to Qana as a tragedy, but there was zero criticism in the *Bulletin* of Israel's actions in the April war/ Operation Grapes of Wrath (*Bulletin of the EU* 4-1996: 59). Instead five new trends emerged in the *Bulletin* in 1996. First, there were more and more appeals to Arafat to do more to fight terrorism (see, for example, *Bulletin of the EU* 1/2-1996: 79, 3-1996: 70). Second, there was relatively little criticism of Israel for human rights violations during this period. Instead, there was more and more questioning of Israel's commitment to the peace process and signed agreements. Third, criticism of Israel and the Palestinians now tended to be more and more proportionate in the sense that both sides were equally criticized when outbreaks of violence occurred. One example of this came in October 1996 after Israel opened a tunnel at the Western Wall that led to massive riots and violence, resulting in the death of seventy Palestinians and seventeen Israeli soldiers. The EU responded by calling

> upon both the Israeli authorities and the Palestinians to exercise the utmost restraint and to refrain from any actions or words which might lead to further violence. It urges both sides to avoid resorting to disproportionate force, in particular the use of firearms, tanks and helicopter gunships. (*Bulletin of the EU* 10-1996: 66)

With increased violence there followed Israeli closures of the Palestinian territories, which in turn had very negative effects for the Palestinian economy; so, fourth, the lifting of closures and other restrictions became a new point for criticism by the EU of Israel (see, for example, *Bulletin of the EU* 3-1996: 70, 6-1996: 18). Fifth, for the first time in the *Bulletin*, the EU singled out Iran for its negative role in the peace process. In March 1996, the EU stated that it was 'deeply concerned at the absence of specific Iranian condemnation of the terrorist bombings in Israel' (*Bulletin of the EU* 3-1996: 70). Iran was further criticized for its 'irresponsible declarations' about the bombings in Israel. Finally, the EU called

> on Iran to condemn once and for all acts of terrorism, whoever by and for whatever end, and to respect its commitment to refrain from any action which could undermine the peace process or legitimize terrorism. (*Bulletin of the EU* 3-1996: 70)

Throughout 1996, there were repeated calls by the EU in the *Bulletin* on the parties to re-engage themselves in the peace process, to respect and implement fully all the agreements already reached, and to resume negotiations on the final status issues as soon as possible (see, for example, *Bulletin of the EU* 6-1996: 18). The Florence European Council of June 1996 stated that 'the Peace Process is the only path to security and peace for Israel, the Palestinians and the neighbouring States' (*Bulletin of the EU* 6-1996: 18).

There were also some good developments taking place during this period. The Palestinian National Council was widely praised by the EU for its decision, taken by an overwhelming majority, to amend the Palestinian Charter so that it would no longer deny the right of the State of Israel to exist (*Bulletin of the EU* 4-1996: 60). This constituted a confirmation of the strong desire by the Palestinians to fulfil their undertakings, it showed how widespread the support for peace was among the Palestinians, and how limited the following was of those who were opposed to it through violent means and terrorist actions, according to a presidency statement on behalf of the EU (*Bulletin of the EU* 4-1996: 60).[5] In October 1995, an EU special envoy to the peace process was appointed for the first time. The role fell to Ambassador Miguel Angel Moratinos, whose mandate included establishing and maintaining

---

[5] There has been a debate ever since on whether or not the charter actually was changed. The ambiguity has remained even after the PA reaffirmed it would nullify the clauses in the 1998 Wye River Memorandum.

close contact with all the parties to the peace process, observing the peace negotiations, contributing where requested to the implementation of international agreements, and promoting compliance with basic norms of democracy, including respect for human rights and the rule of law (*Bulletin of the EU* 10-1996: 81).

At the yearly UNGA meeting in September 1996, Ireland's Foreign Minister and current President of the Council, Dick Spring, said that the Union was deeply concerned about the current lack of progress in the negotiations. He also delivered a very powerful statement against the settlements:

> We call upon the Israeli Government not to pursue the extension of settlements. Continued expansion of settlements does more than any other issue to erode Palestinian confidence in the peace process. It undermines the ability of both the Palestinian Authority and society at large to deter extremists and trouble-makers. (*Bulletin of the EU* 9-1996: 98)

A long declaration by the Council on the peace process on 1 October 1996 called 'on Israel to 'match its stated commitment to the peace process with concrete actions to fulfil its obligations, as well as to refrain from any action likely to create mistrust about its intentions' (*Bulletin of the EU* 10-1996: 66). For the first time, the EU called on the Israeli government to 'prevent its forces from re-entering autonomous areas in Zone A, contrary to the spirit and the letter of the Interim Agreement' (*Bulletin of the EU* 10-1996: 66). The declaration, moreover, asserted that the Fourth Geneva Convention was fully applicable to East Jerusalem, as it was to other territories under occupation (*Bulletin of the EU* 10-1996: 66). Also, for the first time, but without threatening punitive measures, the Council stressed the importance of the EU–Israel association agreement, which was 'based on a common commitment to the peace process' (*Bulletin of the EU* 10-1996: 66). It finally praised the security partnership between Israel and the PA as 'one of the main achievements of the peace process' (*Bulletin of the EU* 10-1996: 66). There was an additional shorter declaration on the peace process in the same issue of the *Bulletin*, which stated that the Council 'also strongly supported the United States' active and constructive role in the peace process and wished to see the European Union associate itself with efforts contributing to the advancement of the peace process in an effective and complementary way' (*Bulletin of the EU* 10-1996: 81).

The year ended with another long and very negative EU declaration on the peace process. The Dublin European Council was 'gravely concerned by the continuing deterioration in the peace process' (*Bulletin of the EU* 12-1996: 33). It singled out the settlements for 'eroding confidence in the peace process' (*Bulletin of the EU* 12-1996: 33). The optimism generated by the establishment of Palestinian self-rule had dissipated and instead been replaced by discontent and violence, stated the declaration (*Bulletin of the EU* 12-1996: 33).

The EU–PA Interim Association Agreement

An interim association agreement on trade and cooperation was concluded between the EU and the PLO on behalf of the PA in February 1997. It was based on respect for human rights and covered all economic and trade relations between the EU and the PA. Among other things, the agreement established the conditions for the liberalization of trade between the EU and the West Bank/ Gaza Strip. It also established a regular political dialogue between the two sides (*Bulletin of the EU* 1/2-1997: 90–1). A key problem of the interim association agreement with the PA ever since the signing has been Israel's restrictions on Palestinian movement and access, which has contributed to making EU–PA trade very limited.[6] As the largest donor to the PA, these restrictions quickly became a key point of friction between the EU and Israel. A clear example of this came in September 1997 at the annual UNGA meeting where the EU was represented by Jacques Poos, Foreign Minister of Luxembourg:

> We ask that Israel discontinue certain measures adopted towards the Palestinians, which we consider to be counter-productive. In particular, we ask that Israel transfer all of the tax revenue it owes to the Palestinian Authority. It is not in the interests of peace to weaken the Palestinian

---

[6] There are no figures in the *Bulletin* for EU–PA trade during the peace process, but the 2018 figure for goods was around €200 million, less than 1 per cent of the EU–Israel trade, which stood at €34.4 billion for goods in 2018. For more information about EU–PA trade, see <https://ec.europa.eu/trade/policy/countries-and-regions/countries/palestine/>. For information about EU–Israel trade, see <https://ec.europa.eu/trade/policy/countries-and-regions/countries/israel/>.

economy, administration and leadership and to feed the feelings of frustration and humiliation of an entire people. (*Bulletin of the EU* 9-1997: 86)

In 1997 it was also decided by the Council to support the PA in its efforts to counter terrorism. ECU 3.6 million was provided for a three-year period. In particular, specific training would be provided for the Palestinian police in order to ensure that the security and police services concerned were fully aware of the principles of human rights in the implementation of their activities in the territories under the PA's control (*Bulletin of the EU* 4-1997: 85). The year before, the European Parliament had called on the PA to improve its standards as regards respect for human rights and fundamental freedoms in its territories (*Bulletin of the EU* 11-1996: 87). Also in 1997, the European Parliament made it known that they deplored the decision by the Israeli government to approve construction plans in the Har Homa (also known as Jabal Abu Ghneim) settlement in East Jerusalem. This particular settlement became a symbol for the whole peace process, casting into doubt Israel's willingness to abide by the spirit of the Oslo process. The Parliament considered the approved construction plans in Har Homa 'to be part of the resumption of the Israeli policy of colonizing the Occupied Territories of Gaza and the West Bank, which would have a negative impact on the peace negotiations' (*Bulletin of the EU* 3-1997: 77).

What Can the EU Do?

In October 1997, the peace process reached what the EU called a 'total impasse' (*Bulletin of the EU* 10-1997: 85). Two months later, the Luxembourg European Council stated that the EU remained deeply concerned about the lack of progress in implementing all the commitments in the Israeli–Palestinian interim agreements, including the Hebron Protocol,[7] and by the continuing deadlock on the Syrian and Lebanese tracks (*Bulletin of the EU* 12-1997: 15). The Luxembourg European Council endorsed a long list of guidelines for an EU policy aimed at facilitating progress in the

[7] The Protocol Concerning the Redeployment in Hebron, also known as the Hebron Protocol or Hebron Agreement, was signed in January 1997 by Benjamin Netanyahu and Yasser Arafat under US supervision. It concerned the partial redeployment of Israeli military forces from Hebron in accordance with the 1995 Oslo II Agreement.

peace process and restoring confidence between the parties. The guidelines included:

- Continuing to use all the EU's political and moral weight to ensure that agreements already reached are fully implemented on the basis of reciprocity.
- Proposing adopting a code of conduct to avoid unilateral steps by the parties.
- Proposing a Permanent Security Committee as a mean of institutionalizing security cooperation, which may even include the US and the EU.
- Working towards the removal of obstacles to Palestinian economic development and to facilitate the free movement of people and goods.
- Enhancing its support to Palestinian institutions in East Jerusalem.
- Stressing the importance of people-to-people programmes as an essential mean of reinforcing dialogue and restoring mutual confidence between the parties at the level of civil society.
- Continuing to monitor closely developments on the ground through its own human rights, Jerusalem, and settlements watch instruments.
- Readiness to contribute to the final status negotiations by offering specific suggestions to the parties on the remaining issues at stake.
- Reviewing its financial support with the aim of ensuring greater effectiveness in achieving the objectives of the peace process.
- Underlining the importance of concluding negotiations in the nine committees created by the interim agreements.
- Insisting on the revival of regional economic cooperation as a mean of promoting social and economic development.
- Reiterating the importance which the EU attaches to the relaunching of negotiations on the Syrian and Lebanese tracks; seeking the restoration of a comprehensive process on the basis of 'land for peace' and demanding the full implementation of UNSC resolutions 242, 338 and 425.
- Strongly supporting US efforts to revive the peace process and expressing the EU's willingness to work closely with the US and to maintain close contact with Russia and the regional parties (*Bulletin of the EU* 12-1997: 15–16).

The EU continued to explore how it could best contribute to the peace process. A 1998 Commission communication to the Council and the Parliament on 'The role of the European Union in the peace process and its future assistance to the Middle East' noted that EU and Member States' assistance to the Palestinian economy had not brought about an economic upswing or raised the living standards in the occupied territories (*Bulletin of the EU* 1/2-1998: 103). The Council had in the same issue of the *Bulletin* 'expressed its deep concern at the serious decline of the Palestinian economy' (*Bulletin of the EU* 1/2-1998: 103). At the same time, the communication stressed 'that this assistance has nevertheless helped avoid the total collapse of the economy and Palestinian institutions and helped keep the peace process alive' (*Bulletin of the EU* 1/2-1998: 103).

The discussion on Israeli products' rule of origin came up again in May 1998 when the *Bulletin* reported that the Commission suspected that Israeli products originating in the occupied territories (Gaza, West Bank, East Jerusalem and the Golan Heights) were being exported to the EU as if they had originated in Israel (*Bulletin of the EU* 5-1998: 89). The report in the *Bulletin* pointed out that, in line with international law, the EU considered none of these territories to be part of the State of Israel. The agreement concerning Israeli products' rule of origin 'applied to the territory of Israel within its pre-1967 borders, and that products originating in the Palestinian Territories were covered by the EC-PLO interim association agreement' (*Bulletin of the EU* 5-1998: 89). Finally, the report stated that the EU would take steps to verify these allegations and bring violations to an end if they were confirmed (*Bulletin of the EU* 5-1998: 89). The discussion continued in the next issue of the *Bulletin*, June 1998, where the Council noted that the application of origin and related issues needed to be clarified and resolved at the technical level in constructive dialogue with Israel (*Bulletin of the EU* 6-1998: 99).

At the end of 1998, the *Bulletin* published the Council's conclusions on future assistance to the West Bank and Gaza Strip. The conclusions noted that the EU (including the European Investment Bank and the Member States) had been the main donor to the Palestinians, providing around 54 per cent of the total assistance between 1994 and 1998. For the coming period, 1999–2003, the Council announced a pledge of ECU 400 million in grants with the aim of improving the prospects for viable Palestinian self-determination (*Bulletin of the EU* 11-1998: 83). According to the EU, this would mean

> reconstructing physical, social and economic infrastructures, building up the institutions needed for an efficient, transparent and accountable Palestinian administration, and facilitating direct Palestinian access to Israel and the rest of the world. In this context Gaza airport, Gaza seaport, Gaza industrial park and safe passages were essential. (*Bulletin of the EU* 11-1998: 83)

The Need for a Palestinian State gets EU-Mainstreamed

The 1980 Venice Declaration had fallen short of explicitly calling for a Palestinian state and it took almost another two decades before the EU was ready to explicitly support the idea of a Palestinian state. At the Amsterdam European Council of 1997, the EU for the first time called

> on the people of Israel to recognise the right of the Palestinians to exercise self-determination, without excluding the option of a State. The creation of a viable and peaceful sovereign Palestinian entity is the best guarantee of Israel's security. (*Bulletin of the EU* 6-1997: 22)

This somewhat ambiguous call for a Palestinian state was repeated in the Cardiff European Council of 1998, which, at the same time, called 'upon the Palestinian people to reaffirm their commitment to the legitimate right of Israel to live within safe, recognized borders' (*Bulletin of the EU* 6-1998: 15). It was not until the Berlin Declaration of 1999 that the EU explicitly endorsed the idea of a Palestinian state:

> The European Union reaffirms the continuing and un-qualified Palestinian right to self-determination, including the option of a State, and looks for-ward to the early fulfilment of this right. It appeals to the parties to strive in good faith for a negotiated solution on the basis of the existing agree-ments, without prejudice to this right, which is not subject to any veto. The European Union is convinced that the creation of a democratic, viable and peaceful sovereign Palestinian State on the basis of existing agreements and through negotiations would be the best guarantee of Israel's security and Israel's acceptance as an equal partner in the region. The European

Union declares its readiness to consider the recognition of a Palestinian State in due course in accordance with the basic principles referred to above. (*Bulletin of the EU* 3-1999: 21–2)

The PA's plan to declare independence unilaterally by 4 May 1999, which eventually did not materialize, led the European Parliament in March 1999 to predict 'stormy times ahead for the peace process'. The Parliament, however, recognized 'the basic right of the Palestinians to found their own State' (*Bulletin of the EU* 3-1999: 94).

The strong case for path-dependency in the EC/EU's declarations is very clear with the adoption of the need for a Palestinian state, which has been present ever since 1999 in basically all EU declarations on the conflict. A year and a half after the Berlin Declaration, just weeks before the second intifada broke out, a presidency statement on behalf of the EU declared that

> the right of the Palestinian people to build a sovereign, democratic, viable and peaceful State may not be brought into question. This right is established. There remains the choice of timing which belongs to the Palestinian people. (*Bulletin of the EU* 9-2000: 69)

The Wye River Memorandum, Final Status Issues and the Sharm el-Sheikh Memorandum

The first of these two agreements, the Wye River Memorandum, was signed in October 1998 in Washington and sought to implement the Oslo II and subsequent agreements. It called for more land to be transferred to the PA in three phases in return for the Palestinian side combatting terror, prohibiting incitement, and reaffirming that it had nullified the problematic parts of the PLO charter. As had become the norm, the agreement was warmly welcomed by the EU (*Bulletin of the EU* 10-1998: 62). The EU called the agreement a 'breakthrough' and looked forward to its 'speedy implementation' (*Bulletin of the EU* 10-1998: 63). It went on to call for starting negotiations without delay on the final status issues and added that the EU 'has much to offer to the success of the peace process and is determined to continue playing its full part, enhancing it in all its aspects' (*Bulletin of the EU* 10-1998: 63). But as had happened several times before during the peace process, the optimism that a new agreement generated was soon replaced by pessimism. It was no different this time. Already by December 1998, the Israeli government announced that it would suspend the implementation of the Wye River Memorandum and not proceed with the second phase of the redeployment from the West Bank. The EU deeply regretted this and accused Israel of imposing new conditions on the Palestinians which went beyond the Wye River Memorandum (*Bulletin of the EU* 12-1998: 109).

When the end of the interim period was approaching in the spring of 1999, the European Council's Berlin Declaration of March 1999 urged the parties to agree on an extension. The EU called 'in particular for an early resumption of final status negotiations in the coming months' with a target period of concluding the final status negotiations within a year. The declaration also urged both parties to refrain from activities which prejudged the outcome of those final status negotiations (*Bulletin of the EU* 3-1999: 21). The 4 May 1999 deadline for solving the final status issues and completing an agreement was missed, but in September 1999 Israel and the PLO signed the Sharm el-Sheikh Memorandum. It was a similar agreement to Wye in several aspects, stipulating further Israeli redeployment, more territory to the PA, combatting terror and incitement. Most importantly, the Sharm el-Sheikh Memorandum stipulated that a framework agreement on the final status issues was to be achieved by February 2000 and permanent agreement by September 2000. The standard ritual followed: the EU welcomed the agreement and congratulated the parties for concluding the difficult negotiations (*Bulletin of the EU* 9-1999: 69). The European Parliament also welcomed the agreement, 'which it believed was a fundamental step towards achieving a definitive peace' (*Bulletin of the EU* 10-1999: 76). However, at the same time, the Parliament regretted that the EU, 'one of the main financial contributors to the peace process, still failed to play a meaningful political role in this process' (*Bulletin of the EU* 10-1999: 76).

The Syrian and Lebanese Tracks

Just like the Israeli–Palestinian conflict – which unquestionably was the main track of the peace process – saw constant ups and downs, so did the Syrian and Lebanese tracks. The EU was much less involved in these, but sometimes mentioned them in its declarations on the peace process. The Cardiff European Council of June 1998, for example, expressed its grave concern at the lack of progress on the Syrian and Lebanese tracks and underlined the need for a continuing effort to reinvigorate them in order to achieve a comprehensive peace based on the principle of 'land for peace' and the relevant UNSC resolutions. Moreover, the European Council called 'for the full and unconditional withdrawal of Israeli forces from southern Lebanon' (*Bulletin of the EU* 6-1998: 15). In August 1998, a presidency statement on behalf of the EU urged Israel not to implement a newly approved plan to expand the settlements on the Golan Heights:

> If such a plan is implemented it would represent a significant setback to the efforts to resume the Israeli–Syrian negotiations. It would also constitute a further complication for the implementation of the principle 'land for peace' and raise questions about Israel's commitment to the peace process. (*Bulletin of the EU* 7/8-1998: 83)

In this context, the EU also reiterated 'its position that settlements in the occupied territories are illegal and in contravention of international law' (*Bulletin of the EU* 7/8-1998: 84). When Ehud Barak was elected Prime Minister of Israel in May 1999, the EU welcomed his campaign promises to resume negotiations with Syria and withdraw the Israeli forces from Lebanon (*Bulletin of the EU* 6-1999: 17). In December 1999, the European Council welcomed the courageous decision of President Assad and Prime Minister Barak to resume negotiations on the Syrian track. It looked forward to an early agreement between Israel and Syria, which should pave the way for resuming negotiations and for a solution also on the Lebanese track (*Bulletin of the EU* 12-1999: 15). But no agreements were reached either with Syria or Lebanon. Instead, Israel unilaterally withdrew its forces from south Lebanon in May 2000, ending its eighteen-year occupation, except for in the still-disputed Sheba Farms area. The withdrawal was welcomed by the EU (*Bulletin of the EU* 5-2000: 67).

The Failed Camp David Summit

The first target date of the Sharm el-Sheikh Memorandum to conclude a framework agreement on the final status issues in February 2000 was missed, which the Council 'expressed regret and concern' for (*Bulletin of the EU* 1/2-2000: 108). Three communities in the Jerusalem area (Abu Dis, Al-Azariya and Sawahara) were transferred to the PA in May 2000, a move which the EU welcomed (*Bulletin of the EU* 5-2000: 67). In June 2000, the European Council issued a declaration which stated that 'a real opportunity exists to attain a just, lasting and comprehensive peace in the Middle East, based on the principles established within the framework of Madrid, Oslo and subsequent agreements and in accordance with relevant UN resolutions' (*Bulletin of the EU* 6-2000: 18). The next month, the Camp David summit took place in the US where President Clinton negotiated with Barak and Arafat for two weeks without reaching an agreement. Surprisingly, there is no mention at all in the *Bulletin*'s July/August 2000 issue of these negotiations, which is very strange since the *Bulletin* followed the peace process very closely, even those aspects of it, like the US-led negotiations, where the EU was not directly involved. In the September 2000 issue of the *Bulletin*, there is a declaration on the peace process where the EU welcomed the role and personal commitment of President Clinton and Secretary of State Madeleine Albright (*Bulletin of the EU* 9-2000: 69). The declaration encouraged them to remain mobilized and to continue unremittingly their mediation efforts. The declaration went on to state that there still was

> a chance for peace in order to achieve, in the weeks ahead, a mutually satisfactory agreement between Israelis and Palestinians. The European Union continues to place itself in this perspective. The European Union renews its support to President Arafat and Prime Minister Barak and calls on the parties, at this decisive moment in time, to have the political courage to make the final effort that will enable them to reach an historic agreement. (*Bulletin of the EU* 9-2000: 69)

The EU was right that this was indeed 'a decisive moment in time'. But instead of peace, the second intifada broke out two weeks after this declaration was issued.

Conclusions

The Oslo peace process was met with intense interest from the EC/EU, something the coding schedule of this book clearly attests to. The EU was probably the biggest supporter of the peace process and contributed around 50 per cent of the total aid to the Palestinians during the peace process. However, the EU's vision of peace in the Middle East through regional cooperation did not materialize. Only one track of the multilateral peace process was successful: the Israel–Jordan track. The Israel–Palestinian track, the Israel–Syria track, the Israel–Lebanon track, the Israel–wider Arab world track – all failed, even if some progress was made, especially on the Israel–Palestinian track, and a significant change also happened on the Israel–Lebanon track with the unilateral Israeli withdrawal in 2000. In retrospect, it is striking how the EU nevertheless continued to talk about peace in the Middle East through regional cooperation all the way up to the outbreak of the second intifada. The Feira European Council of June 2000, for example, included a long section on the EU's vision for the Mediterranean region. The declaration praised the adoption of the EU's new 'Euro-Mediterranean Charter for Peace and Stability', which it said 'should be a deciding factor in the post-conflict process in the Mediterranean' (*Bulletin of the EU* 6-2000: 34–5).

Despite all the obstacles, a Palestinian entity with limited self-rule was created in the West Bank and Gaza Strip during the peace process; the territory it controlled in Areas A and B was progressively expanded through the different agreements the parties signed. But many obstacles undermined the peace process. In particular, the EU singled out the settlements for 'eroding confidence in the peace process' (*Bulletin of the EU* 12-1996: 33), but Palestinian terrorism also got a much harder treatment than before from the EU. This was a trend that intensified further after the outbreak of the second intifada.

Another distinguishing feature of this chapter is the EU's stated willingness, repeated over and over again during the 1990s, to use all of its power – political, economic and normative – and its technical expertise to help the peace process. In reality, as the chapter shows, it almost never used this power. It was not an important part of the high-level negotiations on any of the tracks of the peace process, which often took place in the US and often without direct involvement of the EU. Perhaps even more importantly, there was a very clear unwillingness or inability by the EU to use any kind of punitive measures, primarily against Israel, and to a lesser degree also against the Palestinians.

5

2000–9:

THE ISRAELI–ARAB CONFLICT
IN THE 9/11 ERA

To avoid any equating of terrorism with the Arab and Muslim world, the European Council considers it essential to encourage a dialogue of equals between our civilisations, particularly in the framework of the Barcelona process but also by means of an active policy of cultural exchange. (*Bulletin of the EU* 10-2001: 114)

While the outbreak of the second intifada mortally wounded the EU's vision of peace in the Middle East through regional cooperation, the events that followed definitely killed it, at least for the foreseeable future. The 2001 9/11 attacks, the 2003 invasion of Iraq, the 2004–5 terror attacks in Madrid and London, the 2006 war in Lebanon – all contributed to make the EU's vision of peace in the Middle East through regional cooperation look like a distant dream from the past decade. This development, however, did not stop the EU from continuing talking about peace in the Middle East through regional cooperation, even if it was quite clear after the 9/11 attacks that the Middle East was headed for more conflicts, rather than less. One clear result of the peace process and the period that followed 9/11 was that the EU started more and more to talk about a distinct Israeli–Palestinian conflict, rather than a wider Israeli–Arab conflict. Among other things, this meant that the Israeli–Lebanese/Hezbollah conflict and the Israeli–Syrian conflict became more and more separated from the Israeli–Palestinian track.

97

Iran's ascending role in the Middle East also contributed to this. Another clear result of 9/11 was that a 'war on terrorism narrative' became much more prominent in the EU's declarations, which in turn led to more sympathy/less criticism of Israel and less sympathy/more criticism of the Palestinians during the 2000s. This culminated with the 2008–9 Gaza war, which passed without criticism of Israel in the *Bulletin*.

The EU's vision of a just peace in the conflict also developed during the 2000–9 period, from the second intifada to the first Gaza war. The main development was that the 2002 Seville Declaration for the first time mentioned the 1967 borders and some of the final status issues in relation to the two-state solution. Besides the intifada, five diplomatic initiatives stood in focus during this period: the 2002 Arab Peace Initiative, the 2003 US-led 'road map', the 2005 unilateral Israeli withdrawal from Gaza, the 2006–8 Olmert-Abbas talks, and the 2007 Annapolis conference in the US. As had been the case with similar initiatives in the past, the EU had no major role in any of them, even if it played important side roles in relation to some, often before or after they took place. After the intifada wound down in 2004, much of the EU's focus shifted from emergency assistance to rebuilding and developing Palestinian institutions in preparation for future statehood. But many obstacles were in place, from the continued Israeli occupation to the intra-Palestinian split between Hamas and Fatah.

The Outbreak of the Second Intifada

The EU's first reaction to the intifada, which broke out on 28 September 2000, came in a presidency statement on 2 October. Expressing its concern 'at the continued bloody clashes in Jerusalem and in the territories', the EU called 'on the leaders of both parties to take all necessary measures to ensure that the violence ceases and that new provocative action is avoided' (*Bulletin of the EU* 10-2000: 76–7). In another meeting on 9 October, the EU stated that 'in this critical period no effort must be spared to prevent fear, hatred and violence from gaining the upper hand, so that the dialogue for peace may resume as soon as possible' (*Bulletin of the EU* 10-2000: 77). The EU, moreover, stated that it was 'convinced that two peoples who must coexist have no other option than immediately to resume the negotiation path to peace, to which Israelis and Palestinians have both, in recent weeks, overcome so many obstacles hitherto considered insurmountable' (*Bulletin of the EU* 10-2000: 77). Finally, the EU stated that it would 'do everything in its power to prevent further escalation' (*Bulletin of the EU* 10-2000: 77).

Among the things the EU did was to participate in an emergency summit held in Sharm el-Sheikh, Egypt, on 17 October 2000. At the summit, it was decided to establish a fact-finding committee to determine the cause of the intifada, whose findings were published in the Sharm el-Sheikh Fact-Finding Committee Report, also known as the Mitchell Report (*Bulletin of the EU* 10-2000: 115). The EU very much supported the Mitchell Report (*Bulletin of the EU* 5-2001: 78), whereas the European Parliament

> applauded the fact that the EU, in the person of its High Representative for the CFSP [Javier Solana], was present at the Sharm-el-Sheikh Summit, and regarded this as a first step towards raising substantially the Union's diplomatic and political profile in the negotiation process. (*Bulletin of the EU* 10-2000: 115)

The Euro–Arab dialogue held a meeting the following month, November 2000, where the situation in the Middle East and the announcement of the establishment of the Sharm el-Sheikh Fact-Finding Committee were discussed. However, the *Bulletin* reported that it was impossible to issue a final communiqué because of the lack of consensus on the Israeli–Arab conflict (*Bulletin of the EU* 11-2000: 90). Another chance to stop the intifada came during President Clinton's last days in office at the Taba summit in Egypt in late January 2001, in which the EU's special representative, Miguel Moratinos, also participated.[1] The European Council saluted 'President Clinton's efforts at a breakthrough in the peace process' and stated that it looked forward to working closely with the incoming Bush administration (*Bulletin of the EU* 1/2-2001: 119). The same issue of the *Bulletin* also congratulated Ariel Sharon for his victory in the election for Prime Minister of Israel (*Bulletin of the EU* 1/2-2001: 100).

---

[1] Although not reported by the *Bulletin*, it is worth mentioning that Ambassador Moratinos wrote an unofficial non-paper on the negotiations at Taba, which both Israelis and Palestinians acknowledged was a relatively fair description. Moratinos' (2001) non-paper can be found at the Economic Cooperation Foundation's (ECF) database of documents related to the Israeli–Palestinian conflict: <https://ecf.org.il/ media_items/966>.

Balancing Criticism During the Second Intifada

After the outbreak of the second intifada, which was actually not referred to as an intifada until December 2001 by the *Bulletin* (*Bulletin of the EU* 12-2001: 25), there was a clear shift in the *Bulletin*'s statements towards balancing criticism of Israeli and Palestinian misbehaviour. The EU had in a presidency statement blamed Israel for the outbreak of the intifada, stating that the 'lack of progress in the peace process, including the settlements issue, is the source of the Palestinian community's frustration and the violence' (*Bulletin of the EU* 11-2000: 76). As usual, the European Parliament went one step further and condemned what it called 'Mr Sharon's act of provocation [a visit by then Israeli opposition leader Ariel Sharon under heavy security to the Temple Mount/Haram al-Sharif in Jerusalem], which had sparked off the conflict' (*Bulletin of the EU* 10-2000: 89). In the first two years of the intifada, there was massive criticism of Israeli policies. These included:

- extrajudicial killings (*Bulletin of the EU* 1/2-2001: 101);
- illegal incursions into PA-controlled territories (*Bulletin of the EU* 4-2001: 60);
- use of excessive and disproportionate force (*Bulletin of the EU* 4-2001: 60);
- expanding settlements, in particular the Har Homa/Jabal Abu Ghneim settlement, because they change the physical character and demographic composition of the occupied territories (*Bulletin of the EU* 4-2001: 59);
- house demolitions (*Bulletin of the EU* 7/8-2001: 71);
- closure of the Orient House (the PLO headquarters) in Jerusalem (*Bulletin of the EU* 7/8-2001: 71);
- closures and restrictions imposed on the Palestinian people (*Bulletin of the EU* 12-2001: 25);
- restrictions in the freedom of movement of the Palestinian leadership (*Bulletin of the EU* 9-2002: 67);
- the systematic destruction of Palestinian infrastructures, including those financed by the EU (*Bulletin of the EU* 10-2002: 92);
- collective punishment, including deportations of members of Palestinian families (*Bulletin of the EU* 10-2002: 92);

- failure to give full access to international personnel necessary for humanitarian projects in the Palestinian territories (*Bulletin of the EU* 10-2002: 92);
- a deteriorating humanitarian situation in the West Bank and Gaza, which was making life increasingly intolerable for ordinary Palestinians and fuelling extremism (*Bulletin of the EU* 12-2002: 14).

In addition, the European Parliament stated that 'the disproportionate use of force by the Israeli Army and collective punishment were not in accordance with the principles of the association agreement in force between the European Union and Israel' (*Bulletin of the EU* 5-2001: 78). However, there was never any suggestion in the *Bulletin* during this time of suspending the association agreement with Israel or of any other punishment.

Of all points of criticism against Israel, it was by far its use of extrajudicial killings that garnered most attention from the EU during the second intifada. In February 2001, a presidency statement deplored 'the practice of so-called "eliminations" or extra-judicial killings of Palestinians carried out by Israeli security forces' (*Bulletin of the EU* 1/2-2001: 101). The declaration reiterated the EU's strongly held opinion that Israel's policy in this regard was unacceptable and contrary to the rule of law. A démarche reflecting this concern was made to the Israeli Foreign Ministry, which confirmed the existence of such a policy (which the Israeli side called 'targeted killings'). Extrajudicial killings were also an obstacle to peace and could provoke further violence, according to the EU (*Bulletin of the EU* 1/2-2001: 101). Israel's policy of extrajudicial killings climaxed in March–April 2004 with the killings of Hamas's top leaders Sheikh Ahmed Yassin in March and his successor, Abdel Aziz al-Rantisi, the following month (*Bulletin of the EU* 3-2004: 15). Besides being contrary to international law, the Council also stated that extrajudicial killings contributed to the 'cycle of retaliatory violence', which led the parties even further away from a negotiated settlement (*Bulletin of the EU* 3-2004: 15). Sometimes, Israeli extrajudicial killings and Palestinian terrorism were condemned together in the same sentence (see, for example, *Bulletin of the EU* 7/8-2001: 71).

However, for the first time in the *Bulletin*, there was now also strong and persistent criticism of the Palestinian side for its use of terrorism, in particular suicide bombings, against Israel. In the summer of 2001, after a series of suicide bombings against Israel, the EU condemned them 'in the strongest terms' (*Bulletin of the EU* 7/8-2001: 71), further noting that:

> These acts, in particular those targeted at Israeli civilians, are hateful and repugnant in the extreme. Terrorism is a serious threat to the stability of the region. It must be resisted with the utmost rigour. The European Union also condemns any assistance to the organisations which engage in terrorism, whether this be financial aid, arms supplies or training. The European Union calls on the Palestinian Authority to do its utmost to arrest and bring to justice the perpetrators, instigators and sponsors of acts of terror. (*Bulletin of the EU* 7/8-2001: 71)

After the 9/11 attacks in the US, the EU expressed on several occasions that it rejected any equation of terrorism with the Arab and Muslim world. The EU also called for a dialogue of civilizations with the Arab and Muslim world, between equals (see, for example, *Bulletin of the EU* 10-2001: 114). During the peace process of the 1990s, the EU had routinely condemned terrorism against Israel, but often, with a few exceptions, without naming Hamas or Palestinian Islamic Jihad as being responsible for the attacks. This practice continued in the beginning of the second intifada but changed after 9/11 when the Laeken European Council in December 2001 called on the PA to dismantle Hamas' and Islamic Jihad's terrorist networks, arresting and prosecuting all suspects, and issuing a public appeal in Arabic for an end to the armed intifada (*Bulletin of the EU* 12-2001: 25). The same declaration also stated that Israel needed the PA and its elected President, Yasser Arafat, as a partner both to eradicate terrorism and to work with towards peace. 'Its capacity to fight terrorism must not be weakened', stated the declaration (*Bulletin of the EU* 12-2001: 25). Finally, the Laeken European Council stated the EU's 'reaffirmation and full recognition of Israel's inalienable right to live in peace and security within internationally recognised borders' (*Bulletin of the EU* 12-2001: 25).

During 2001, several attempts, all supported by the EU, were made to stop the intifada; besides the Sharm el-Sheikh Fact-Finding Committee Report (the Mitchell Report), there were the Jordanian–Egyptian Initiative and the Tenet Cease-Fire Plan (*Bulletin of the EU* 5-2001: 78, 12-2001: 25).

The EU's High Representative, Javier Solana, also presented his own report, which, among other things, called for rebuilding confidence, improving the situation on the ground, restoring cooperation between the civil societies, and maintaining the aid to the PA (*Bulletin of the EU* 6-2001: 17). In relation to these different plans, a presidency statement from December 2001 stated that the EU was convinced that setting up a third-party monitoring mechanism would serve the interests of both parties, and that the EU was prepared to play an active role in such a mechanism (*Bulletin of the EU* 12-2001: 25). The same statement also attached 'great importance to an economic recovery programme focused on Palestine as a way of encouraging peace' (*Bulletin of the EU* 12-2001: 25). A couple of months earlier, the European Parliament had called for 'the deployment of an international observer mission in the occupied territories and urged the Member States to launch a suitable initiative within the UN' (*Bulletin of the EU* 7/8-2001: 8).

2002 – The Second Intifada Peaks

When the second intifada peaked in the spring of 2002, the Barcelona European Council of 15–16 March 2002 issued a long declaration on the conflict, which stated that the Middle East was 'in the grip of an extremely grave crisis'. The declaration stated that there was no military solution to the conflict and called 'on both sides to take immediate and effective action to stop the bloodshed' (*Bulletin of the EU* 3-2002: 20). It condemned the indiscriminate terrorist attacks over the past weeks and stated that the PA, as the legitimate authority, bore full responsibility for fighting terrorism with all the legitimate means at its disposal. The PA's capacity to fight terror must not be weakened, stated the declaration (*Bulletin of the EU* 3-2002: 20). Israel was called on to immediately withdraw its military forces from the PA's areas, stop extrajudicial executions, lift the closures and restrictions, freeze settlements, and respect international law. Both parties must respect international human rights standards, refrain from using excessive force, and not hinder medical and humanitarian personnel in their work, stated the declaration (*Bulletin of the EU* 3-2002: 20). The declaration ended with a pledge that the EU would

make a full and substantial economic contribution to peace-building in the region, with the aim of improving the living conditions of the Palestinian people, of consolidating and supporting the PA, of strengthening the economic basis of the future State of Palestine and of promoting development and regional economic integration. In this perspective, the European Union stands ready to contribute to the reconstruction of the Palestinian economy as an integral part of regional development. (*Bulletin of the EU* 3-2002: 20)

After a long series of Palestinian suicide bombs in March 2002, the second intifada reached it absolute climax with the Israeli offensive in the Jenin refugee camp and other Palestinian cities in the beginning of April 2002. As the Jenin refugee camp and other places were under Israeli siege, a presidency statement from the EU called 'for medical and humanitarian organisations to have immediate access to the Palestinian population', as called for in the newly adopted UNSC resolution 1405, which stated its concern for the dire humanitarian situation of the Palestinian population (*Bulletin of the EU* 4-2002: 63). Because of the Israeli siege, conflicting reports came out from the Jenin refugee camp about the level of destruction and number of deaths there. The EU therefore reiterated the call in UNSC resolution 1405 'to obtain detailed information on the events that took place in the Jenin refugee camp' (*Bulletin of the EU* 4-2002: 63). On 10 April 2002, the European Parliament adopted a resolution calling on the Council and the Commission to suspend the association agreement between the EU and Israel. The Parliament's resolution also called on the Council to impose an arms embargo on Israel and the Palestinian territories (*Bulletin of the EU* 4-2002: 75). However, there were no suggestions in the Council's declarations of any types of punishments against either Israel or the Palestinians.

A major concern for the EU during the second intifada was how to avoid the economic and institutional collapse of the PA (see, for example, *Bulletin of the EU* 3-2001: 18). This became an even more pressing issue when the intifada peaked in 2002 and the EU began fearing for Arafat's physical safety. During the peak of the violence in April 2002, the EU warned Israel 'against any use of force against the headquarters of the Palestinian Authority in Ramallah which could endanger the physical safety of President Arafat and others on the premises' (*Bulletin of the EU* 4-2002: 63). The European Parliament's resolution from 10 April, which had called for suspending the association agreement with Israel, also called for freedom of movement for the Palestinian President and deplored Israel's refusal to allow a high-level EU delegation to meet with him (*Bulletin of the EU* 4-2002: 75).

The violence continued over the summer of 2002. In September, the EU issued a long presidency statement on the Middle East peace process. The declaration deplored 'that civilians on both sides continue to suffer from violence: horrors of terror for ordinary people in the streets of Israel, brutality of occupation for the ordinary people in the Palestinian territories' (*Bulletin of the EU* 9-2002: 67). The declaration was heavily focused on terrorism: it urged the Palestinians to work with the US and regional partners to reform PA's security services 'in order to fight terror that has so severely undermined the legitimate aspirations of the Palestinian people (*Bulletin of the EU* 9-2002: 67). At the same time, the declaration criticized the ongoing Israeli siege of Arafat's compound in Ramallah as being counter-productive. 'Force cannot defeat force' and 'restricting freedom of movement of the Palestinian leadership does not contribute to fighting terror', stated the declaration (*Bulletin of the EU* 9-2002: 67). The declaration also expressed sympathy for the Palestinian victims of a bomb attack (presumably by Israeli terrorists) on a schoolyard in Yatta, outside Hebron. 'Deliberately targeting children in their school is a particular odious act', stated the EU declaration (*Bulletin of the EU* 9-2002: 67). The declaration, moreover, welcomed a promise by Fatah that it would prevent any attacks against Israeli civilians and called on other Palestinian groups to do the same (*Bulletin of the EU* 9-2002: 67).

In December 2002, the Copenhagen European Council called 'upon the Israeli and Palestinian people to break the endless cycle of violence' (*Bulletin of the EU* 12-2002: 14). In unusually blunt language, the EU reiterated 'its strong and unequivocal condemnation of all acts of terrorism. Suicide attacks do irreparable damage to the Palestinian cause' (*Bulletin of the EU* 12-2002: 14). The same declaration also called 'upon Israel to stop excessive use of force and extra-judicial killings, which do not bring security to the Israeli population' (*Bulletin of the EU* 12-2002: 14). It went on to state that violence and confrontation must give way to negotiations and compromise and that all efforts should now be directed at translating the two-state solution into reality (*Bulletin of the EU* 12-2002: 14). However, in this context, the EU was alarmed by the continuing illegal settlement activities, which threaten to render the two-State solution physically impossible to implement. The expansion of settlements and related construction, as widely documented including by the European Union's Settlement Watch, violates international law, inflames an already volatile situation, and reinforces the fear of Palestinians that Israel is not genuinely committed to end the occupation. It is an obstacle to peace. The European Council urges the Government of Israel to reverse its settlement policy and as a first step immediately apply a full and effective freeze on all settlement activities. It calls for an end to further land confiscation for the construction of the so-called security fence. (*Bulletin of the EU* 12-2002: 14)

This was one of the strongest statements by the EU against the Israeli settlements during the second intifada.

The Seville Declaration

Another landmark resolution in the EU's diplomatic history in the Israeli–Arab conflict was the Seville Declaration of June 2002. The declaration stated that the crisis in the Middle East had 'reached a dramatic turning point. Further escalation will render the situation uncontrollable. The parties on their own cannot find a solution' (*Bulletin of the EU* 6-2002: 22). The European Council therefore suggested the early convening of an international conference, which, among other things, would confirm the parameters of a solution to the conflict and establish a realistic and well-defined timescale for achieving it (*Bulletin of the EU* 6-2002: 22). In line with the spirit of the time, the declaration was very harsh against Palestinian terrorism, stating that 'the peace process and the stability of the region cannot be hostage to terrorism. The fight against terrorism must go on; but so at the same time must the negotiation of a political solution' (*Bulletin of the EU* 6-2002: 22). The Seville Declaration also included a major innovation with regards to the two-state solution. For the first time ever, an EU declaration stated that the two-state solution should be based on the 1967 borders; if necessary, with minor adjustments agreed by the parties:

The objective is an end to the occupation and the early establishment of a democratic, viable, peaceful and sovereign State of Palestine, on the basis of the 1967 borders, if necessary with minor adjustments agreed by the parties. The end result should be two States living side by side within secure and recognized borders enjoying normal relations with their neighbours. In this context, a fair solution should be found to the complex issue of Jerusalem, and a just, viable and agreed solution to the problem of the Palestinian refugees. (*Bulletin of the EU* 6-2002: 22)

This was also the first time the EU addressed the final status issues of Jerusalem and refugees within the framework of a two-state solution. The Seville Declaration, moreover, stated that it was essential to reform the PA, especially the security sector, and hold Palestinian elections (*Bulletin of the EU* 6-2002: 22). It went on to state that military operations in the occupied territories must end, so must restrictions on freedom of movement, plus that 'walls will not bring peace' – the first reference by the EU in the *Bulletin* to the barrier/wall that Israel was building (*Bulletin of the EU* 6-2002: 22).

Member of the Quartet on the Middle East

The Seville Declaration ended with the EU stating that it would pursue every opportunity for peace within the newly established Quartet on the Middle East and contribute fully to peace-building and reconstruction in the Palestinian territories (*Bulletin of the EU* 6-2002: 22). The other three members of the Quartet were the UN, the US and Russia. The Quartet's mandate was to help mediate the negotiations and to support Palestinian economic development and institution-building. In July 2002, the Council stressed the need for the Quartet to establish a road map for peace between Israel and the PA in order to achieve a final agreement within three years (*Bulletin of the EU* 7/8-2002: 95). The following month, the Quartet decided to start working on a three-phased plan known as the 'road map', which was supposed to end with the creation of a Palestinian state as part of a permanent agreement by 2005. The *Bulletin* reported that the plan was 'in line with the EU's proposals' (*Bulletin of the EU* 9-2002: 77). The Copenhagen Declaration of December 2002 stated that the European Council attached 'the highest priority to the adoption on 20 December this year by the Middle East Quartet of a joint road map with clear timelines for the establishment of a Palestinian State by 2005' (*Bulletin of the EU* 12-2002: 14). The implementation of the road map was supposed to be based on parallel progress in the security, political and economic fields, closely monitored by the Quartet, according to the EU declaration (*Bulletin of the EU* 12-2002: 14).

As the publication of the road map was initially delayed, the Brussels European Council of 20–1 March 2003 stated that 'it must be published and implemented immediately' (*Bulletin of the EU* 3-2003: 22). The Quartet's work on the road map coincided with the period leading up to the invasion of Iraq, with the Brussels European Council taking place just five days before the invasion. In the Brussels Declaration, the European Council stated that

> the Iraqi crisis makes it all the more imperative that the other problems of the region be tackled and resolved. The Israeli–Palestinian conflict, in particular, remains a cause of great concern. (*Bulletin of the EU* 3-2003: 22)

This was a remarkably similar statement to the one issued by the EC before the 1990–1 Gulf war, when the EC responded to Iraq's invasion of Kuwait by stating that it was determined to multiply its efforts aimed at resolving the other conflicts of the region, most notably the Israeli–Arab conflict (*Bulletin of the EC* 9-1990: 83). The Brussels Declaration went on to state the EU's 'full support for the international community's vision of two States living side by side in peace and security, on the basis of the 1967 borders. All those involved share a historic responsibility for turning this vision into reality' (*Bulletin of the EU* 3-2003: 22). As the EU had done many times during the peace process of the 1990s, the Brussels Declaration stated that the Union 'has and will continue to spare no effort to achieve peace in the Middle East, to the benefit of the peoples of the region but also for international peace and stability' (*Bulletin of the EU* 3-2003: 22).

The road map was finally released on 30 April 2003. It consisted of three phases:

- Phase one was to end the violence and return to the pre-intifada territorial status quo.
- Phase two was to create a Palestinian state with provisional borders.
- Phase three was to negotiate a permanent agreement.

The plan was accepted by both sides, albeit with a long list of Israeli reservations. The Thessaloniki European Council of 19–20 June 2003 welcomed the road map as 'a historic opportunity for peace in the Middle East' (*Bulletin of the EU* 6-2003: 19). It further stated that the EU was 'determined that this opportunity for peace should not be missed' (*Bulletin of the EU* 6-2003 :19).

After the road map was issued, the European Council regularly reiterated its determination to contribute to all aspects of its implementation. In particular, the European Council stressed the need and urgency of setting up a credible and effective third-party monitoring mechanism (*Bulletin of the EU* 10-2003: 19). In the following years, the European Council reaffirmed several times its belief that the road map represented the only route to achieving a negotiated two-state solution and its determination to pursue vigorously the course set out in the road map, including the two sides' obligations (see, for example, *Bulletin of the EU* 6-2004: 21–2).

Reforming the PA, Dealing with Hamas

When the EU began calling for the road map to be established in the summer of 2002, it simultaneously stressed the need for the PA to reform 'in all sectors in preparation for statehood, notably in the framework of free and fair elections' (*Bulletin of the EU* 7/8-2002: 95). A key part of the reforms was President Arafat's decision to appoint a Prime Minister for the first time, Mahmoud Abbas, which was welcomed by the EU as a step in the right direction (*Bulletin of the EU* 1/2-2003: 8). Another key part was reforming the PA's security sector (*Bulletin of the EU* 9-2003: 66). The EU often called on the PA during this period to concretely demonstrate its determination in fighting terrorism and consolidating its security forces under the clear control of a duly empowered Prime Minister and Interior Minister (*Bulletin of the EU* 10-2003: 18).

The Thessaloniki European Council of 19–20 June 2003 marked the beginning of a new EU policy vis-à-vis Hamas. Up until then, the EU had very rarely mentioned Hamas in its declarations, save for a few condemnations of its terror attacks against Israel. In the Thessaloniki Declaration, the European Council stated:

> The European Union unequivocally condemns terrorism and will contribute to efforts aimed at cutting off support, including arms and financing,

to terrorist groups. It is also ready to help the Palestinian Authority in its efforts to stop terrorism, including its capacity to prevent terrorist financing. The Union demands that Hamas and other groups declare immediately a ceasefire and halt all terrorist activity, and recalls that the Council is urgently examining the case for wider action against Hamas fund-raising. It is essential that all concerned, in particular the countries of the region, condemn terrorism and assist in efforts to eradicate it. (*Bulletin of the EU* 6-2003: 19)

It is clear that the EU, after the outbreak of the second intifada and the 9/11 attacks in the US, underwent a profound transformation in how it regarded Palestinian terrorism. From not having mentioned at all the major Palestinian terror attacks against Israel in the 1970s, the EU came to see 'the fight against all forms of terrorism' as 'paramount in the quest for a just and comprehensive peace in the Middle East' (*Bulletin of the EU* 7/8-2003: 80).

After a particularly deadly Hamas suicide bomb in Jerusalem in August 2003, the EU issued a presidency statement calling the attack 'evil' (*Bulletin of the EU* 7/8-2003: 80). The next month, after new suicide bombings in Israel, the EU started the process of putting the political branch of Hamas on its terror list. On the symbolically important date of 11 September 2003, a presidency statement from the EU read:

The European Union thus considers the authors of these acts as enemies of peace and strongly urges the Palestinian Authority to take all necessary concrete measures against those terrorist organisations that are opposed to any political dialogue and undermine all the efforts to restore hope and to bring peace, security and better conditions of life to the region. It is in this context and in the framework of the global fight against terrorism that the EU decided, on September 5 and 6 at the informal ministerial meeting of Riva del Garda, to begin procedures leading to the insertion of the political branch of Hamas in the European list of terrorist organisations. (*Bulletin of the EU* 9-2003: 66)

In October 2003, the Brussels European Council stated that 'terrorist attacks against Israel have no justification whatsoever' (*Bulletin of the EU* 10-2003: 18). The Brussels European Council of June 2004 stated that 'violence and terror have no place in the search for a just and lasting peace in the Middle East' (*Bulletin of the EU* 6-2004: 22).

The Barrier/Wall

The EU initially had a hard time finding agreed-upon language for the structure that Israel started to build in 2002 along the Green Line and in some parts beyond it. It was alternatively referred to as a wall that will not bring peace (*Bulletin of the EU* 6-2002: 22), 'the so-called security fence' (*Bulletin of the EU* 12-2002: 14), 'the dividing wall' (*Bulletin of the EU* 7/8-2003: 102), 'the security wall' (*Bulletin of the EU* 9-2003: 66) and finally, 'the separation barrier' (*Bulletin of the EU* 6-2005: 24). Regardless of the naming of the structure, the EU was consistent in its criticism of it, in particular of the parts built beyond the Green Line. The strongest EU statement against the barrier/wall came in the Brussels European Council of 16–17 October 2003:

> The European Council is particularly concerned by the route marked out for the so-called security fence in the Occupied West Bank. The envisaged departure of the route from the 'green line' could prejudice future negotiations and make the two-State solution physically impossible to implement. It would cause further humanitarian and economic hardship to the Palestinians. Thousands of Palestinians west of the fence are being cut off from essential services in the West Bank; Palestinians east of the fence will lose access to land and water resources. (*Bulletin of the EU* 10-2003: 19)

Two months later, in December 2003, the EU stated that it was 'alarmed by the creation of a closed zone between this "fence" and the Green Line' (*Bulletin of the EU* 12-2003: 17). In the summer of 2005, the Council stated that the construction of the separation barrier in the occupied Palestinian territory, including in and around East Jerusalem, was contrary to the relevant provisions of international law (*Bulletin of the EU* 6-2005: 24).

Besides the criticism by the EU of the barrier/wall, another common point of criticism of Israel in the road map-period was the call on Israel to freeze all settlement activity (including natural growth of settlements) and dismantle settlements/outposts built after March 2001, as stipulated by the road map (*Bulletin of the EU* 10-2003: 19).

Israel's 2005 Withdrawal from Gaza and Parts of the Northern West Bank

The European Council was supportive of the proposal for an Israeli withdrawal from the Gaza Strip and the northern West Bank from the very beginning these plans began to surface. The thinking in the EU was that such a withdrawal could represent a significant step towards the implementation of the road map, provided that it took place in accordance with the following principles, outlined by the Council on 23 February 2004:

- that it took place in the context of the road map;
- that it was a step towards a two-state solution;
- that it did not involve a transfer of settlement activity to the West Bank;
- that there was an organized and negotiated handover of responsibility to the PA;
- that Israel facilitated the rehabilitation and reconstruction of Gaza. (*Bulletin of the EU* 3-2004: 15)

In April 2004, the Council stated the EU's readiness 'to work on concrete measures to make a success of Israel's disengagement from Gaza' (*Bulletin of the EU* 4-2004: 115). The Council reiterated its view in October 2004 that an Israeli withdrawal from the Gaza Strip and parts of the northern West Bank could represent a significant step towards the implementation of the road map if it was a full and complete withdrawal and implemented in accordance with the five elements laid down by the European Council in March 2004, and not an attempt to replace the road map and the two-state solution it encompassed (*Bulletin of the EU* 10-2004: 86). Several times during the period leading up the withdrawal, the EU stated that although it was 'encouraged by the prospect of the dismantling of settlements', it called 'on Israel to observe its obligations, to freeze all settlement activity, and to dismantle outposts' (*Bulletin of the EU* 4-2005: 64). Two months before the disengagement, the Brussels European Council of June 2005, commended

> the political courage shown by the leaders of the two sides with regard to the withdrawal from Gaza and certain parts of the northern West Bank.

The Council calls on countries in the region to facilitate the Palestinian Authority's efforts to establish control in its territory and to step up their political and economic support. It stresses the importance of a successful disengagement, including for the advancement of the peace process. The European Council confirms the European Union's support for the Quartet's Special Envoy for disengagement, Mr James Wolfensohn, and its determination to work in close cooperation with him to ensure the success of the project. To ensure the social and economic viability of Gaza, the European Council stresses the need for access to the outside, particularly through the borders with Egypt and through a port and an airport, and to establish a meaningful link with the West Bank. (*Bulletin of the EU* 6-2005: 24)

After the withdrawal took place in August 2005, the Council 'commended Israel's armed forces and police for the smooth and professional way in which settlers were evacuated and the Palestinian Authority and people for maintaining a peaceful environment during the evacuation' (*Bulletin of the EU* 10-2005: 72). However, the same statement also expressed the Council's 'grave concern about the ongoing expansion of Israeli settlements in the West Bank and the continuing construction of the separation barrier' (*Bulletin of the EU* 10-2005: 72). The European Commission stated that the disengagement had generated momentum that the EU should strive to maintain in order to revitalise the implementation of the road map. Furthermore, the Commission also assessed the need to increase the EU's financial assistance to the Palestinians over the period 2006–8. It also recalled the central role played by the European Neighbourhood Policy, which both Israel and the PA had joined (*Bulletin of the EU* 10-2005: 72).

As part of the momentum generated by the Israeli withdrawal, the Council decided in November 2005 to launch an urgent Common Security and Defence Policy (CSDP) mission, the European Union Border Assistance Mission at Rafah (EUBAM Rafah), to monitor the operations at the Rafah border crossing between Gaza and Egypt (*Bulletin of the EU* 11-2005: 72). According to the Council, the mission reflected the strong commitment of the EU to support the parties as they worked together for a lasting, negotiated settlement (*Bulletin of the EU* 12-2005: 17).

The Rule of Origin Dispute Continues

Related to the question of settlements, the issue of Israeli products' rule of origin dragged on during the decade, sowing the seeds for what in the next decade would be a huge issue of differentiation in the EU's relations with Israel. In November 2001, the European Commission confirmed 'its doubts about the validity of the certificates of origin issued by the Israeli authorities for goods produced in the Occupied Territories of the West Bank, Gaza Strip, the Golan Heights and East Jerusalem' (*Bulletin of the EU* 11-2001: 108). The Commission 'recommended European importers and the customs authorities of the Member States to take precautionary measures such as the lodging of guarantees' (*Bulletin of the EU* 11-2001: 108). A year later, in October 2002, at the third EU–Israel Association Council meeting, the *Bulletin* reported that 'the parties also examined – without reaching an agreement – the issue of the origin rules of products exported by Israel from colonies on Palestinian territory' (*Bulletin of the EU* 10-2002: 92). In that meeting, the EU

> reiterated the importance it attached to the correct application of the Association Agreement, in particular its territorial scope, and called on Israel to continue talks with a view to finding a mutually acceptable technical solution. The European Union acknowledged that Israel's security concerns were legitimate, but reiterated that they must be addressed with full respect for human rights and the rule of law. (*Bulletin of the EU* 10-2002: 92)

In June 2005, the European Council issued a very strong declaration against the settlements, calling 'for the abolition of financial and tax incentives and direct and indirect subsidies, and the withdrawal of exemptions benefiting the settlements and their inhabitants' (*Bulletin of the EU* 6-2005: 24). The Council went on to stress 'the need for a halt to Israeli settlement activities in the Palestinian territories. This implies a complete cessation of construction of dwellings and new infrastructures such as bypass roads' (*Bulletin of the EU* 6-2005: 24).

Further Reform of the PA, More Help from the EU

PA President Yasser Arafat died in November 2004. The European Council expressed its condolences to the Palestinian people and commended the approach of the current leadership to organize a smooth transition. It concluded that immediate action was needed to support the presidential election, improve security and give financial backing to the PA (*Bulletin of the EU* 11-2004: 88). In particular, the Council underlined its readiness to support the electoral process in the Palestinian territories. It called on the PA to organize elections in accordance with international standards under the authority of an independent electoral commission and simultaneously called upon Israel to facilitate these elections (*Bulletin of the EU* 11-2004: 13). In December 2004, the Council stated that the EU 'will support the electoral process financially, technically and politically', and also provide an observer mission (*Bulletin of the EU* 12-2004: 19).

The 2005 Palestinian Presidential election – the first to be held since 1996 – took place in January 2005. It was boycotted by Hamas and Palestinian Islamic Jihad, and was therefore easily won by Mahmoud Abbas. The EU congratulated Abbas for his victory and paid 'tribute to the Palestinian people and government for the commitment to democracy that they have just demonstrated' (*Bulletin of the EU* 1/2-2005: 91). The EU's election observation mission confirmed that the elections had proceeded in a satisfactory manner given the difficult circumstances. The mission also welcomed the considerable turnout of voters (*Bulletin of the EU* 1/2-2005: 91).

Almost simultaneously, as EUBAM Rafah was launched, the Council decided to launch another CSDP mission in the West Bank to help train the Palestinian civil police. EUPOL COPPS (official title, the EU Co-ordinating Office for Palestinian Police Support) began operating on 1 January 2006 (*Bulletin of the EU* 11-2005: 73). For a long time before EUPOL COPPS was established, the EU had expressed its readiness to support the PA in taking responsibility for law and order, and in particular, in improving the capacity of its civil police and law enforcement capacity in general (*Bulletin of the EU* 3-2004: 15). Both these CSDP missions raised the EU's profile on the ground in the Israeli–Palestinian conflict.

The 2006 Elections

In December 2005, a month before the elections to the Palestinian Legislative Council, the European Council stated that 'those who want to be part of the political process should not engage in armed activities, as there is a fundamental contradiction between such activities and the building of a democratic state' (*Bulletin of the EU* 12-2005: 17). The Council urged 'groups who have engaged in terrorism to abandon this course and engage in the democratic process' (*Bulletin of the EU* 12-2005: 17). The Council, moreover, urged Israel to cooperate fully with the PA in preparing the elections, especially concerning freedom of movement for all candidates, election workers and voters, particularly in East Jerusalem (*Bulletin of the EU* 12-2005: 17). To the surprise of many, including outside third parties like the EU, Hamas won 74 of the 132 seats in the Palestinian Legislative Council. The Council deemed the elections 'free and fair' (*Bulletin of the EU* 1/2-2006: 133), while the European Parliament 'declared its respect of the results of the election', which were monitored by the EU's election observation missions and followed 'respected international standards', according to the Parliament (*Bulletin of the EU* 1/2-2006: 133).

Both the Council and the Parliament responded to Hamas's victory by placing a number of demands on the group: renounce violence, disarm, recognize Israel's right to exist, accept existing agreements, and commit itself to the principle of peaceful negotiations aiming at a two-state solution (*Bulletin of the EU* 1/2-2006: 133). Three months after the elections, the Council noted with grave concern the failure of the new Palestinian government to commit itself to the three main principles laid out by the Council and the Quartet after the elections: non-violence, recognition of Israel's right to exist, and acceptance of existing agreements (*Bulletin of the EU* 4-2006: 85). Because of the Palestinian government's failure to adhere to these principles, the Council declared in April 2006 that it was reviewing the EU's assistance to the Palestinians, but still promised that it would continue to provide necessary assistance to meet the basic needs of the Palestinian population (*Bulletin of the EU* 4-2006: 85).

To avoid channelling money to the new Palestinian Hamas-led government, the Quartet asked the European Commission in May 2006 to set up a 'Temporary International Mechanism' (TIM) to ensure direct delivery of assistance to the Palestinian people (*Bulletin of the EU* 5-2006: 94). Even non-EU members participated in the TIM (*Bulletin of the EU* 6-2006: 20).

The 2006 Lebanon War

A new war between Israel and Hezbollah broke out in July 2006 after Israeli soldiers were killed and captured in a Hezbollah attack on the Israeli side of the Israel–Lebanon border. Three weeks before the war, another Israeli soldier had been captured on the Israeli side of the Gaza border. The Council responded to the 2006 Lebanon war by expressing 'its utmost concern at the Lebanese and Israeli civilian casualties and human suffering, the widespread destruction of civilian infrastructure and the increased number of internally displaced persons following the escalation of violence' (*Bulletin of the EU* 7/8-2006: 108). It condemned both sides: Hezbollah for its rocket attacks and Israel for 'the death of innocent civilians, mostly women and children, by Israeli air strikes such as that on the Lebanese village of Qana' (*Bulletin of the EU* 7/8-2006: 108). The *Bulletin*'s coverage of the 2006 Lebanon war, including the Council's declarations, is noteworthy because it was the first war since 1967 when the EU did not place heavy criticism or political demands on Israel.[2] As mentioned before in this chapter, the EU's less Israeli-critical approach had begun earlier, but the 2006 Lebanon war was a very clear example of this emerging trend.

Various Other Initiatives to Resolve the Conflict During the 2000s

During and after the second intifada, various non-EU initiatives were presented to break the deadlock in the Israeli–Arab conflict, all of which were strongly supported by the EU. The most well-known of these was the Saudi-sponsored 2002 Arab Peace Initiative (API), which was presented and endorsed at the height of the second intifada in March 2002 during the Arab League's summit in Beirut, then re-presented and re-endorsed at the Arab League's 2007 summit in Riyadh. The Arab Peace Initiative called

---

[2] The EU's less Israeli-critical approach is very much in contrast to how the leading human rights organizations covered the war. See, for example, Amnesty International's (2006) *Israel/ Lebanon Out of All Proportion – Civilians Bear the Brunt of the War* and Human Rights Watch's (2007) *Israel/Lebanon: Israeli Indiscriminate Attacks Killed Most Civilians.*

for the resolution of the Israeli–Arab conflict and a normalization of relations between Israel and the Arab countries in exchange for full Israeli withdrawal from the West Bank (including East Jerusalem), Gaza, the Golan Heights, and resolution of the Palestinian refugee issue according to UNGA resolution 194. The EU welcomed the Arab Peace Initiative as 'a unique opportunity to be seized in the interest of a just, lasting and comprehensive solution to the Arab–Israeli conflict' (*Bulletin of the EU* 3-2002: 21). Over the years, the EU has repeatedly praised the API and called for it to be reinvigorated (see, for example, *Bulletin of the EU* 12-2008: 15). It is also worth noting that the API is very close to the EU's own conception of a just peace in the Israeli–Arab conflict.

Another initiative that was close to the EU's conception of a just peace in the conflict was the 2003 Geneva Initiative, which only dealt with the final status issues of the Israeli–Palestinian conflict. A presidency statement on behalf of the EU stated that the EU considered the Geneva Initiative 'as a valuable contribution by the civil society in support of the Quartet's Roadmap' (*Bulletin of the EU* 12-2003: 122).

The EU also welcomed the 2006–8 talks between Israeli Prime Minister Ehud Olmert and PA President Abbas (*Bulletin of the EU* 12-2006: 16, 1/2-2007: 135–6). Around the same time, in 2007, the US convened a large conference on the Israeli–Arab conflict at Annapolis. The EU was represented by its High Representative for Common Foreign and Security Policy, Javier Solana, and many of the Member States' Foreign Ministers also participated. Before the conference, the Council 'reiterated its strong support for the upcoming international meeting at Annapolis' (*Bulletin of the EU* 11-2007: 126). After the conference, the Council welcomed the joint understanding 'to immediately launch good-faith bilateral negotiations in order to conclude a peace treaty before the end of 2008' (*Bulletin of the EU* 12-2007: 162). The Council underlined 'the EU's determination to accompany this new momentum by supporting the parties in their negotiations in a sustained and active manner and through working closely with international partners' (*Bulletin of the EU* 12-2007: 162).

Intra-Palestinian Divisions and Hamas's Takeover of Gaza

At the Brussels European Council of June 2006, the European Council began calling 'on all Palestinian political forces to engage in a national dialogue aimed primarily at putting an end to inter-Palestinian confrontation and establishing law and order' (*Bulletin of the EU* 6-2006: 20). It also called on the Palestinian government and President Abbas to disarm groups engaged in violence and terror (*Bulletin of the EU* 6-2006: 20). Later that year, in November 2006, the Council called on the Palestinians to form a unity government with a platform accepting the Quartet's three principles and expressed its willingness to engage with such a government (*Bulletin of the EU* 11-2006: 119). The same issue of the *Bulletin* also included a resolution by the European Parliament calling on Israel to end the blockade of Gaza (*Bulletin of the EU* 11-2006: 120–1). In March 2007, the European Council welcomed the agreement reached between the Palestinian factions in Mecca on the formation of a Palestinian national unity government (*Bulletin of the EU* 3-2007: 13). But further split rather than unity awaited the Palestinians, as the Mecca agreement soon collapsed. Further confrontations between Fatah and Hamas over control of Gaza led to a complete Hamas takeover of the coastal enclave in June 2007. The Council reacted strongly to Hamas's takeover:

> The Council expressed its deep concern regarding the extremely serious events in Gaza and condemned in the strongest possible terms the violent coup perpetrated by Hamas militias, in particular attacks against and the destruction of the legitimate security services of the Palestinian Authority, the summary execution of many of its members, the attacks against hospitals and the cruel treatment of captives. (*Bulletin of the EU* 6-2007: 156–7)

The same declaration further expressed the EU's 'full support for President Abbas' and stated that 'the EU will resume normal relations with the Palestinian Authority immediately' (*Bulletin of the EU* 6-2007: 156–7).

The trouble in Gaza continued. In July 2007, the Council 'strongly condemned the firing of Qassam rockets into Israeli territory' (*Bulletin of the EU* 7/8-2007: 125). In October 2007, the European Parliament adopted a resolution on the humanitarian situation in Gaza, calling it 'catastrophic' (*Bulletin of the EU* 10-2007: 116). The Parliament noted that

> as a result of the embargo on the movement of people and goods, the massive devastation of public facilities and private homes, the disruption of hospitals, clinics and schools, the partial denial of access to proper drinking water, food and electricity, and the destruction of agricultural land, the humanitarian crisis in the Gaza Strip has reached a catastrophic level. (*Bulletin of the EU* 10-2007: 116)

After Salam Fayyad was appointed Palestinian Prime Minister in 2007, and as he gained popularity in the international community, the EU became more and more involved in state-building in the West Bank in preparation for future Palestinian statehood (*Bulletin of the EU* 12-2007: 134–5, 162). In December 2008, two weeks before the Gaza war, the Council called 'for the creation of a Palestinian state, comprising the West Bank and Gaza, which is viable, independent, democratic and sovereign, living in peace and security alongside Israel, within secure and recognised borders' (*Bulletin of the EU* 12-2008: 143). However, in the same statement, the Council also called 'for a major change in the situation on the ground in accordance with the undertakings given in the context of the roadmap' (*Bulletin of the EU* 12-2008: 143). The month before, November 2008, the European Parliament had adopted a resolution criticizing Israel for evicting the al-Kurd family from their home in East Jerusalem. The Parliament's resolution further stated that it did not recognize Israeli courts' jurisdiction in East Jerusalem (*Bulletin of the EU* 11-2008: 125).

Continued Centrality of the Israeli–Arab Conflict in the EU's Foreign Policy

Throughout the 2000s, both during and after the second intifada, there were many references in the *Bulletin* emphasizing the centrality of the Israeli–Arab conflict in the EU's foreign policy. In February 2001, the European Parliament adopted a resolution which stated 'that a solution to the Middle East conflict was an essential condition for achieving peace and stability in the region' (*Bulletin of the EU* 1/2-2001: 118). The language was even stronger in the European security strategy, which was adopted by the European Council in December 2003 (*Bulletin of the EU* 12-2003: 8). The Middle East was one of the strategy's focus areas (*Bulletin of the EU* 12-2003: 8). It defined resolution of the Israeli–Arab conflict as 'a strategic priority for Europe', without which 'there will be little chance of dealing with other problems in the Middle East'.[3] In June 2004, the European Council endorsed a report from the Presidency, the Commission and its High Representative for the Common Foreign and Security Policy (CFSP) on the EU's strategic partnership with the Mediterranean and the Middle East, which sought to establish 'a common zone of peace, prosperity and progress in the Mediterranean and the Middle East' (*Bulletin of the EU* 6-2004: 17). The Council noted, however, 'that it will not be possible to fully build a common zone of peace, prosperity and progress unless a just and lasting settlement of the Arab–Israeli conflict is found' (*Bulletin of the EU* 6-2004: 17). In June 2005, the European Council stressed

> the global strategic importance of peace, stability and prosperity in the Mediterranean. This is the context in which the European commitment to the resolution of the Middle East conflict must be seen. The European Union is firmly resolved to continue its action with a view to achieving this goal. (*Bulletin of the EU* 6-2005: 23)

And so it continued over the decade. In December 2006, the European Council 'noted with concern that the Middle East is faced with one of the worst crises in years. The Israeli–Arab conflict is at the heart of this crisis' (*Bulletin of the EU* 12-2006: 16). In October 2008, the European Council stated that 'the Middle East peace process will remain a top priority for the European Union in 2009' (*Bulletin of the EU* 12-2008: 15). As the Union had stated many times in the past, it stated even this time that 'the EU will do all it can both practically and politically to drive the peace process forward next year' (*Bulletin of the EU* 12-2008: 15).

The 2008–9 Gaza War

However, instead of driving the peace process forward, a war in Gaza drove it backward. The EU's less Israeli-critical approach of the 2000s, which

---

[3] These two quotes are from the European security strategy (2003: 8)

was visible during the second intifada and the 2006 Lebanon war, became even clearer during the 2008–9 Gaza war. The war was met with very lame reactions by the EU, almost without criticism of both Israel and Hamas in the *Bulletin*. Without assigning blame, the Council deeply deplored 'the loss of life during this conflict, particularly the civilian casualties. The Council reminded all parties to the conflict to fully respect human rights and comply with their obligations under international humanitarian law' (*Bulletin of the EU* 1/2-2009: 152). The Council, moreover, expressed the EU's readiness to reactivate EUBAM Rafah as soon as conditions allowed, and also to examine the possibility of extending the mission to other cross-ings in Gaza (*Bulletin of the EU* 1/2-2009: 152). The EU's lame reaction to the 2008–9 Gaza war was in stark contrast to how the EC/EU had historically reacted to Israeli–Arab/Palestinian wars and other outbreaks of violence between the parties. It was also in stark contrast to how the UN and many human rights organizations reacted to the 2008–9 Gaza war.[4] Even the European Parliament adopted relatively mild resolutions. In its first resolution on the war, the Parliament 'expressed its shock at the suf-fering of the civilian population in Gaza and strongly deplores the fact that civilian and UN targets have been hit during the attacks' (*Bulletin of the EU* 1/2-2009: 151).

A consequence of the Gaza war was that the EU froze a much-expected upgrade of the EU–Israel Action Plan, which was a part of the European Neighbourhood Policy. Before the 2008–9 war, the *Bulletin* had reported about the planned upgrade in several issues. At the eighth EU–Israel Association Council, held on 16 June 2008, the *Bulletin* reported that the EU was 'pleased with the developing partnership, in particular on the very demanding question of human rights' (*Bulletin of the EU* 6-2008: 135). It also reported that 'the request made by Israel some time ago to upgrade relations with the EU was welcomed by all Member States' (*Bulletin of the EU* 6-2008: 135). In October 2008, the *Bulletin* reported that the European Commission wished 'to gradually strengthen its cooperation with Israel, both at the political and sectoral levels' (*Bulletin of the EU* 10-2008: 127). In particular, the Commission wanted to reinforce the EU–Israel politi-

---

[4] See, for example, United Nations Fact-Finding Mission on the Gaza Conflict (2009).

cal dialogue through the establishment of a fully fledged subcommittee on human rights, instead of the informal working group (*Bulletin of the EU* 10-2008: 127).

Conclusions

The decade between the outbreak of the second intifada in 2000 and the first Gaza war in 2008–9, with the 2006 Lebanon war in between, was a very violent period in the Israeli–Arab conflict. Yet all these wars were overshadowed by the 9/11 attacks in the US and then incorporated into what became known as 'the global war on terror'. Among other things, this led to a clear change in how the EU reacted to Palestinian terror attacks against Israel. On several occasions in the 2000s, the EU issued declarations saying that it would oppose all sides in the conflict who have recourse to violence and support all those who strive for peace, at one point in 2003 even declaring that its relations to parties not conducive to dialogue and negotiations would be negatively affected (see, for example, *Bulletin of the EU* 10-2003: 18, 6-2005: 24). This policy, however, was only applied to Hamas. With the benefit of hindsight, it is clear that the EU's policy vis-à-vis Hamas must be seen in the light of the 9/11 attacks and the 'war on terrorism' narrative. There was, nevertheless, an ocean of discrepancy between placing Hamas on a terror list as the EU did a few years before and the Palestinians voting to place the same group in their government.

The EU's shift towards being more critical of the Palestinians and less critical of Israel during the 2000s is something which the academic EU literature has not sufficiently recognized. The shift is visible across all the EU institutions' statements in the *Bulletin*. It is likely, as the EU stated in 2002, that suicide bombings did 'irreparable damage to the Palestinian cause' (*Bulletin of the EU* 12-2002: 14) and 'severely undermined the legitimate aspirations of the Palestinian people' (*Bulletin of the EU* 9-2002: 67). It is also likely that the EU's independent room for manoeuvre was curtailed by its membership of the Quartet, which, in addition, probably led it to be less critical of Israel and more critical of the Palestinians.

During the 2000s, until 2009, the EU's vision of a two-state solution was further developed and consolidated. The EU was also much more involved than before in peace-building and state-building on the ground through its

EUBAM Rafah and EUPOL COPPS missions, and through its massive support for the Palestinian state-building project under Prime Minister Salam Fayyad.

6

2009–19:

UPHOLDING THE SACRED FLAME OF THE TWO-STATE SOLUTION[1]

Solving the Israeli–Palestinian conflict is also a fundamental European interest. Because of the impact it has on our direct neighbourhood – and our own inner-cities. The only way out is the two state solution. (Javier Solana, the EU's High Representative for the Common Foreign and Security Policy, speaking at the Ditchley Foundation's annual lecture, Oxfordshire, 11 July 2009)

Beginning with the election of US President Barak Obama and ending with two years of Donald Trump's presidency, the decade between 2009 and 2019 was a tumultuous period, to say the least, for the Israeli–Arab conflict and for the EU's involvement in it. In between the elections of the two American Presidents, momentous events such as the 2011 Arab Spring, the 2014 rise of Islamic State, the 2015 nuclear agreement with Iran, and the still ongoing Syrian civil war – deeply affected both the conflict and maybe the EU even more. Add to that massive internal upheavals in the EU in light of Brexit and the refugee crisis, two more wars in Gaza and continued rule throughout the decade by both Israeli Prime Minister Benjamin Netanyahu, who re-assumed office in March 2009, and PA President Mahmoud Abbas, whose four-year mandate ended as the decade began. To further complicate

---

[1] The phrase 'the sacred flame of the two-state solution' was originally used by a European diplomat in an interview with *European Voice* (Gardner 2013).

the picture, President Trump shook up both the Israeli–Arab conflict and the EU by moving the American embassy to Jerusalem, cutting funds to the Palestinians, exiting the nuclear deal with Iran, and declaring in the same week as he was inaugurated that he did not care if the EU split apart or stayed together (interviewed by *The Times* 2017).

While this period ended with high uncertainty about where both the conflict and the EU were heading, it is easy to forget today that it started with a lot of optimism in Europe about what President Obama could do for the conflict. Unsurprisingly, the EU and many of the Member States were among the foremost believers. As it had done so many times before in crisis situations in the Middle East, the Council of the European Union responded to the 2011 Arab Spring by stating that 'the fundamental changes across the Arab world have made the need for progress on the Middle East Peace Process all the more urgent' (Council of the European Union 2011) Optimism about progress in the conflict was further reinforced by Prime Minister Fayyad's plan for a Palestinian state, which was supposed to be established in 2011. Both no state was established and the hesitant twenty-seven Member States of the EU could not decide on a common position on either the 2011 or 2012 Palestinian bid for statehood. After this, much of the EU's work vis-à-vis the conflict shifted from focusing on Palestinian state-building to differentiation – the policy of excluding settlement-linked entities and activities from the internationally recognized Israel in the EU's relations with Israel. This became a major issue in the middle of the 2010s with huge potential, but the unofficial differentiation strategy has so far changed very little on the ground in the conflict.

Israel's Prime Minister Benjamin Netanyahu developed his own differentiation strategy between the EU and individual Member States, focusing on cultivating close relations with some Member States, in part to weaken the EU's role in the conflict. It seems to have been a successful strategy so far, as the EU (writing in September 2019) has not been able to formulate Foreign Affairs Council conclusions on the conflict since June 2016. While High Representative Federica Mogherini continues to emphasize the stubbornness of the EU in relation to the two-state solution, the situation on the ground in the Palestinian territories, together with the fragmentation of the EU's policy vis-à-vis the conflict, the election of Trump, and the rise of various right-wing, nationalist or populist governments and parties in Europe, means that there currently is high uncertainty about where both the conflict is heading and the EU's role in it.

Jerusalem as the Future Capital of Two States

In December 2009, just after the *Bulletin* had ceased to exist, the Swedish presidency led the Council to issue a major declaration calling for Jerusalem to be the capital of a future Palestinian state:

> The Council recalls that it has never recognised the annexation of East Jerusalem. If there is to be a genuine peace, a way must be found through negotiations to resolve the status of Jerusalem as the future capital of two states. The Council calls for the reopening of Palestinian institutions in Jerusalem in accordance with the Roadmap. It also calls on the Israeli government to cease all discriminatory treatment of Palestinians in East Jerusalem. (Council of the European Union 2009)

This was a major development in the EU's vision of a just peace in the conflict, which then constantly was repeated in future declarations. Before the Council issued the declaration on Jerusalem in December 2009, a draft version containing even more explicit formulations on Jerusalem had been leaked to the Israeli press (Ravid 2009). This was the beginning of a new trend which would become more prevalent during the decade – that Israel managed, often through its allies among the Member States, to soften critical EU drafts, which were then leaked to the Israeli press.

Obama and the Two-State Solution

Both Obama's many European supporters and his many American and Israeli detractors agreed that he had a European approach to the Israeli–Arab conflict.[2] In his 2009 speech in Cairo, symbolically titled 'A New Beginning', Obama stated that the US did 'not accept the legitimacy of continued Israeli

---

[2] For example, Swedish Foreign Minister Carl Bildt said in 2011 that Obama was 'very much on the European line' (quoted in Associated Press 2011), whereas John Bolton said in 2013 that Obama bought in to what he said was 'the "European line" that if you make progress between Israel and the Palestinians "sweetness and light" will break out in the region, and every other problem from Iran to terrorism will be easier to solve' (quoted in Keinon 2011a).

settlements . . . It is time for these settlements to stop' (Obama 2009). He went on to state: 'So let there be no doubt: the situation for the Palestinian people is intolerable. America will not turn our backs on the legitimate Palestinian aspiration for dignity, opportunity, and a state of their own' (Obama 2009). In a long address on the Middle East and North Africa at the State Department in 2011, Obama stated:

> So while the core issues of the conflict must be negotiated, the basis of those negotiations is clear: a viable Palestine, and a secure Israel. The United States believes that negotiations should result in two states, with permanent Palestinian borders with Israel, Jordan, and Egypt, and permanent Israeli borders with Palestine. The borders of Israel and Palestine should be based on the 1967 lines with mutually agreed swaps, so that secure and recognized borders are established for both states. The Palestinian people must have the right to govern themselves, and reach their potential, in a sovereign and contiguous state. (Obama 2011)

The European Council welcomed Obama's speech (Council of the European Union 2011) and so did High Representative Catherine Ashton, who said that Obama's 'ideas and objectives find a clear echo in the work the EU is doing' (Ashton 2011a). It is important to note that Obama spoke about the settlements in terms of their illegitimacy, typically avoiding invoking international law, whereas the EU since 1979 has stated that they are illegal and contrary to international law (*Bulletin of the EC* 6-1979: 93).

The EU was excluded from the US-led negotiations in 2010 between the parties, which led the French Foreign Minister Bernard Kouchner to say that it was 'too bad' that the EU was 'locked out of the peace process', whereas Solana's successor as the EU's High Representative, Catherine Ashton's spokesperson responded that 'for the EU as a whole, the focus is on a successful outcome of the talks (and not) on the choreography or who goes to Washington' (quoted in Associated Press 2010). A similar development occurred with the US-led 2013–14 talks in Washington.

Fayyad and his Plan for a State

The December 2009 Council of the European Union's declaration stated the EU's full support for Palestinian Prime Minister Salam Fayyad's plan

'Palestine, Ending the Occupation, Establishing the State', seeing it 'as an important contribution' to the Palestinian state-building process (Council of the European Union 2009). The declaration also stated that the EU would work 'for enhanced international support for this plan' (Council of the European Union 2009). Fayyad's plan for a state, which was supposed to lead to a Palestinian state by September 2011, created much needed political momentum for the Palestinians during 2009–11. Senior EU officials almost outbid each other in praising Fayyad and his plan for a state. In July 2010, High Representative Ashton said that the EU will 'work side by side with him [Fayyad] and his government to lay the foundations for a Palestinian State' (Ashton 2010). A month earlier, in June 2010, Tomas Dupla del Moral, Director of the Middle East and South Mediterranean Department in the European Commission, said 'we are proud of our joint achievements during the past three years and we see steady progress in the PNA's efforts to fulfil their ambitious state-building agenda that we support whole-heartedly' (quoted in EU–PA joint committee 2010). The former head of the EU's Technical Assistance Office for the West Bank and Gaza Strip, Christian Berger, hailed the Fayyad plan as 'music to our ears' (quoted in Bröning 2011: 104). In addition, Fayyad's technocratic idea of state-building for peace was also clearly reflecting the EU's own history and identity as a technocratic peace project. However, Berger also said, around the same time in 2010, that the EU's 'support can only be sustained if there is a clear indication that a Palestinian state will be established in a foreseeable future' (quoted in DPA 2010).

Fayyad's state-building project was heavily centred on creating security, both for Palestinians and, no less important, for Israel as well. His tough measures quickly made him the darling of the Western actors involved in the conflict, but critics were equally quick to point out that human rights and civil liberties suffered from the measures taken to restore security. The EU repeatedly criticized the PA for the problematic human rights situation in the Palestinian territories in its Progress Reports between 2008 and 2013, but the Union was careful not to criticize Fayyad personally for any of these violations (European Commission 2008, 2009, 2010, 2011, 2012, 2013a). Fayyad's technocratic approach marked a radical break from the strategies employed by the late PLO leader Yasser Arafat, and to a lesser extent by his successor as PA President, Mahmoud Abbas. But this inevitably meant that

Fayyad's plan for a state did not solve – and was not even close to solving – any of the final status issues (borders, settlements, refugees, security, and Jerusalem). Nor did it deal in any serious way with Area C, which was only mentioned twice in Fayyad's plan for a state (PNA 2009). Area C is the 60 per cent of the West Bank under full Israeli control where the settlements are located, the same territory that the Palestinians need to make a future Palestinian state contiguous and economically viable. As the EU Heads of Missions concluded in an internal report in mid-2011,

> the increasing integration of Area C into Israel proper has left Palestinian communities in the same area ever more isolated. During the past year there has been a further deterioration of the overall situation in Area C. If current trends are not stopped and reversed, the establishment of a viable Palestinian state within the pre-1967 borders seems more remote than ever. (EU HoMs Report 2011: 1)

Despite all the obstacles, the state-building period between 2009 and 2011 marked a honeymoon period between Fayyad's government and large parts of the international community, in particular the EU. Expectations quickly started to build up and all eyes were focused on September 2011 when the Palestinian state was supposed to be established. In the first half of 2011, all the involved international institutions, with the notable exception of the US government, published reports that unanimously stated that the Palestinians were ready for statehood (Ashton 2011b; UNSCO 2011; IMF 2011; The World Bank 2011). Ashton (2011b) said that 'today Palestinian institutions compare favourably with those in established states'. Fayyad and his international backers, most notably the EU, had managed to make the PA function above the threshold for what was expected of a state. This was a considerable achievement given all the constraints, but the technocratic achievements were never accompanied by any similar political achievements. The Palestinian state-in-the-making was in many aspects a technocratic success that turned out to be a political failure.

Europe's Moment – the Palestinians Bid for Statehood at the UN

In 2010–11, when it became clear that the Palestinians were planning to seek recognition at the UN for a Palestinian state, the EU and its Member States quickly emerged as the crucial battlefields for whether the bid would succeed or not. The US was not enthusiastic about the prospect of a Palestinian state that did not have Israel's support. President Obama therefore declared in his speech at the State Department in May 2011 that the US would not support any unilateral Palestinian declaration for statehood (Obama 2011). This took much of the momentum out of the bid for statehood that the PA had planned to submit to the UN in September 2011. Instead, both the Israeli and Palestinian leaderships openly declared that they would measure the outcome by the stance adopted by the EU members. Some Palestinians even implied that they were only interested in a resolution enjoying EU support (International Crisis Group 2011: 32). The EU had, arguably, never before in its five-decades-long involvement in the Israeli–Arab conflict been in such a pivotal position. The International Crisis Group (2011: 32) called it 'Europe's moment', a chance for the EU to really use its normative power as leverage in the conflict. The argument was that the EU – as the largest bloc of liberal democracies, which were neither part of the Palestinians' non-Western automatic majority, nor automatically allied with Israel and the US – was the 'key diplomatic prize' in itself, but also an actor that could influence how other countries voted (Persson 2017a: 1422).

As mentioned in Chapter 4, the European Council had in its Berlin Declaration from 1999 expressed its 'readiness to consider the recognition of a Palestinian State in due course' (*Bulletin of the EU* 3-1999: 22). A year later, just before the second intifada broke out, a presidency statement had stated that the right of the Palestinian people to build a sovereign state 'may not be brought into question. This right is established. There remains the choice of timing which belongs to the Palestinian people' (*Bulletin of the EU* 9-2000: 69). But the paradoxical reality was that, as the Palestinian Authority progressed towards statehood, from the mid-1990s to the early 2010s, the EU and its Member States became less and less ready to recognize a Palestinian state. In late 2009, during the Swedish presidency, both Swedish Foreign Minister Carl Bildt and High Representative Solana said that it was premature to recognize a Palestinian state. Bildt told Reuters:

> I would hope we would be in a position to recognize a Palestinian state but there has to be one first. So I think that is a bit premature . . . We would be

ready to recognize a Palestinian state but conditions are not there as of yet. (quoted in Reuters 2009)

In December 2009, the Council's commitment to recognize a Palestinian state was downgraded to 'when appropriate' (Council of the European Union 2009). The 'when appropriate' was then repeated in Council Conclusions in 2010 and 2011 (Council of the European Union 2010, 2011). In early 2010, French Foreign Minister Kouchner and his Spanish counterpart, Miguel Moratinos (the former special envoy to the MEPP), wrote a joint article in *Le Monde* where they stated that Europe had collectively pledged to recognize a Palestinian state. The two Foreign Ministers hinted at favouring recognizing Palestine, but fell short of actually calling for it (Kouchner and Moratinos 2010). When PA President Abbas submitted the Palestinian application to the UNSC on 23 September 2011 for recognition of a Palestinian state, deliberations immediately stalled. In the end, the Palestinians could not get the necessary nine out of fifteen votes it needed for a vote in the UNSC. Most EU members were hesitant and did not openly declare their positions on the Palestinian bid; of the few that actually did, most seemed, in fact, to be against the Palestinians (Ravid 2011).

A year later, in 2012, the Palestinians went back to the UN, this time to the UNGA and sought non-member observer status. This meant that the twenty-seven Member States had to declare their positions: fourteen Member States voted in favour, twelve abstained, and only the Czech Republic opposed the bid.

The divisions in the EU over the 2012 Palestinian bid for statehood at the UNGA were deep, between the big three (France, Germany, the UK) and between West/old and East/new Europe within the EU.

Two years later, in October 2014, Sweden became the first EU member to recognize Palestine. Cyprus and Malta had previously recognized Palestine, before they joined the EU. The Czech Republic, Slovakia, Hungary, Romania, Bulgaria and Poland had also recognized Palestine, but that was when they were part of the Warsaw Pact during the Cold War. Later that year, in December 2014, the European Parliament recognized Palestine with 498 MEPs voting for, 88 against, with 111 abstentions (European Parliament 2014a). Both before and even more so after Sweden's recognition, there have

Table 6.1 The EU Member States' votes on the Palestinians' 2012 UNGA bid

In favour	Abstained	Opposed
Austria	Bulgaria	Czech Republic
Belgium	Estonia	
Denmark	Germany	
Cyprus	Hungary	
Finland	Latvia	
France	Lithuania	
Greece	Netherlands	
Ireland	Poland	
Italy	Romania	
Luxembourg	Slovakia	
Malta	Slovenia	
Portugal	United Kingdom	
Spain		
Sweden		

been countless reports and rumours that other EU members were about to follow, even that the Quartet might do it, but no other Member State has done it so far (see, for example, Ynet 2011; Maan 2018a). However, the Swedish recognition created a certain momentum for the Palestinians, as parliaments in a number of other EU Member States (among them Ireland, the United Kingdom, France, Portugal, Spain and Italy) adopted resolutions supporting Palestinian statehood and urging their governments to follow Sweden's lead (Persson 2014). Around the same time, and contradicting what had previously been understood to be the EU's 'collective pledge' to recognize Palestine, the new High Representative, Federica Mogherini, stated in her first speech to the European Parliament in November 2014: 'You know very well that the recognition of a state is not within the competences of the European Union.' In the same speech, she also stated that her first trip as High Representative had been to Israel–Palestine (Mogherini 2014). Just like the EC being completely against equating Zionism with racism in 1975, Mogherini took a strong position against the BDS (Boycott, Divestment and Sanction) movement, even if she also stated that the right to boycott Israel, including through BDS, was protected by the Charter of Fundamental Rights of the European Union (Mogherini 2016).

It is indeed noteworthy that two decades after the Berlin Declaration, the EU has not yet recognized Palestine, despite being the leading third party in the Palestinian state-building process and despite (together with the UN, the IMF and the World Bank) deeming the Palestinian Authority technically ready for statehood in 2011. When PA President Abbas appealed to the EU for recognition of a Palestinian state during his 2018 visit to Brussels, some EU diplomats followed Mogherini's line and told the press that recognition 'is up to national governments to make, not for the EU as a whole' (quoted in Barigazzi 2018). Other EU diplomats, again contradictory, said that EU recognition could only 'come as part of a peace settlement' (quoted in Reuters 2018).

Two More Wars in Gaza

A limited war between Israel and Hamas erupted in Gaza in November 2012 and lasted a week. High Representative Ashton issued two statements during the war. In the first from 16 November, she blamed 'the rocket attacks by Hamas and other factions in Gaza' for starting the crisis (Ashton 2012a). She further stated that the rocket attacks were 'totally unacceptable' and 'must stop', and that 'Israel has the right to protect its population from these kinds of attacks', but urged Israel to ensure that its response was proportionate (Ashton 2012a). In her second statement from 21 November, the day the war ended, she 'strongly condemned the rocket attacks on Israel from the Gaza Strip' (Ashton 2012b), and deplored 'the summary executions of seven Palestinians in the Gaza Strip over the past two days by armed groups there. These represent the grossest violation of human rights' (Ashton 2012b). She did not criticize Israel at all. The same pattern repeated itself in the EU's Foreign Affairs Council Conclusions from 19 November 2012, which stated:

> The European Union strongly condemns the rocket attacks on Israel from the Gaza Strip which Hamas and other armed groups in Gaza must cease immediately. There can be no justification for the deliberate targeting of innocent civilians. Israel has the right to protect its population from these kinds of attacks; in doing so it must act proportionately and ensure the protection of civilians at all times. The EU stresses the need for all sides to fully respect international humanitarian law. (Council of the European Union 2012a)

A much bigger war broke out between Israel and Hamas two years later in the summer of 2014, following a period of growing tensions. This war lasted longer and led to many more casualties on both sides. The Council of the EU adopted two Foreign Affairs Council resolutions on the war, High Representative Ashton issued eight statements, the European Parliament adopted two resolutions, and other top EU officials also commented on the war. Both the 2014 Gaza war and the previous war in 2012 are clear examples of what this book calls the EU's more Palestinian-critical/less Israeli-critical approach, which began during the second intifada. In the two Foreign Affairs Council resolutions, there is no criticism whatsoever of Israel, though the Council stated in its first Foreign Affairs Council resolution from 22 July 2014 that the EU was 'appalled by the human cost of the Israeli military operation in Shuja'iyya [a neighbourhood in Gaza city]' (Council of the European Union 2014a). Instead, as was the case with the 2012 war, the EU strongly condemned

> the indiscriminate firing of rockets into Israel by Hamas and militant groups in the Gaza Strip, directly harming civilians. These are criminal and unjustifiable acts. The EU calls on Hamas to immediately put an end to these acts and to renounce violence. All terrorist groups in Gaza must disarm. The EU strongly condemns calls on the civilian population of Gaza to provide themselves as human shields. (Council of the European Union 2014a)

The FAC resolution further stated that 'this tragic escalation of hostilities confirms again the unsustainable nature of the status quo with regard to the situation in the Gaza Strip' (Council of the European Union 2014a). It also once again confirmed the EU's readiness to reactivate the EUBAM Rafah mission in Gaza (Council of the European Union 2014a).

High Representative Ashton's statements followed a similar pattern as the FAC resolutions, even though on 31 July 2014 she condemned the Israeli shelling of an UNRWA school in Gaza and of a market in the Shuja'iyeh district:

> It is unacceptable that innocent displaced civilians, who were taking shelter in designated UN areas after being called on by the Israeli military to evacuate their homes, have been killed. These incidents must be investigated with immediate effect. (Ashton 2014)

The European Parliament's resolutions on the war from 17 July 2014 and 18 September 2014 also followed the EU's less Israeli-critical approach (European Parliament 2014b, 2014c), again in contrast to the leading human rights organizations' reports on the war.[3]

The Foreign Affairs Council resolution from 22 July 2014 was a long declaration that also included the EU's positions on the two-state solution. As had been the case many times in the past during wars and crisis situations, the EU stated that the current crisis and the regional context made a solution to the conflict more necessary than ever (Council of the European Union 2014a). The declaration went on to state that 'the only way to resolve the conflict is through an agreement that ends the occupation which began in 1967, that ends all claims and that fulfils the aspirations of both parties. A one state reality would not be compatible with these aspirations' (Council of the European Union 2014a). This was the first time the Council had explicitly talked about the 'one state reality' of the conflict. In order to achieve a resolution, the declaration stated that the EU believed that clear parameters defining the basis for negotiations were key elements for a successful outcome. The declaration outlined four such parameters:

- An agreement on the borders of the two states, based on the 4 June 1967 lines with equivalent land swaps as may be agreed between the parties. The EU will recognize changes to the pre-1967 borders, including with regard to Jerusalem, only when agreed by the parties.
- Security arrangements that, for Palestinians, respect their sovereignty and show that the occupation is over; and, for Israelis, protect their security, prevent the resurgence of terrorism, and deal effectively with security threats, including with new and vital threats in the region.
- A just, fair, agreed, and realistic solution to the refugee question.
- Fulfilment of the aspirations of both parties for Jerusalem. A way must be found through negotiations to resolve the status of Jerusalem as the future capital of both states. (Council of the European Union 2014a)

---

[3] See, for example Amnesty International's (2014) *Families under the Rubble: Israeli Attacks on Inhabited Homes* and Human Rights Watch's (2014) *Israel/Palestine: Unlawful Israeli Airstrikes Kill Civilians: Bombings of Civilian Structures Suggest Illegal Policy.*

In addition, the declaration stated that 'the preservation of the viability of the two-state solution must remain a priority. The developments on the ground make the prospect of a two-state solution increasingly unattainable' (Council of the European Union 2014a). The developments on the ground that the declaration was referring to were continued settlement expansion, especially in sensitive areas such as Har Homa, Givat Hamatos and E1; settler violence; the worsening of living conditions for Palestinians in Area C; demolitions – including of EU-funded projects; evictions and forced transfers; and increasing tensions and challenges to the status quo on the Temple Mount/Haram al-Sharif. A fundamental change of policy on these negative developments was 'necessary to prevent the irreversible loss of the two-state solution', stated the declaration (Council of the European Union 2014a). Finally, the declaration underlined 'that the future development of the relations between the EU and both the Israeli and Palestinian partners will also depend on their engagement towards a lasting peace based on a two-state solution', and that 'the EU's continued support to Palestinian state-building requires a credible prospect for the establishment of a viable Palestinian state, based on respect of the rule of law and human rights' (Council of the European Union 2014a).

In the Foreign Affairs Council resolution that was adopted on 15 August 2014, the Council reiterated its offer to reactivate and even expand EUBAM Rafah (Council of the European Union 2014b). The resolution also stated that the Gaza Strip constituted

> an integral part of the territory occupied in 1967 and will be part of a future State of Palestine. The situation in the Gaza Strip cannot and must not be seen separately from the broader challenges and developments on the ground that continue to make the prospect of the two-state solution increasingly difficult to attain. (Council of the European Union 2014b)

A More Legalistic EU Approach to the Conflict

The over two-decades-long rule of origin dispute concerning Israeli products from the occupied territories was settled, at least for the time being, in 2010 when the European Court of Justice ruled in what was called the 'Brita case' that 'Member States may refuse to grant the preferential treatment' to Israeli products made in the settlements (Infocuria 2010: art. 74:

1). This in turn created the necessary legal framework for the differentiation strategy. In 2012, the Council issued two major declarations against the Israeli settlements, preparing the ground for a more legalistic EU approach to the conflict. In May 2012, the Council declared to 'fully and effectively implement existing EU legislation and the bilateral arrangements applicable to settlement products. The Council underlines the importance of the work being carried out together with the Commission in this regard' (Council of the European Union 2012b). The same declaration also expressed the EU's 'deep concern about developments on the ground which threaten to make a two-state solution impossible' (Council of the European Union 2012b). These developments were:

- the marked acceleration of settlement construction;
- the ongoing evictions and house demolitions in East Jerusalem, changes to the residency status of Palestinians, the expansion of Givat Hamatos and Har Homa, and the prevention of peaceful Palestinian cultural, economic, social or political activities in East Jerusalem;
- the worsening living conditions of the Palestinian population in Area C and serious limitations for the PA to promote the economic development of Palestinian communities in Area C, as well as plans of forced transfer of the Bedouin communities, in particular from the wider E1 area;
- the risk of jeopardising the major achievements of the PA in state-building if the current financial difficulties are not addressed by a common effort of the PA, Israel, and donors. (Council of the European Union 2012b)

The declaration further noted that 'social and economic developments in Area C are of critical importance for the viability of a future Palestinian state, as Area C is its main land reserve' (Council of the European Union 2012b). In December 2012, the Council went one step further, expressing

> its commitment to ensure that – in line with international law – all agreements between the State of Israel and the European Union must unequivocally and explicitly indicate their inapplicability to the territories occupied by Israel in 1967, namely the Golan Heights, the West Bank including East Jerusalem, and the Gaza Strip. Recalling its Foreign Affairs Council

Conclusions adopted in May 2012, the European Union and its Member States reiterate their commitment to ensure continued, full and effective implementation of existing European Union legislation and bilateral arrangements applicable to settlement products. (Council of the European Union 2012c)

The 2013 Settlements Guidelines

In July 2013, the European Commission issued new guidelines against the Israeli settlements in the West Bank, East Jerusalem and the Golan Heights. The new guidelines, which were supposed to go into effect on 1 January 2014, prohibited grants, prizes or funding from the EU to the settlements in these territories. Most significantly, the guidelines included a clause stipulating that the occupied territories were not part of the State of Israel (European Commission 2013b). Few in Europe took notice of the guidelines against the settlements when they were issued during the summer holiday season in 2013, but they immediately created a political storm in Israel. Prime Minister Netanyahu was, for example, quoted in the Israeli press as saying that Israel's failure to stop them represented his country's biggest diplomatic failure since he entered politics three decades ago (Ravid 2013). The Israeli government initially responded to the European Commission that it would be unable to sign the upcoming €80 billion Horizon 2020 research project if the guidelines remained in place. Israel was the only non-European country that offered to participate fully in Horizon 2020, and was expected to contribute about €600 million to the project, receiving more than €1 billion in return (Lis 2013). Underscoring that research and development had become an issue of the highest strategic importance for EU–Israeli relations, Manuel Trajtenberg, then chairman of the Israeli Planning and Budgeting Committee of the Council for Higher Education, told the ministers during the government's deliberations over how to respond to the guidelines that if Israel gave up its share in Horizon 2020, it would be 'the end of the world, a blow that even the devil never invented' (quoted in Verter 2013). After significant pressure, not least from the academic community, the Israeli government finally accepted the guidelines with some reservations. In the compromise that was reached, Israel was allowed to insert a clause that stated that it did not recognize the EU clause stipulating that the occupied territories were not part of Israel. A unilateral statement by Israel was attached to the Horizon 2020 agreement, which stated 'that references to Commission Notice No 2013/C-205/05 [the settlement guidelines] should not be construed as prejudicing Israel's principled position against it' (Unilateral Statement by Israel 2014: 1).

In the debate surrounding the settlements guidelines, it was clear that they represented a new policy tool for the EU vis-à-vis Israel, potentially very effective, as it is hard for a small post-industrialized, high-tech oriented country like Israel to flourish in the twenty-first century if it is excluded from major international research projects. As such, the guidelines represented a powerful combination between what political scientists call hard and soft power (Nye 2004). They had both realpolitikal and normative underpinnings. It is also worth noting that there never were any discussions in the *Bulletin* of linking Israel's participation in previous research agreements (FP6, FP7) to any kind of conditionality. Just as the 2011–12 Palestinians' bids for statehood at the UN represented Europe's moment in the conflict, the 2013 settlement guidelines represented another such moment for the EU. The long-sought and suddenly acquired 'player status' for the EU in the conflict after the settlement guidelines were issued was much welcomed and clearly visible in an interview then EU ambassador to Israel, Andrew Standley, gave to *The Jerusalem Post*, where he said that it was time to put to rest the misconception in Israel that the EU was only a 'payer not a player' whose job was to write checks to the Palestinians and not do much more than that:

> If you want to see the silver lining in the [settlement guidelines] cloud, it is that it has brought into the forefront and attention of the wider Israeli public just how important Israel's cooperation with Europe is. People have been focusing very much on the scientific and technological cooperation – how important that is to Israel. And that is not the characteristic of someone who is a payer, not a player. (quoted in Keinon 2013)

Later in 2013, Dutch Foreign Minister Frans Timmerman bluntly stated that 'for the European Union and the Netherlands, Israel ends at the Green Line' (quoted in Hass 2013). A year later, in 2014, Lars Faaborg-Andersen, the EU ambassador to Israel, told Israeli media that the EU was effectively 'disengaging from the settlements' (quoted in Bechor 2014).

Differentiation in Everything but the Name[4]

As a term, differentiation is not accepted EU language, even if the European Parliament (2015) has used it, as has individual Member States like Sweden (Wallström 2015). Other Member States like Germany have used the term 'distinction' (Federal Foreign Office 2018). Nevertheless, there is a clear differentiation strategy in play vis-à-vis Israel in everything but name, which since 2013 has taken a number of different forms. According to the think tank the European Council on Foreign Relations (ECFR), seventeen Member States have issued business advisories warning businesses of the legal and financial consequences involved in doing business with entities linked to Israel's occupation (Lovatt and Toaldo 2015: 7). In 2014, the European Commission implemented a policy of non-recognition of Israeli veterinary supervision beyond the Green Line, which effectively banned these products from entering the EU (EUbusiness 2014). In April 2015, the Foreign Ministers from sixteen Member States sent a letter to the new High Representative, Federica Mogherini, asking her to push forward the process of labelling goods produced in Israeli settlements that were sold in the EU (Ravid 2015). Later in 2015, the European Commission adopted labelling guidelines of settlement products (European Commission 2015). There was a crucial difference though between, on the one hand, the guidelines and the suspension of veterinary inspection and, on the other, the labels, as the two former were wholly owned by the European Commission, while it was up to the members to decide on labelling settlement products, which immediately exposed the divisions within the EU. Some members, notably Hungary, bluntly said: 'We do not support that decision' (Hungarian FM Szijjártó quoted in Ahren 2015). Greece and the Czech Republic expressed similar reservations (Lovatt 2016: 6–7). In July 2015, a strongly worded Foreign Affairs Council (FAC) resolution reiterated the EU's

> strong opposition to Israel's settlement policy and actions taken in this context, such as building the separation barrier beyond the 1967 line,

---

[4] The term differentiation was coined by the think tank ECFR in 2014. ECFR's Hugh Lovatt defines the concept as 'a variety of measures taken by the EU and its member states to exclude settlement-linked entities and activities from bilateral relations with Israel' (Lovatt 2016: 2).

demolitions and confiscation – including of EU funded projects – evictions, forced transfers including of Bedouins, illegal outposts, settler violence and restrictions of movement and access. These actions seriously threaten the two state solution. Settlement activity in East Jerusalem seriously jeopardizes the possibility of Jerusalem serving as the future capital of both states. The EU will continue to closely monitor developments on the ground and their broader implications and remains ready to take further action in order to protect the viability of the two state solution. (Council of the European Union 2015)

In public and in the press, many top EU officials have tried to downplay the significance of the differentiation strategy, often by referring to it as a technical rather than a political issue. For example, Andrew Standley, the former EU ambassador to Israel, referred to the 2013 settlement guidelines as 'a bump in the road' (quoted in Keinon 2013) and the European Commission's Vice President Valdis Dombrovskis told the press in 2015 that the labels on Israeli settlement products were merely 'a technical issue, not a political stance' (quoted in De La Baume 2015). A European Commission's spokesperson told the Israeli press that the labels on settlement products would simply 'ensure the uniform application of the rules concerning the indication of origin of Israeli settlement products. The aim is to ensure effective implementation of existing EU legislation' (quoted in Lazaroff 2015).

Even if it is difficult to establish the exact causal mechanisms involved, there is strong evidence suggesting that the EU's differentiation strategy has had a legitimizing and encouraging effect. Many other actors in the conflict – from the Chinese government, to the UN Human Rights Council, to the leading human rights organizations Amnesty International and Human Rights Watch, to the New Israel Fund, to American liberal Zionist groups – have all expressed support for the EU's differentiation strategy or have implemented it themselves. In addition, and probably encouraged by the EU's more formal differentiation, there seemed in 2016–17 to be a growing trend of what might be called more 'grassroots differentiation' where the PA, civil society organizations, and other activists involved were trying to get organizations like FIFA and companies like Airbnb, PayPal, Hewlett Packard, and others to suspend their activities with Israeli entities beyond the Green Line

(Persson 2018a). The differentiation strategy was further mainstreamed in December 2016 when the UNSC adopted resolution 2334 which called upon all states 'to distinguish, in their relevant dealings, between the territory of the State of Israel and the territories occupied since 1967' (UNSC 2016).

Earlier in 2016, pressure from Israel had managed to soften the wording of an EU Foreign Affairs Council resolution that originally had used the term 'distinction'. The draft resolution had stated that 'the EU will continue to unequivocally and explicitly make the distinction between Israel and all territories occupied by Israel in 1967' (Ravid 2016).[5] In the final wording of the resolution, the term 'distinction' had been deleted. The resolution stated:

> The EU and its Member States are committed to ensure continued, full and effective implementation of existing EU legislation and bilateral arrangements applicable to settlements products. The EU expresses its commitment to ensure that – in line with international law – all agreements between the State of Israel and the EU must unequivocally and explicitly indicate their inapplicability to the territories occupied by Israel in 1967. This does not constitute a boycott of Israel which the EU strongly opposes. (Council of the European Union 2016a)

In 2017, Israel signed the 'ENI CBC Med agreement' for cross-border cooperation in the Mediterranean basin, which excluded Israeli projects that originate beyond the Green Line (Landau 2017). In 2018, in his first major interview with the Israeli press, the new EU ambassador to Israel, Emanuele Giaufret, was asked whether the EU was planning more steps in the future against settlement building. He answered, No (Eichner 2017).

A Special Privileged Partnership with both Israel and Palestine

In December 2013, in the middle of the crisis over the settlement guidelines and Israel's participation in Horizon 2020, the Council of the European Union offered both Israel and the future Palestinian state a Special Privileged Partnership in the event of the parties reaching a final peace agreement (Council of the European Union 2013). The proposed Special Privileged Partnership would include the following incentives:

---

[5] For a full analysis of this, see Pardo and Gordon (2018).

- increased access to the European markets;
- closer cultural and scientific ties;
- facilitation of trade and investment;
- promotion of business-to-business relations;
- enhanced political dialogue with both states;
- enhanced security cooperation with both states. (Council of the European Union 2013)

In the declaration, the Council reiterated that it was 'in its fundamental interest to see an end to the conflict' (Council of the European Union 2013). But what really stood out from the proposal were its vagueness and the lukewarm response it received from both Israel and the Palestinians (see, for example, Ahren 2013). The 2014 Israeli Foreign Policy Index showed that only 15 per cent of Israel's Jewish population and 10 per cent of its Arab population had heard about the proposal (Mitvim 2014). In 2014, the Council of the European Union reiterated its offer to both parties of a package of European political, economic and security support, and of a Special Privileged Partnership with the EU in the event of a final peace agreement. The EU was convinced, stated the declaration, 'that this support and partnership, anchoring both the State of Israel and a future State of Palestine in an ever closer relationship with Europe, will provide a strategic framework for their stable, secure and prosperous development' (Council of the European Union 2014a).

The 2016 EU Global Strategy

In the summer of 2016, the EU released its global strategy (hereafter EUGS) for foreign and security policy. The key concept of the global strategy was resilience, both within and outside the Union (EUGS 2016). On the surface, the Israeli–Arab conflict seemed to fit quite well into the EUGS's new focus on resilience as an old, protracted, unresolved conflict with no quick fix that regularly lapsed back to violence. The fact that the EU and its predecessor, the EC, had been involved in this conflict for five decades was in itself a form of resilience. Many questions remained, however, of how the strategy with its resilience approach would be implemented in practice. But the most striking aspect was how different the language in the EUGS was from the 2003 EU security strategy, which had stated in its introduction: 'Europe has never been so prosperous, so secure nor so free. The violence of the first half of the 20th Century has given way to a period of peace and stability unprecedented in European history' (European security strategy 2003: 1). In 2016, the world had become more contested and conflictual, both within the EU and in its surrounding regions to the east and south. Nathalie Tocci (2017: 488) has described this process as a development from a context 'of a ring of friends to a union on fire'. This new assessment was the baseline for the EUGS's focus on resilience.

Major turmoil in Europe, the US and the Middle East had all contributed to make the whole Israeli–Arab conflict less of a burning priority. The downgrading of importance for the conflict was clearly visible in the EUGS, where it was mentioned only in one passage on pages 34–5, with quite weak language:

> On the Palestinian–Israeli conflict, the EU will work closely with the Quartet, the Arab League and all key stakeholders to preserve the prospect of a viable two-state solution based on 1967 lines with equivalent land swaps, and to recreate the conditions for meaningful negotiations. The EU will also promote full compliance with European and international law in deepening cooperation with Israel and the Palestinian Authority. (EUGS 2016: 34–5)

This was, of course, in stark contrast to the security strategy, which had stated that resolution of the Israeli–Arab conflict was considered as 'a strategic priority for Europe', without which 'there will be little chance of dealing with other problems in the Middle East' (European security strategy 2003: 8).

Resilience in the Wake of Donald Trump

The EUGS was less than six months old when Donald Trump won the 2016 US presidential election. While it was and still is difficult to discern where he stands on many issues, he clearly did not share the enthusiasm for multilateralism that is at the core of the EU's identity and of its engagement with the world. The EUGS (2016: 10) had stated that the 'EU will strive for a strong UN as the bedrock of the multilateral rules-based order and develop globally coordinated responses with international and regional organisations'.

Trump early on made the Israeli–Arab conflict a strategic priority and told the press that it would be 'the ultimate deal' for him to achieve peace in the conflict. He very symbolically went to the Middle East (Saudi Arabia, Israel and Palestine) on his first presidential trip abroad. On this trip, during a press conference with PA President Mahmoud Abbas in Bethlehem, Trump (2017) said that 'I also firmly believe that if Israel and the Palestinians can make peace, it will begin a process of peace all throughout the Middle East'. All of this – the conflict's strategic priority, eagerness for a resolution, and the conflict's role for wider peace in the region – were in line with the standard EU narrative of the conflict. On many other occasions, however, President Trump did not play an EU tune in his approach to the conflict at all. At times, it seemed as if he was in favour of the so-called outside-in approach (Israeli–Arab normalization first, Israeli–Palestinian peace later) rather than the inside-out approach, which he embraced in his speech in Bethlehem. He did not take a clear stand in favour of the two-state solution with a Palestinian state alongside Israel. Moreover, he recognized Jerusalem as Israel's capital and moved the American embassy there without any reciprocal gestures to the Palestinians. He then proceeded to cut US funds to UNRWA and other types of assistance to the Palestinians, except support for the Palestinian security sector.

The resilience approach has been clearly visible so far in High Representative Mogherini's reactions to Trump's announcement on recognizing Jerusalem and moving the US embassy there. In a speech to the European Parliament a week after Trump's announcement on Jerusalem, she spoke of the peace process as being in the 'the darkest hours':

> The region and the world count on Europe – count on the European Union – to stay engaged with a clear, united message and clear, determined work and this is exactly what we are doing in the clearest and most united manner. (Mogherini 2017a)

In that speech, she also seemed to make a point out of the fact that the EU, in contrast to the Trump administration, was both a 'credible' and 'predictable' partner, with whom both Israel and the Palestinians knew where it stood. At a press conference a day before her speech at the European Parliament, Mogherini said that Israeli Prime Minister Netanyahu could keep his expectations for others that they would follow President Trump's decision to move their embassies to Jerusalem because the EU's Member States would not follow (Mogherini 2017b). However, the Czech Republic, Hungary, Romania and Bulgaria have all mulled over moving their embassies to Jerusalem (see, for example, *Times of Israel* 2018). On 21 December 2017, the UNGA voted by a large majority to declare the unilateral US recognition of Jerusalem as Israel's capital 'null and void' (UNGA 2017; for voting, see *Al Jazeera* 2017). No EU Member State voted against the resolution, six abstained (Croatia, Czech Republic, Hungary, Latvia, Poland and Romania), while the rest voted in favour. Again, the division between West/old and East/new Europe within the EU was laid bare for all to see.

The EU has clearly sided with the PA over the US and Israel in that the framework for the peace process must be multilateral and inclusive. 'Nothing without the United States, nothing with the United States alone', Mogherini (2018a) said at a press conference of the International Donor Group for Palestine (Ad Hoc Liaison Committee, AHLC) in January 2018. The EU again applied the resilience approach in response to Trump after he decided to cut US funding to UNRWA in early 2018. In a major speech in March 2018, Mogherini argued that continued EU support for UNRWA was of crucial importance for three reasons: for the future of all Palestinian refugees, for the viability of the two-state solution, and for stability and security in the region. She also said that the EU and its Member States contribute about half of UNRWA's budget (Mogherini 2018b).

Trump's Recognition of the Golan Heights

In March 2019, Trump's administration recognized the occupied Golan Heights as part of Israel. When this book went to press, six months later, no other country had followed. Without condemning or criticizing Trump, Mogherini responded to Trump's recognition of the Golan Heights with a very short statement that only said, 'The position of the European Union as regards the status of the Golan Heights has not changed. In line with the international law and UN Security Council resolutions 242 and 497, the European Union does not recognise Israeli sovereignty over the occupied Golan Heights' (Mogherini 2019a). In mid-April 2019, three weeks after the recognition, Mogherini was more critical in a speech to the European

Parliament. She stated that 'might makes right' was not a good principle on which to base foreign policy (Mogherini 2019b). She went on to state:

> The idea that you can change borders with the use of military force is a dangerous one in Europe, in the Middle East, elsewhere. And this is why our position on the Golan Heights has been so clear, because we believe that international rules, international law and international standards must be upheld and that this is a principle that is in the interest of everybody to uphold in a very consistent and coherent manner. If you think of the situation in the Middle East but also if you think of the situation in Europe or elsewhere, international law affirms it very clearly: borders cannot be changed by military force. And this is a principle behind which the EU will continue to firmly stand and in a united manner. (Mogherini 2019b)

During the first two and a half years of Trump's administration, his so-called peace plan for the Israeli–Palestinian conflict was repeatedly postponed. All leaks to the press in this period hinted at a 'mini-Palestine' with limited or no sovereignty on much less territory than the Palestinian Authority wanted, with all or most of the settlements remaining, with no refugees returning, and with limited or no control over East Jerusalem (Persson 2018b). Eventually, in June 2019, the Trump administration decided to release the economic part of the 'deal of the century' at a workshop in Bahrain. The economic part of the deal vaguely promised $50 billion to the conflict, but many questions, such as where exactly the money would come from, remained unanswered. At the workshop, the EU was represented by its new special representative to the Middle East peace process, Susanna Terstal, who played a low-key role there. Back home in Brussels, an EU spokesperson told the press that the special representative attended the workshop 'without any commitment from our side to support it or participate in' Trump's peace plan (quoted in Rettman 2019a).

More of the Member States, Less of the EU

A trend that became more and more prevalent during the 2010s was the inability of the EU to act together on the Israeli–Arab conflict. This was already clear during the Palestinian bids for statehood at the UN in 2011–12, it was clear with the 2015 labels on settlement products and with Trump's diplomacy in the conflict during 2017–18. France had its own so-called 'French initiative' in 2016, which sought to facilitate negotiations between the parties, but did not lead anywhere (Gouvernement.fr 2016). Between June 2016 and September 2019 when this book went to press, the EU was not able to formulate new Foreign Affairs Council resolutions on the Israeli–Arab conflict (Council of the European Union 2016b). Instead, Member States, including grassroots activists in the Member States, have advanced the differentiation strategy. In 2017, five EU Member States (Belgium, Germany, the Netherlands, Portugal and Slovenia) of the UN Human Rights Council helped pass a comprehensive resolution on the Israeli settlements containing some of the strongest language on differentiation to date (UN Human Rights Council 2017; see also Dajani and Lovatt 2017: 10). This included calling upon all states

- to distinguish, in their relevant dealings, between the territory of the State of Israel and the territories occupied since 1967, including not to provide Israel with any assistance to be used specifically in connection with settlements in these territories by, inter alia, refraining from trade with settlements, consistent with their obligations under international law;
- to implement the Guiding Principles on Business and Human Rights in relation to the Occupied Palestinian Territory, including East Jerusalem, and to take appropriate measures to help ensure that businesses domiciled in their territory and/or under their jurisdiction, including those owned or controlled by them, refrain from committing, contributing to, enabling or benefiting from the human rights abuses of Palestinians;
- to provide guidance to individuals and businesses on the financial, reputational, and legal risks, including the possibility of liability for corporate involvement in gross human rights abuses and the abuses of the rights of individuals, of becoming involved in settlement-related activities, including through financial transactions, investments, purchases, procurements, loans, the provision of services, and other economic and financial activities in or benefiting Israeli settlements. (UN Human Rights Council 2017)

Another example of how Member States now lead the differentiation strategy is the passing in Ireland's senate of a bill in 2018 prohibiting 'the import and sales of goods, services and natural resources originating in illegal settlements in occupied territories' (Landau 2018).

The lack of a common EU line vis-à-vis the conflict has also been visible in several votes in UNESCO on controversial issues connected to the conflict. For example, France, Slovenia, Spain and Sweden voted for a controversial 2016 resolution on Jerusalem's holy sites, while the United Kingdom, Germany, the Netherlands, Estonia and Lithuania voted against, with Greece and Italy abstaining (UNESCO 2016). In May 2017, Sweden voted as the only EU Member State for another controversial resolution on Jerusalem, while Germany, Greece, Italy, Lithuania, the Netherlands and United Kingdom voted against, with Estonia, France, Spain and Slovenia abstaining (UNESCO 2017; for voting, see Ravid 2017a). In September 2018, eight Member States (all Western European: Belgium, France, Netherlands, Poland, Sweden, United Kingdom, Germany and Italy) declared their opposition to Israel's planned demolition of the Bedouin village of Khan al-Ahmar, east of Jerusalem, and urged Israel to reconsider its decision (Maan 2018b). High Representative Mogherini also called upon the Israeli authorities to reconsider their decision to demolish Khan al-Ahmar:

> The European Union and its Member States have repeatedly stated their long-standing position on Israel's settlement policy, illegal under international law, and actions taken in that context, including the demolitions of Palestinian communities and possible forced transfers of population. The community of Khan al-Ahmar is located in a sensitive location in Area C, of strategic importance for preserving the contiguity of a future Palestinian state. As repeatedly stressed, the consequences of a demolition of this community and the displacement of its residents, including children, against their will, would be very serious and would severely threaten the viability of the two-state solution and undermine prospects for peace. (Mogherini 2018c)

The European Parliament adopted a resolution on 13 September 2018 concerning the threat of demolition of Khan al-Ahmar and other Bedouin villages. It stated that 'the forcible transfer of residents of an occupied territory, unless the security of the population or imperative military reasons so demand, is prohibited under the Fourth Geneva Convention, and constitutes a grave breach of international humanitarian law' (European Parliament 2018). The same resolution also stated that Israel bore 'full responsibility for providing the necessary services, including education, healthcare and welfare, for the people living under its occupation, in line with the Fourth Geneva Convention' (European Parliament 2018). At the plenary session of the European Parliament on the threat of demolition of Khan al-Ahmar and other Bedouin villages, Mogherini stated that

> this is the situation on the ground: new settlements for Israelis are built, while Palestinian homes in the same area are demolished. This will only further entrench a one-state reality, with unequal rights for the two peoples, perpetual occupation and conflict. The two-state solution is today under serious threat – more than ever before – and yet there is no realistic and viable alternative that would end the conflict and achieve a just and lasting peace. This is also mainly, I would say, in Israel's interest. This is why the European Union does not and will not give up on a negotiated two-state solution. (Mogherini 2018d)

In December 2018, a joint statement by eight Member States (Belgium, France, Germany, Italy, Netherlands, Poland, Sweden and the UK) called upon the Trump administration to base its upcoming peace plan on the internationally agreed parameters for a just and lasting peace in the Middle East. These parameters were international law, relevant UN resolutions and previous agreements. 'Any peace plan that fails to recognize these internationally agreed parameters would risk being condemned to failure', the eight Member States argued (EU MS Joint statement 2019). Six months later, in May 2019, all Member States except for Hungary urged Israel not to deport Human Rights Watch's Israel and Palestine Director Omar Shakir (Rettman 2019b).

Even if the EU in 2018–19 had a hard time displaying a united position on the conflict, the normative power of the EU and its Member States was still significant. The latest example of this came in December 2018 when the US and Israel were leading a push at the UNGA to condemn Hamas. The underlying logic was that European backing would significantly boost the chances of approval by the 193-nation body. Openly acknowledging the EU's normative power, Israel's UN Ambassador, Danny Danon said that 'for us it's very symbolic to have this resolution presented with the support of the

EU' (quoted in France24 2019). All twenty-eight EU Member States voted in favour of the resolution (UNGA 2018).

Conclusions

The Palestinian state-building process was always and still is a gamble for the EU. If it pays off and a Palestinian state is eventually established, the EU will be widely credited for its persistent support of the PA. If no state is established, the EU will be accused of having pursued a misguided peace-building strategy, directly or indirectly contributing to the occupation instead of Palestinian statehood. When the moments of truth arrived at the UNSC in 2011 and the UNGA in 2012, the Member States hesitated whether or not to support Palestinian statehood. The same hesitation can now be seen in the Member States' deliberations over whether or not to unilaterally recognize Palestine. Nothing remains today of what was previously understood to be the EU's 'collective pledge' to recognize Palestine. Further improvements can certainly be made in the Palestinian state-building process, but with the PA since 2011 performing above the threshold for what can be expected of a functioning state, it is unclear what strategic objectives the EU-supported state-building process now can achieve in the Palestinian territories, except for upholding what is often referred to as the status quo, which President Trump so clearly has tried to undermine during his first two and a half years in office.

With no Palestinian state in sight, the EU shifted much of its attention in the conflict after 2011–12 towards what became known as the differentiation strategy. Even if the EU does not use the term itself, or the related term 'distinction', there has been a clear differentiation strategy in place since the settlement guidelines were issued in 2013. Like so many previous EU strategies in the conflict, the differentiation strategy has enormous potential and is a normatively successful strategy, but with little political or economic impact so far on the ground in Israel–Palestine. The fact that the EU is currently going through its worst period of inglorious disarray in the conflict has, among many other things, meant that the differentiation strategy has not developed further on the EU level.[6] The EU has stubbornly defended the

---

[6] 'Inglorious disarray' was the title of Rory Miller's (2011) book on Europe, Israel and the Palestinians since 1967.

two-state solution, but there is, as there always has been, little appetite for punitive measures against Israel in the EU. It also seems clear that President Trump's vision of a two-state solution is far below the EU's expectations of what a viable Palestinian state should look like.

7

CONCLUSIONS:
THE PAST FIFTY YEARS – AND THE NEXT?

We Europeans excel at declarations . . . it is compensation for our scarcity
of action. (Miguel Moratinos, former EU special envoy to the Middle East
peace process, interviewed in Eldar 2010)

There are a number of different types of conclusions that can be drawn from
this study and that will be elaborated upon in this last chapter. The EC/EU's
positions on the conflict have naturally evolved over the decades, but there
have been both a clear path-dependency and normative power attached to
them. Once new terminology was introduced, it often remained and often
became real policies. Other actors often followed and adopted the EU's
positions, or were at least influenced by them. The Israeli–Arab conflict has
indeed been much more important than other conflicts for the EU because
of the four reasons outlined in the introduction: (1) the conflict has been
central to the formation of the EU's foreign policy; (2) the conflict has had a
persistent unique place in the EU's foreign policy; (3) the EU's involvement
in the conflict has been based on major strategic factors; and (4) the EU has
for a long time been part of the conflict. But whereas these arguments were
true for several decades, basically up until the early 2010s, it is clear today
that several of them no longer apply or need to be revised. Moreover, there
are a number of additional conclusions that can be drawn from this study:
the EU has tremendous potential leverage in the conflict, but the biggest

rhetoric–reality gap has been between the EU's repeatedly stated willingness to use all of its power to reach a solution in the conflict and the reality of this never happening. Another interesting conclusion is what this book has called the EU's more Palestinian-critical/less Israeli-critical approach, which began during the 2000s and is still ongoing.

The Policy Departures

This book has specifically focused on the policy departures of the EU in the conflict since 1967 – when, how, and why they took place. In this regard, there are three broad policies that stand out in particular: (1) the decades-long legitimization of the Palestinians, including the PLO, and their right to a state alongside Israel in the form of a two-state solution to the conflict; (2) the firm recognition of Israel's right to exist in security and prosperity within internationally recognized borders without being subjected to terror or boycotts; and (3) among the five final status issues (borders, settlements, refugees, security, and Jerusalem), the settlements issue has been singled out by the EU since the late 1970s as an especially serious obstacle to the peace process. Five decades of EC/EU declarations on the conflict have cumulatively created relatively clear EU positions on the final status issues, which can be read on the European External Action Service's (EEAS) website. Nothing similar exists on the US Department of State's website or on the websites of the Russian or Chinese Foreign Ministries – or on the websites of the Israeli and Palestinian Foreign Ministries for that matter. In fact, it is often hard to know where many other actors in the international community really stand on the final status issues of the conflict. The 2002 Arab Peace Initiative would be one of few exceptions here. But as the former High Representative, Javier Solana, correctly noted during the second intifada, the EU has had enormous problems throughout its involvement in the conflict to move from A to B even if it knows where Z is – the solution at the end of the road (quoted in Taylor 2003: 154).

Legitimizing the Palestinians and the Two-state Solution

Resolving the conflict through a two-state solution has been the EU's most important policy in the Israeli–Arab conflict since the late 1990s. The idea of a Palestinian state alongside Israel has been present in almost all major

Table 7.1 The EU's positions today on the final status issues

Borders	The EU considers that the future Palestinian state will require secure and recognized borders. These should be based on a withdrawal from the territory occupied in 1967 with minor modifications mutually agreed, if necessary, in accordance with UNSC resolutions 242, 338, 1397, 1402 and 1515 and the principles of the Madrid Process.
Israeli settlements	The EU has repeatedly confirmed its deep concern about accelerated settlement expansion in the West Bank, including East Jerusalem. This expansion prejudges the outcome of final status negotiations and threatens the viability of an agreed two-state solution. The EU considers that settlement building anywhere in the occupied Palestinian Territory, including East Jerusalem, is illegal under international law, constitutes an obstacle to peace, and threatens to make a two-state solution impossible.
Jerusalem	The EU considers that the peace negotiations should include the resolution of all issues surrounding the status of Jerusalem as the future capital of two states. The EU will not recognize any changes to the pre-1967 borders, including with regard to Jerusalem, other than those agreed by the parties. The EU supports institution building work in East Jerusalem, notably in the areas of health, education and the judiciary.
Palestinian refugees	The EU supports a just, viable and agreed solution on this question. We will respect an agreement reached between the two Parties on this point. Since 1971 the EU has been providing significant support to the work of agencies providing vital services to the Palestinian refugees (UNRWA). It is committed to adapting this support as appropriate, in pursuit of a just and equitable solution to the refugee issue.
Security	The EU condemns all acts of violence which cannot be allowed to impede progress towards peace. The EU recognizes Israel's right to protect its citizens from attacks and emphasizes that the Israeli government, in exercising this right, should act within international law. Through its EUPOL COPPS mission, the EU supports the reform and development of the Palestinian police and judicial institutions. EU–Israel cooperation on the fight against terrorist financing and money laundering or other aspects of soft security as well as on security research represents a non-negligible practical EU contribution to Israel's security. Security arrangements should, for Palestinians, respect their sovereignty and show that the occupation is over, and, for Israelis, protect their security, prevent the resurgence of terrorism and deal effectively with new and emerging threats.

Source: EEAS MEPP, *EU Positions on the Middle East Peace Process*.

EU declarations on the conflict ever since, thus making it one of the clearest examples of the path-dependency in the EU's declarations. At the same time, the EU has since the early 2000s repeatedly stated that developments on the ground in the form of the barrier/wall and settlement construction threaten to make the two-state solution physically impossible to implement.

The current High Representative, Federica Mogherini, has been a stubborn defender of the two-state solution in her statements and she sees no alternative to it (see, for example Mogherini 2018d). But while the EU's legitimization of the Palestinians and the two-state solution has shown remarkable consistency over the decades, as Table 7.2 shows, the EU's vision of a just peace in the conflict has been constantly evolving. There is nothing suggesting that it will not continue to evolve in the future as well. The EU already has gone, and certainly will continue to go, to great lengths to defend the two-state solution in its statements. One possibility, however, is that the EU will start legitimizing a 'mini-Palestine' not based on the 1967 borders, which Donald Trump seems to be doing. Another possibility is that the EU will accept a Palestinian entity with limited sovereignty, which seems to be Netanyahu's vision of peace. The issue of Israeli annexation of parts of the West Bank loomed large over the September 2019 Israeli election, but no decision has been made on the issue when this book went to press in October 2019.

The Sacrosanct Existence of Israel

Israel's right to live in security and prosperity within recognized borders has been mentioned in almost all declarations by the EC/EU on the conflict since 1971. The EC early on took a clear stand against boycotts against Israel in the 1970s, which continued during the 1980s and in the early years of the 1990s, when the Community repeatedly urged the Arab states to end their boycott of Israel. This pattern repeated itself with the EU's strong stand against the BDS movement in the 2000s and 2010s. Regarding terrorism against Israel, the pattern was rather different. There were surprisingly few condemnations during the 1970s and 1980s when the worst terror attacks against Israel took place, stronger condemnations during the peace process of the 1990s and much stronger condemnations during the second intifada of the 2000s. Israel was given a 'special status' in its relations with the Union in 1994 and was in 2013 offered a Special Privileged Partnership by the Council of the European Union in the event of reaching a peace agreement with the Palestinians. Israel has been described by top EU officials like former High Representative Javier Solana as being a member of the EU in all but name and as being 'closer to the EU than any other country in the world outside Europe' (quoted in

Table 7.2 The EC/EU's legitimization of the Palestinians and the two-state solution

Year	EU Institution/forum	Policy departure (the most important part in bold)
1971	EPC Foreign Ministers statement	First declaration by the EC's Foreign Ministers on the Israeli–Arab conflict. **No mentioning of the Palestinians.** Same with UNSC resolution 242.
1971	European Commission	The EC begins supporting UNRWA.
1973	EPC Foreign Ministers statement	The **first mentioning of 'the Palestinians'** in an EC declaration. The EC Foreign Ministers recognize that in the establishment of a just and lasting peace account must be taken of the **legitimate rights of the Palestinians**.
1975	EPC report to the European Parliament	Max van der Stoel, Chairman of political cooperation among the Nine, talks for the first time in the *Bulletin* about the Palestinians as a **people** with **legal rights** to **express its national identity in concrete terms**. This happened in an EPC report to the European Parliament.
1976	Euro–Arab dialogue	Both sides [European and Arab] explain their views on the question of **Palestine** and on the Middle East crisis. They noted with great interest the statements made by each side, and recognized that **a solution to the question of Palestine** based on the recognition of the legitimate rights of the Palestinian people is **a crucial factor** in the achievement of a just and lasting peace. A very rare mentioning of the term 'Palestine' by the EC at the time.
1977	Euro–Arab dialogue	The European side restates its view that a solution to the conflict in the Middle East will be possible only if the legitimate right of **the Palestinian people** to give effective expression to **its national identity is translated into fact**. The European side is also opposed to any moves to **alter unilaterally the status of Jerusalem**. This was the first time the EC raised the status of Jerusalem as part of the conflict.
1977	London European Council	A solution to the conflict in the Middle East will be possible only if the legitimate right of the Palestinian people to give effective expression to its national identity is translated into fact, which would take into account **the need for a homeland** for the Palestinian people. The Nine consider that **the representatives of the parties to the conflict including the Palestinian people, must participate** in the negotiations in an appropriate manner to be worked out in consultation between all the parties concerned. In the context of an overall settlement, **Israel must be ready to recognize the legitimate rights of the Palestinian people**; equally, t**he Arab side must be ready to recognize the right of Israel** to live in peace within secure and recognized boundaries.

Table 7.2 *continued*

Year	EU Institution/forum	Policy departure (the most important part in bold)
1979	EPC Foreign Ministers statement	The EC regards the peace treaty between Israel and Egypt as a **correct application** of the principles of UNSC resolution 242, but envisages the peace treaty **not as a separate peace** but as a first step in the direction of a comprehensive settlement **with representatives of the Palestinian people included.**
1980	Venice European Council	Art. 6: A just solution must finally be found to the Palestinian problem, which is not simply one of refugees. The Palestinian people must be placed in a position to **exercise fully their right to self-determination.** Art. 7: The peace settlement which the nine Member States are endeavouring requires the involvement and support of all the parties concerned. **The PLO will have to be associated with the negotiations.**
1980	'The Thorn Mission' following the Venice Declaration	Gaston Thorn, President of the Council and of the EPC, **meets PLO leader Yasser Arafat** in Tunis. This is the first mentioning in the *Bulletin* of an EC official meeting Arafat within an EC context.
1982	Brussels European Council	The European Council states that the Palestinian people should have the opportunity to **exercise their right to self-determination with all that this implies**, and that the Member States believe that for negotiations to be possible the Palestinian people must be able to commit themselves to them and thus to be represented at them.
1989	Madrid European Council	In the Madrid Declaration of June 1989, considered by the EC to be its most important advance on the conflict since the Venice Declaration, the EC states for the first time that the peace negotiations should be based on a **'land for peace'** principle and **mutual recognition**. These two principles later formed the basis of the Oslo peace process.
1993	European Commission	The President of the European Commission, Jacques Delors, welcomes the agreement on mutual recognition between Israel and the PLO as a major step towards lasting peace in the Middle East which **lays the ground for Palestinian autonomy** in the Gaza Strip and Jericho.
1997	European Council European Commission European Parliament MS Parliaments	An interim association agreement on trade and cooperation is concluded between the EU and the PLO on behalf of the PA.
1997	Amsterdam European Council	At the Amsterdam European Council of 1997, the EU for the first time called on the people of Israel to recognize the right of the Palestinians to exercise self-determination, **without excluding the option of a State**. The creation of a viable and peaceful **sovereign Palestinian entity** is the best guarantee of Israel's security.

Table 7.2 *continued*

Year	EU Institution/forum	Policy departure (the most important part in bold)
1998	Cardiff European Council	The somewhat ambiguous call for a Palestinian state is repeated in the Cardiff European Council of 1998.
1999	Berlin European Council	The European Union reaffirms the continuing and **unqualified Palestinian right to self-determination, including the option of a state**, and looks forward to the early fulfilment of this right. It appeals to the parties to strive in good faith for a negotiated solution on the basis of the existing agreements, without prejudice to this right, which is not subject to any veto. The European Union is convinced that the creation of **a democratic, viable and peaceful sovereign Palestinian State** on the basis of existing agreements and through negotiations would be the best guarantee of Israel's security and Israel's acceptance as an equal partner in the region. The European Union **declares its readiness to consider the recognition of a Palestinian State in due course** in accordance with the basic principles referred to above.
1999	European Parliament	The European Parliament considers it essential, in recognition of **the basic right of the Palestinians to found their own State**, that the international guarantors of the Oslo agreements solemnly reaffirm their commitment to all the objectives of the peace process.
2000	Presidency statement on behalf of the EU	Just weeks before the second intifada broke out, a presidency statement on behalf of the EU declares that the right of the Palestinian people to build a sovereign, democratic, viable and peaceful state **may not be brought into question**. This right **is established**. There remains **the choice of timing which belongs to the Palestinian people**.
2002	Seville European Council	For the first time ever, an EU declaration states that the two-state solution should be based on the 1967 borders, if necessary with minor adjustments agreed by the parties. This is also the first time the EU addresses the final status issues of Jerusalem and refugees within the framework of a two-state solution.
		The objective is an end to the occupation and the early establishment of a democratic, viable, peaceful and sovereign State of Palestine, **on the basis of the 1967 borders, if necessary with minor adjustments agreed by the parties**. The end result should be two States living side by side within secure and recognized borders enjoying normal relations with their neighbours. In this context, **a fair solution** should be found to the complex issue of Jerusalem, and a just, viable, and an **agreed solution** to the problem of the Palestinian refugees.

Table 7.2 *continued*

Year	EU Institution/forum	Policy departure (the most important part in bold)
2003	Brussels European Council	The European Council is particularly concerned by the **route marked** out for the so-called security fence in the Occupied West Bank. The envisaged departure of the route from the green line could prejudge future negotiations and **make the two-State solution physically impossible to implement.**
2009	Council of the European Union	The European Union **will not recognize any changes to the pre-1967 borders** including with regard to Jerusalem, **other than those agreed by the parties.** The Council recalls that it has **never recognized** the annexation of East Jerusalem. If there is to be a genuine peace, a way must be found through negotiations to resolve **the status of Jerusalem as the future capital of two states.** Also, in this declaration, the Council's commitment to recognize a Palestinian state was **downgraded to when appropriate.**
2012	Council of the European Union	Social and economic developments in Area C are of **critical importance for the viability** of a future Palestinian state, as Area C is its **main land reserve.**
2012	Member States	Fourteen Member States vote in favour, twelve abstain and only the Czech Republic opposed the **Palestinian bid for statehood** at the UNGA.
2013	Council of the European Union	The Council of the European Union offers both Israel and the future Palestinian state a **Special Privileged Partnership** in the event of the parties reaching a final peace agreement.
2014	Council of the European Union	The **preservation of the viability of the two-state solution must remain a priority.** The developments on the ground make the prospect of a two-state solution **increasingly unattainable.** A fundamental change of policy on these negative developments is necessary to **prevent the irreversible loss of the two-state solution.** The future development of the relations between the EU and both the Israeli and Palestinian partners will also **depend on their engagement towards a lasting peace based on a two-state solution.** The EU's continued support to Palestinian state-building requires a **credible prospect** for the establishment of a viable Palestinian state, **based on respect of the rule of law and human rights.**
2014	Member States European Parliament	Sweden becomes the first EU Member State **to recognize Palestine.** A number of Members States had already done so before they joined the EU. The European Parliament also **recognizes Palestine** with 498 MEP's voting for, 88 against, with 111 abstentions.

Table 7.2 *continued*

Year	EU Institution/forum	Policy departure (the most important part in bold)
2016	EU Global Strategy	On the Palestinian–Israeli conflict, the EU will work closely with the Quartet, the Arab League and all key stakeholders **to preserve the prospect of a viable two-state solution based on 1967 lines with equivalent land swaps**, and to recreate the conditions for meaningful negotiations.
2018	High Representative Federica Mogherini	This is the situation on the ground: new settlements for Israelis are built, while Palestinian homes in the same area are demolished. This will only further **entrench a one-state reality**, with unequal rights for the two peoples, perpetual occupation and conflict. **The two-state solution is today under serious threat – more than ever before –** and yet there is no realistic and viable alternative that would end the conflict and achieve a just and lasting peace. This is also mainly, I would say, in Israel's interest. **This is why the European Union does not and will not give up on a negotiated two-state solution.**

Pardo 2015: 4). The already very close relations between the EU and Israel make it hard to find positive incentives to offer Israel, as it already enjoys the three main things it wants from the EU: an association agreement, visa-free travel, and full membership in the EU's research programmes (Witney 2013: 6). Israel was the only non-European country offered full participation in Horizon 2020.

Singling Out the Settlements

As this book has shown, the settlements issue has preoccupied the EU's declarations much more than any other of the final status issues. In the late 1970s and early 1980s, the settlements came to be seen as an obstacle to peace, as an illegal measure in contravention of international law, and as the vehicle for taking over the occupied territories by changing its physical and demographic composition. In the late 1980s and early 1990s, the settlements issue was seen by the EC/EU as a test for Israel's commitment to the peace process. Later in the 1990s, together with Palestinian terrorism, it was seen by the EU as the main reason undermining the peace process. During the second intifada in the early 2000s, the settlements were seen as inflaming an already volatile situation and threatening to render the two-state solution physically

Table 7.3 The EC/EU's main policy departures related to Israel's right to live in peace and security

Year	EU Institution/forum	Policy departure (the most important part in bold)
1967	European Parliament	The first EP resolution after the war **expresses grave concern** at the situation where the existence of a State [Israel] is being threatened.
1975	European Council European Commission European Parliament	A new EEC–Israel Agreement is signed in May 1975.
1975	Member States European Parliament	All nine EC Member States **vote against** the UNGA resolution **equating Zionism with racism**. The European Parliament terms the resolution **incomprehensible and absurd**. All party groups in the Parliament are against it.
1977	European Council European Commission European Parliament	The 1975 EEC–Israel agreement is followed up in 1977 by the signing of additional protocols between the Community and Israel. The *Bulletin* described this upgrade **as a unique contribution** by the EC **to the economic and social development of Israel**.
1977	European Parliament	A rapporteur from the European Parliament reports that the House **unequivocally opposes any boycott** against firms having business contacts with Israel and welcomes Israel's request that the Commission establish a permanent delegation there.
1981	'The Thorn Mission' following the Venice Declaration	Gaston Thorn, President of the Council and of the EPC, states at the UNGA that the Arab countries and the Palestinians **must explicitly recognize Israel's right to exist**.
1982	EC at the yearly UNGA meeting	Speaking on behalf of the Community and the Member States, Uffe Ellemann-Jensen, Denmark's Foreign Minister, tells the Assembly: 'Our commitment to the right of Israel to live in security and peace **is absolute and unwavering**'.
1989	Madrid European Council	The European Council calls upon the Arab countries to **establish normal relations** of peace and cooperation with Israel.
1991	European Political Cooperation	The Community and its Member States **strongly condemn** Saddam Hussein's Scud missile attack on Israel, calling the attacks **non-provoked and entirely unjustified**, further stating that Israel's right to security constitutes **one of the fundamental principles of the policy** of the Community and its Member States in the Middle East.
1992	Lisbon European Council	The European Council calls upon the members of the Arab League to lift the boycott of trade against Israel, which is **incompatible with the spirit of the peace process**.

Table 7.3 *continued*

Year	EU Institution/forum	Policy departure (the most important part in bold)
1994	Essen European Council	The European Council concludes that Israel, on account of its high level of economic development, should enjoy **special status** in its relations with the EU on the basis of reciprocity and common interests.
1995	European Council European Commission European Parliament MS Parliaments	EU–Israel association agreement based on respect for human rights and democracy is concluded for an indefinite period.
2001	Laeken European Council	The European Council states the EU's reaffirmation and full recognition of Israel's **inalienable right** to live in peace and security within internationally recognized borders. It also calls on the PA to dismantle Hamas' and Islamic Jihad's terrorist networks, arresting and prosecuting all suspects, and issuing a public appeal in Arabic for an end to the armed intifada against Israel.
2003	Presidency statement on behalf of the EU	The European Union reaffirms that the fight against all forms of terrorism **is paramount** in the quest for a just and comprehensive peace in the Middle East.
2003	Brussels European Council	The European Council states that terrorist attacks against Israel **have no justification whatsoever**.
2006	European Council European Parliament	Both the Council and the Parliament **demand** that Hamas renounce violence, disarm, recognize Israel's right to exist, accept existing agreements, and commit itself to the principle of peaceful negotiations aiming at a two-state solution.
2013	Council of the European Union	The Council of the European Union offers both Israel and the future Palestinian state a **Special Privileged Partnership** in the event of the parties reaching a final peace agreement.
2016	High Representative Federica Mogherini	Mogherini takes a strong position **against the BDS (Boycott, Divestment and Sanction) movement** even if she also states that the right to boycott Israel, including through BDS, is protected by the Charter of Fundamental Rights of the European Union.

impossible to implement. In the 2010s, the settlements became the main issue behind the EU's differentiation strategy.

It is important to note that when the EC began to oppose the settlements in 1977, there were around 5,000 Israeli settlers in the West Bank, according to the Israeli settlement watchdog group Peace Now (Peace Now, *Settlements 101*). As Table 7.4 shows, it is of course utterly ironic that the EC's language

Table 7.4 The EC/EU's main policy departures vis-à-vis the settlements

Year	EU Institution/forum	Policy departure (the most important part in bold)
1977	Euro–Arab dialogue	The EC **opposes** settlements for the first time, also states that the **Fourth Geneva Convention is applicable** to the occupied territories (before Likud comes to power).
1977	EC at the yearly UNGA meeting	Speaking on behalf of the Community and the Member States, Henri Simonet, Belgium's Foreign Minister, refers to the settlements as **illegal measures** taken recently by Israel in the occupied territories, which constitute an **additional obstacle** in the process of negotiation which should lead to a peaceful solution.
1977	EC Foreign Ministers report to the Parliament	The report, presented by Simonet, describes the settlements as a **policy of colonizing the occupied territories** (after Likud has won the election).
1979	European Political Cooperation	The EC **singles out the issue of the Israeli settlements** as impeding the pursuit of a comprehensive settlement. According to the Foreign Ministers, the settlements were problematic because of two reasons: (1) **Israel's claim to eventual sovereignty over the occupied territories**, which is incompatible with resolution 242 establishing **the principle of the inadmissibility of the acquisition of territory by force**; (2) the Israeli government's policy of establishing settlements in the occupied territories **is in violation of international law.**
1980	Venice European Council	Art. 9: The Nine are deeply convinced that the Israeli settlements constitute **a serious obstacle** to the peace process in the Middle East. They consider that these settlements, **as well as modifications in population and property in the occupied Arab territories**, are illegal under international law.
1980	'The Thorn Mission' following the Venice Declaration	Gaston Thorn, President of the Council and of the EPC, calls on Israel to refrain from making any **fait accompli in the occupied territories** in the form of installing further settlements, which can only raise new barriers in the search for an agreement.
1981	EPC Foreign Ministers statement	The Foreign Ministers **strongly deplore** the decision of the government and Knesset of Israel to **extend Israeli law**, jurisdiction, and administration to occupied Syrian territory in the Golan Heights. Such an extension, which **is tantamount to annexation, is contrary to international law, and therefore invalid** in our eyes.
1982	Brussels European Council	Israel will not obtain the security to which it has a right by using force and **creating fait accomplis** but it can find this security by satisfying the legitimate aspirations of the Palestinian people, who should have the opportunity to exercise their right to self-determination with all that this implies.

Table 7.4 *continued*

Year	EU Institution/forum	Policy departure (the most important part in bold)
1983	Brussels European Council	Above all the time has come for Israel to show that it stands ready for genuine negotiations on the basis of UNSC resolution 242 and 338, in the first place **by refraining from enlarging existing settlements or creating new ones**. These settlements are **contrary to international law and a major and growing obstacle** to peace efforts.
1983	EC at the yearly UNGA meeting	Speaking on behalf of the Community and the Member States, Ioannis Kharalabopoulos, Greece's Foreign Minister, tells the Assembly: In the interest of the search for peace, the Ten ask Israel **to abandon its policy of gradual annexation** and of unilaterally creating new facts in the occupied territories, in particular its settlement policy which is contrary to international law and a major and growing obstacle to peace efforts.
1985	EC at the yearly UNGA meeting	Speaking on behalf of the Community and the Member States, Jacques Poos, Luxembourg's Foreign Minister, tells the Assembly that measures taken by Israel in the territories that it has occupied since 1967, which are **aimed at altering the legal, geographical and demographic structure of the territory**, are contrary to international law.
1987	EPC Foreign Ministers statement	First reported protest in the *Bulletin* by the Foreign Ministers against the **establishment of a particular settlement** (Avnei Hefetz) in the West Bank.
1991	Luxembourg European Council	A few months before the Madrid conference, the European Council states that it believes **specifically that the policy of establishing settlements** in the territories occupied by Israel, which is in any case illegal, **is incompatible with the will expressed to make progress with the peace process**.
1992	European Parliament	Resolution calling on the Commission to ensure that the funds provided to Israel from the EC **were not used to finance new building in the Occupied Territories**.
1995	European Parliament	Resolution calling on the Israeli authorities to **prevent all confiscation of land and any further colonization**.
1995	Presidency statement on behalf of the EU	The EU believes that this measure [**land expropriation in East Jerusalem**], **contrary to the spirit of the DoP** and the maintenance of the status quo in the city of Jerusalem, could put the peace process at risk.
1996	EU at the yearly UNGA meeting	Speaking on behalf of the Union and the Member States, Dick Spring, Ireland's Foreign Minister, tells the Assembly: We call upon the Israeli government not to pursue the extension of settlements. **Continued expansion of settlements does more than any other issue to erode**

Table 7.4 *continued*

Year	EU Institution/forum	Policy departure (the most important part in bold)
1996	EU at the yearly UNGA meeting	**Palestinian confidence in the peace process.** It undermines the ability of both the Palestinian Authority and society at large to deter extremists and trouble-makers.
1996	EU statement (Council of Ministers of the EU)	The Union asserts that the **Fourth Geneva Convention is fully applicable to East Jerusalem**, as it is to other territories under occupation.
1996	Dublin European Council	The settlements issue is **eroding confidence** in the peace process.
1998	Presidency statement on behalf of the EU	The EU is concerned about reports of a plan to expand settlements on the Golan Heights. If such a plan is implemented it would **represent a significant setback** to the efforts to resume the Israeli–Syrian negotiations. It would also constitute **a further complication for the implementation of the principle 'land for peace'** and raise questions about Israel's commitment to the peace process.
2002	Copenhagen European Council	The European Council is alarmed at the continuing illegal settlement activities, **which threaten to render the two-state solution physically impossible to implement.** The expansion of settlements and related construction, as widely documented including by the European Union's Settlement Watch, violates international law, inflames an already volatile situation, and reinforces the fear of Palestinians that Israel is not genuinely committed to end the occupation.
2003	Brussels European Council	The European Council calls on Israel to **reverse** its settlement policy and to **dismantle settlements built after March 2001.**
2005	Brussels European Council	The European Council **calls for the abolition of financial and tax incentives and direct and indirect subsidies, and the withdrawal of exemptions** benefiting the settlements and their inhabitants.
2010	European Court of Justice (ECJ)	ECJ rules in the Brita case that Member States **may refuse to grant** preferential treatment to Israeli products made in the settlements.
2012	Council of the European Union	In May 2012, the Council declares to **fully and effectively implement existing EU legislation** and the bilateral arrangements applicable to settlement products.
2012	Council of the European Union	In December 2012, the Council expresses its commitment to ensure that – in line with international law – **all agreements** between the State of Israel and the EU **must unequivocally and explicitly indicate their inapplicability to the territories occupied by Israel in 1967.** The European Union is also **deeply dismayed by and strongly opposes** Israeli plans to expand settlements in the West Bank, including in East Jerusalem, and in particular

Table 7.4 *continued*

Year	EU Institution/forum	Policy departure (the most important part in bold)
2012	Council of the European Union	plans to develop the E1 area. The E1 plan, if implemented, **would seriously undermine the prospects of a negotiated resolution** of the conflict by jeopardizing the possibility of a contiguous and viable Palestinian state and of Jerusalem as the future capital of two states. **It could also entail forced transfer of civilian population.**
2013	European Commission	The European Commission issues **new guidelines** against the Israeli settlements in the West Bank, East Jerusalem, and the Golan Heights, **prohibiting grants, prizes or funding from the EU to the settlements in these territories.**
2013	Member States	Seventeen Member States issue **business advisories** warning businesses of the legal and financial consequences involved in doing business with entities linked to Israel's occupation.
2014	EU ambassador to Israel	Lars Faaborg-Andersen, the EU ambassador to Israel, tells Israeli media that the EU is effectively **disengaging from the settlements**.
2015	Council of the European Union	The EU **reiterates its strong opposition to Israel's settlement policy and actions taken in this context**, such as building the separation barrier beyond the 1967 line, demolitions and confiscation – including of EU-funded projects – evictions, forced transfers including of Bedouins, illegal outposts, settler violence, and restrictions of movement and access. The EU will continue to **closely monitor developments** on the ground and their broader implications and **remains ready to take further action** in order to protect the viability of the two-state solution.
2015	European Commission	The European Commission **adopts labelling guidelines** of settlement products.
2016	Council of the European Union	The EU and its Member States are committed **to ensure continued, full and effective implementation of existing EU legislation** and bilateral arrangements applicable to settlements products. The EU expresses its commitment to ensure that – in line with international law – all agreements between the State of Israel and the EU must unequivocally and explicitly indicate their inapplicability to the territories occupied by Israel in 1967. This does not constitute a boycott of Israel which the EU strongly opposes.
2016	Member States	The UNSC adopts **resolution 2334** calling upon all states 'to distinguish, in their relevant dealings, between the territory of the State of Israel and the territories occupied since 1967'. The three EU Member States in the UNSC at the time (France, United Kingdom, Spain) strongly support the resolution.

was much stronger (terms like colonialization and annexation were used) on the settlements issue four decades ago when they were a fraction of today's 400,000 settlers in the West Bank and 200,000 in East Jerusalem.

The Rhetoric has Mattered

Many critics and even some former top EU officials, as indicated by this chapter's opening quote from Moratinos, see the EU's many hundreds of declarations as a substitute for a more substantive foreign policy vis-à-vis the conflict. There is a lot of truth in what the critics have been saying. There has indeed always been what the academic literature calls a rhetoric–reality gap between the EU's declarations and the reality on the ground in the conflict. But even if this gap is real, it does not negate that the EU's declarations have been much more important that what many analysts think. In line with a constructivist analysis of international relations, the EU's rhetoric has often shaped the reality of the conflict, even if the EU has been nowhere near enforcing a solution to the conflict, and even if many analysts would have liked to see much more from the EU. But the EU's declarations have not been empty rhetoric or just pieces of paper as European, Israeli, Palestinian/Arab and American critics often have said. On the contrary, the many declarations calling for mutual recognition and land for peace helped in legitimizing the Oslo peace process. The same is true for the EC's legitimization of the Palestinians and the PLO during the 1970s, which has long been well acknowledged in the academic EU literature (see, for example, Keukeleire and MacNaughtan 2008: 282; Miller 2011:134). This view is also shared even by some of the harshest critics of the EU's policies in the conflict. For example, Caroline Glick, one of the ideologues of the hard right in Israel, writes in her latest book that 'Europe bears a significant share of the responsibility for shifting U.S. foreign policy toward the PLO' (Glick 2014: 92). She also writes that 'America's embrace of the policy in 1993 would never have happened without years of prior open and subversive European diplomacy, both in Israel and in the United States' (Glick 2014: xx). Another important example would be that the firm condemnation of suicide bombings in the EU's declarations eventually led to the placement of Hamas on the EU's terror list, which in turn has had major consequences for developments in Gaza.

Many of the EU's policy departures – from the legitimization of the

Palestinians during the 1970s to the differentiation strategy in the 2010s – were later adopted by other actors in the international community, which points to an important normative role for the EU in the conflict. The US often adopted the EU's policies on the conflict at a later stage, for example talking with the PLO in the 1980s or advocating for a two-state solution in the 2000s. The idea of the 2003 road map was a European idea from the beginning. Many other actors involved in the conflict, both states and non-state actors, have supported the EU's differentiation strategy or have implemented it themselves. This does not prove direct causality, that other actors changed their policies and did what they did in the conflict only because of the EU without other factors contributing too. But it does point to an important role for the EU as a normative power in the conflict. The fact that both Israelis and Palestinians struggle so hard to influence the EU and its Member States on questions such as recognition of a Palestinian state, the differentiation strategy, or on how the Member States vote on the Israeli–Arab conflict in various UN forums, is further proof of the EU and Member States' important normative role in the conflict. The ability of the EU to shape discourse and set examples in the conflict is clearly visible in the *Bulletin*'s statements on the Israeli–Arab conflict since 1967, even if the harsh reality on the ground in the conflict at the present clearly triumphs over the normative power of the EU.

Related to the normative argument, there is a very strong argument that path-dependency has mattered a lot in the material that I have studied. There were certainly exceptions, but when new terminology was introduced it often remained, and it often became real policies. Concepts such as 'just peace', references to UNSC resolution 242, 'Israel's right to exist', 'legitimate rights of the Palestinians', 'settlements as obstacles to peace', 'land for peace', 'mutual recognition', 'the need for a Palestinian state', 'resolving the conflict through a two-state solution', 'firm condemnations of suicide bombings', and many more have remained in some form since they were first introduced. The main exception to this is that the EC's statements on Israeli settlements were much stronger in the late 1970s and early 1980s than what they are today. It is also important to note that path-dependency creates expectations: if the EU routinely condemns terrorism or settlements, the expectation is that it will continue to do so in the future as well.

Revisiting the Arguments

This book's overarching thesis was that the Israeli–Arab conflict has been more important for the EU than other conflicts for four reasons: (1) because the conflict has been central to the formation of the EU's foreign policy; (2) because the conflict has had a persistent unique place in the EU's foreign policy; (3) because the EU's involvement in the conflict has been based on major strategic factors; and (4) because the EU has for a long time been part of the conflict. While these arguments have been true for several decades, it is clear today that several of them no longer apply or need to be revised. As this book and several other studies have shown, the Israeli–Arab conflict was central to the formation of a united EC foreign policy in the late 1960s and early 1970s. This meant that from the beginning the conflict already had a unique place in the EC's foreign policy, which persisted over the decades, up until a few years into the 2010s. The peak of importance of the Israeli–Arab conflict was probably reached with the EU's 2003 security strategy, which explicitly outlined what had then long been the EU's twin narrative regarding the Middle East: that (1) the Israeli–Arab conflict was the key to deal with other problems in the Middle East; and that (2) resolution of the Israeli–Arab conflict would lead to positive developments elsewhere in the Middle East. This view was shared by the first Obama administration.[1] Donald Trump

---

[1] The centrality of the Israeli–Arab conflict in the first Obama administration can be seen in his 2009 Cairo speech and in many of his closest advisors' thinking. In 2011, his first national security advisor, James Jones, told an Israeli security conference that 'I'm of the belief that had God appeared in front of President Obama in 2009 and said if he could do one thing on the face of the planet, and one thing only, to make the world a better place and give people more hope and opportunity for the future, I would venture that it would have something to do with finding the two-state solution to the Middle East' (quoted in Keinon 2011b). Speaking to reporters after the conference, Jones said Israel's dispute with the Palestinians was the 'knot that is at the center of mass' (quoted in Keinon 2011b). A year earlier, in 2010, General David Petraeus, then head of the US Central Command, gave a much-noted testimony to the Senate Armed Services Committee where he said: 'The enduring hostilities between Israel and some of its neighbors present distinct challenges to our ability to advance our interests in the AOR [Area of Operations]. Israeli–Palestinian tensions often flare into violence and large-scale armed confrontations. The conflict foments anti-American sentiment, due to a perception of U.S. favoritism for Israel. Arab anger over the Palestinian question limits the strength and depth of U.S. partnerships with governments and peoples in the AOR and weakens the legitimacy of moderate regimes in the Arab world.

also repeated this narrative in his 2017 speech in Bethlehem, even if he has contradicted himself many times, both before and after that speech.

Whether or not President Trump really subscribes to the narrative that peace in the Israeli–Arab conflict will lead to peace elsewhere in the Middle East, it is clear that the EU, its top officials and Member States no longer speak about the conflict in this way. There have not been any EU declarations after the 2011 Arab Spring speaking about the Israeli–Arab conflict as the key threat to world peace or European security. Neither does High Representative Federica Mogherini speak about the conflict in the way her predecessor, Javier Solana, spoke about it as a direct threat to the security of European cities. The developments after 2011, with seismic events like the war in Syria and the refugee crisis, the rise and fall of the Islamic State, the signing and exit of the nuclear agreement with Iran, and the major internal upheavals in the EU have all contributed to making the Israeli–Arab conflict less and less of the 'knot that is at the center of mass', as Obama's first national security advisor James Jones described the Israeli–Arab conflict back in 2011. The downgrading of importance for the Israeli–Arab conflict was clearly visible in the EU's 2016 global strategy, where it was mentioned only in one passage with quite weak language. Possible future events like a new Palestinian intifada, a new wave of Islamic terrorism connected to the conflict, changes to the status quo at the Temple Mount/Haram al-Sharif in Jerusalem, Israeli annexation of the West Bank, might shift the conflict back into the centre of the mass again.

The fact that the EU's involvement in the conflict is based partly on strategic factors means that this involvement changes depending on the strategic environment. When more pressing events happen elsewhere in the Middle East, the EU's attention naturally shifts away from the Israeli–Arab conflict. The same is true if the EU's dependence on oil and trade with the region decrease in importance. While the Middle East remains an important trading market for the EU, today the EU is not even remotely as dependent on oil from the Middle East as the EC was back in the late 1960s and early 1970s.

Meanwhile, al-Qaeda and other militant groups exploit that anger to mobilize support. The conflict also gives Iran influence in the Arab world through its clients, Lebanese Hizballah and Hamas' (quoted in Bacevich 2010).

For a variety of reasons, one should be mindful of comparing the EU and its twenty-eight Members States of today with the six to nine Member States the EC had back in the late 1960s and early 1970s. However, according to Eurostat, more than half (55.1 per cent) of the EU Twenty-eight's gross inland energy consumption in 2017 (the latest available figures) came from imported sources. Of these, Russia was by far the biggest supplier, accounting for around 30 per cent of the Union's oil imports and 40 per cent of its gas imports. Norway was second with 11 per cent of the oil imports and 25 per cent of the gas imports. Iraq, Kazakhstan and Saudi Arabia were the third, fourth and fifth most important suppliers of oil to the EU, accounting for around 7–8 per cent each of the Union's oil imports. Algeria and Qatar were the third and fourth most important supplier of gas to the EU, accounting for around 10 and 5 per cent, respectively (Eurostat). Again, mindful of the difficulties of comparing the EU Twenty-eight of today with the EC five decades ago, the fact is that the EU today is much less dependent on oil from the Middle East as compared to the late 1960s and early 1970s. At the same time, it is again important to keep in mind that the Gulf countries, led by Saudi Arabia, still have a variety of leverages around the whole politics of oil (reserves, supply, price, spare capacity), which directly or indirectly can impact the EU.

Regarding the fourth argument, that the EU is part of the conflict, there are no signs at present that this will cease to be the case in the foreseeable future. On the contrary, after President Trump's defunding of Palestinian institutions, there is a clear risk that the EU will once again be 'called upon to pick up the pieces', as the former head of the EU's Technical Assistance Office for the West Bank and Gaza Strip, Christian Berger, described the EU's role in the conflict during the second intifada when Israel destroyed much of the PA's infrastructure and American involvement substantially decreased (quoted in Sheizaf 2014).

Ramifications

Beyond the book's arguments and research questions, five broad ramifications stand out from the analysis of the EU's long involvement in the Israeli–Arab conflict. The first is the EU's inability/unwillingness to use punitive measures in the conflict, despite its tremendous potential leverage over both Israel and the PA. Second, the historical record clearly shows that the EU cannot lead the peace process in place of the US, a fact that is unlikely to change in the Trump era. Third, the EU's more Palestinian-critical/less Israeli-critical approach of the 2000s is something which the academic EU literature has not sufficiently recognized. Fourth, the Palestinian territories are a *sui generis* case for state-building and aid; and finally, the disarray within the EU vis-à-vis the Israeli–Arab conflict has never been greater than today.

- There has indeed been a rhetoric–reality gap in the EU's policies towards the conflict as previous research has established (see, for example, Tocci 2005, 2009). The findings of this book clearly show that this gap has been the widest between the EU's repeated stated willingness to use all of its power to help the peace process and the reality where this has never happened. The EU has never used all of its power in the conflict against any of the warring parties; the only possible exception to this would be the EU's designation of Hamas as a terror group and the ongoing non-contact policy with the group. Other than that, there has always been an almost extreme reluctance to use any kind of punitive measures, primarily against Israel, and to a lesser degree also against the Palestinian Authority. It is not that the EU lacks practical tools in the conflict. The EU has tremendous potential leverage over both Israel and the PA. The EU's economy (in nominal GDP) is fifty times bigger than Israel's and more than 1300 times bigger than the PA's (The World Bank 2019). Yet, the perception has often been that an Israel with American support is too strong to pressure, whereas the PA is too weak to pressure. When it comes to pressuring Israel, the reluctance is probably mostly because of American opposition, rather than because of the legacy of the Holocaust, internal divisions in the EU, domestic pro-Israeli constituencies in the Member States, or pro-Israel lobbying. The EU is simply unwilling to stray too far out of the lines of the US's policy in the Middle East. If an American President – be it Obama, Trump or anyone else in the future – would use all of its leverage to force Israel to end the occupation, the EU would support it whole-heartedly. It is inconceivable that an EU Member State would oppose a comprehensive American initiative to dismantle settlements and end the occupation. When it comes to the Palestinians, a completely different dynamic is at play. With no higher objective than keeping the peace process alive, there are no alternatives for the EU than to support the PA, despite all of its well-known short-comings. Following this logic, it is very difficult for the EU to be tough and use various types of punitive measures against the PA, as weakening the PA would inevitably empower Hamas and other militant Islamists, and thus make a bad situation even worse in the view of the EU. It is important to keep in mind that the EU's vision of a just peace in the conflict is premised on a strong, not a weak PA. Consequently, empowering the militant Islamists or anyone else at the expense of the PA is a situation that the EU absolutely wishes to avoid.

- The historical record clearly shows that the EU cannot lead the peace process in place of the US With some relatively minor exceptions, the EC/EU played at best a marginal role, if indeed it was present at all, in the most important peace negotiations through the years: the 1978–79 Camp David Accords, the 1993–5 Oslo Agreements, the 1994 Israel–Jordan Treaty, the 2000 Camp David Summit, the 2003 road map, the 2007 Annapolis conference, the 2010 proximity talks, and the 2013–14 Obama–Kerry negotiations. There is nothing suggesting that this pattern will change in the Trump era, even if his much-expected peace plan will not lead anywhere.

- Israeli government officials often accuse the EU of being obsessed with Israel while not paying sufficient attention to other, much worse conflicts around the world (see, for example, Ravid 2017b). Hawkish Israeli analysts also say that being anti-Israeli is the only consistent foreign policy that the EC/EU has ever had (see, for example, Glick 2014: 224). As this book has shown, there is merit to the first claim. However, the analysis also shows that the EU became much more critical of the Palestinians and much less critical of Israel during the 2000s, a trend which has continued over the 2010s as well. What this book calls the EU's more Palestinian-critical/less Israeli-critical approach during the 2000s is something which the academic EU literature has not yet sufficiently recognized.

- This study confirms other studies' findings that the Palestinian territories are a *sui generis* case for state-building and foreign aid. The standard figure in the academic literature is that the Palestinian Authority has received over $30 billion in aid since it was established, about half of that coming from the EU and its Member States (Tartir 2018: 366; see also Persson 2015: 130). But however successful Palestinian state-building may be in the short-term perspective, it can never be a replacement for political solutions in the long-term (Le More 2005, 2008; Brown 2010; Persson 2017b; see also European Commission 2017). While the Palestinian state-building process in the West Bank in many ways resembles other state-building processes around the world, with a focus on security first, problematic elections, human rights abuses, local leaders pursuing technocratic measures supported by the many third parties involved – the crucial difference in the Palestinian case is that the state-building process has taken place under a decades-long occupation with seemingly no end in sight. This is indeed a form of contradiction in terms, because state-building is all about achieving sovereignty, but the same is true for an ongoing occupation, which is all about maintaining sovereignty. The Palestinian case is further complicated by the fact that the state-building process takes place in territories (West Bank, East Jerusalem and Gaza) that are physically separated and often hostile to each other. With the PA in the West Bank technically ready for statehood since 2011 and most EU Member States not politically ready to recognize Palestine, it is unclear what strategic objectives the state-building process now can achieve in the West Bank, except for upholding what is often referred to as the status quo – which in reality is not a real status quo, but a constantly deteriorating situation for the Palestinians. At the same time, with the hard lessons learned from the destruction of state institutions, however dysfunctional and unpopular, in Iraq, Syria, Libya and Yemen, it is hard to see how collapsing the PA could be in the interests of the EU, the US, various regional actors or Israel, or even many Palestinians for that matter (see Persson 2017b).

- The inglorious disarray that characterized the EU when Rory Miller wrote his book back in 2011 is nothing compared to the situation that exists today. As has been mentioned before in this book, the EU has not been able to formulate Foreign Affairs Council conclusions on the conflict since June 2016. After the two Palestinian bids for statehood at the UN in 2011–12, there have been several instances in the UNGA, UNESCO and other forums where the Member States have been deeply divided on issues related to the conflict. Israel has successfully cultivated new relations with some Member States, while the Palestinians have so far not been able to convince more Member States to follow Sweden and recognize Palestine. Even if other Member States would recognize Palestine, the critical questions plaguing the EU for the past fifty years will still be there, namely: what commitment and capabilities do the EU really have to help resolve the conflict, end the occupation and create a Palestinian state? With an EU in great internal turmoil and with the rise of various right-wing, nationalist or populist governments and parties in Europe, many of whom are pro-Israeli and anti-Muslim, it seems that the EU's commitment and capabilities to help resolve the conflict are less today than they have been in the past.

The Next Fifty Years of the EU's Involvement in the Conflict

There is often little meaning in speculating about the future when it comes to the Israeli–Arab conflict. But in some cases, it seems as if the future is already here. As of September 2019, twenty-seven US states have enacted legislation against boycotts of Israel, some of it including not just the internationally recognized Israel within the 1967 borders, but also against what is called 'Israeli-controlled territories', another term for the occupied territories (Americans for Peace Now 2017; Jewish Virtual Library). Different types of anti-boycott legislation with similar language have also been prepared in the US Congress during 2018–19, some of which were criticized by the American Civil Liberties Union (ACLU) for violating the First Amendment of the Constitution (Harris 2018; Friedman 2018). It remains to be seen how the legislation in the US will play out against the EU's differentiation strategy, but it seems clear that an area of interest for the future will be to follow 'the legislative turn' on both sides of the Atlantic regarding the Israeli–Arab conflict. A similar legislative turn is also ongoing in the UN Human Rights Council, for example, to obtain information on companies operating in the West Bank.

Another likely future trend that is already emerging is what might be called 'the authoritarian turn' of the Israeli–Arab conflict. Both Israel and Palestine-West Bank were downgraded in 2018 by V-Dem, the world's largest academic democracy ranking project. Its annual democracy report for

2018 downgraded Israel from 'liberal democracy' to 'electoral democracy'. Israel was placed 53/178 on V-Dem's Liberal Democracy Index, three places behind Poland and eight ahead of Hungary (V-Dem 2018: 72). Palestine-West Bank was also downgraded from 'electoral democracy' to 'closed', finishing 132/178, while Palestine-Gaza was ranked 164/178 on the Liberal Democracy Index (V-Dem 2018: 73). Tunisia (44/178) was simultaneously upgraded to become a 'liberal democracy' for the first time, thus replacing Israel as the only liberal democracy in the Middle East (V-Dem 2018: 20). All other Middle Eastern countries trailed far behind, with Lebanon coming a distant third, followed by Iraq and Kuwait (V-Dem 2018: 73). In its report for 2019, V-Dem used a new methodology which restored Israel to a 'liberal democracy', while Tunisia was downgraded to an 'electoral democracy' (V-Dem 2019: 52; see also Persson 2019).

V-Dem's findings when it comes to Israel and the Palestinians mirror those of other similar surveys and indexes over the last years. Freedom House's Freedom in the World 2018 survey also placed Israel (79/100) between Poland (85/100) and Hungary (72/100), but ahead of Tunisia (70/100). All four were, however, considered 'Free' by Freedom House. The Freedom in the World 2018 survey rated the West Bank (28/100) and Gaza (12/100) as 'Not Free' (Freedom House 2018). *The Economist*'s Democracy Index for 2018 rated Israel (7.79/10) clearly ahead of Hungary (6.64/10), Poland (6.67/10) and Tunisia (6.32/10), but still categorized all of them as 'flawed democracies', while Palestine (4.46/10) was categorized as a 'hybrid regime' (*The Economist* 2018). In 2019, Israel, the West Bank and Gaza all received their worst ratings ever from Freedom House since its flagship project Freedom in the World was established almost fifty years ago (Freedom House 2019).[2] A big question for the future is thus where this authoritarian turn will lead Israel, Palestine, and the conflict between them? The loss of democracy might redefine the conflict in the future and also affect the EU's and other third parties' involvement in it.

The EU's close to fifty-year engagement in the Israeli–Arab conflict has seen many ups and downs over the decades and there can be few doubts that

---

[2] It should be noted here that Freedom House has rated Israel since the Freedom in the World programme began in 1973, while it has rated the West Bank and Gaza only since 2011.

the present era is one of the down periods. But this is in no way a guarantee that there will never again be light at the end of the tunnel. Like the present era, the 1980s – from the Lebanon war to the first intifada – was also a very dark era for the Israeli–Arab conflict and for the EC's involvement in it. But it was followed, unexpectedly to most observers, by the much more promising Oslo peace process of the 1990s in which the EU and its Member States played significant roles, often before and after agreements were signed. One of the main lessons to be learnt from the Middle East over the past decade is how difficult it is to identify the paradigm shifts beforehand. Almost no one saw the Arab Spring coming in early 2011; very few predicted beforehand how bad developments in Syria and Libya would be; the refugee crisis took Europe by surprise; very few saw the rise of the Islamic State coming; the secret negotiations between the US and Iran before the nuclear deal came as a surprise to many; and so did Donald Trump's election and his exit from the deal. The best that can be done in circumstances like these is to never rule out that changes, for the better or the worse, can occur.

REFERENCES TO THE *BULLETIN*

8-1967, 12-1969, 6-1970, 7-1970, 8-1970, 1-1971, 4-1971, 6-1971, 8-1971, 11-1971, 12-1971, 5-1972, 10-1972, 3-1973, 5-1973, 10-1973, 11-1973, 12-1973, 3-1974, 4-1974, 5-1974, 6-1974, 10-1974, 12-1974, 1-1975, 4-1975, 5-1975, 6-1975, 7/8-1975, 9-1975, 11-1975, 12-1975, 4-1976, 5-1976, 11-1976, 1-1977, 2-1977, 5-1977, 6-1977, 9-1977, 10-1977, 11-1977, 3-1978, 9-1978, 10-1978, 11-1978, 12-1978, 3-1979, 4-1979, 6-1979, 9-1979, 10-1979, 11-1979, 12-1979, 1-1980, 4-1980, 6-1980, 7/8-1980, 9-1980, 11-1980, 12-1980, 2-1981, 6-1981, 9-1981, 11-1981, 12-1981, 3-1982, 4-1982, 6-1982, 9-1982, 11-1982, 12-1982, 1-1983, 3-1983, 6-1983, 7/8-1983, 9-1983, 12-1983, 3-1984, 12-1984, 1-1985, 4-1985, 6-1985, 9-1985, 10-1985, 12-1985, 3-1986, 9-1986, 10-1986, 12-1986, 2-1987, 7/8-1987, 9-1987, 10-1987, 12-1987, 1-1988, 2-1988, 3-1988, 4-1988, 6-1988, 9-1988, 10-1988, 11-1988, 12-1988, 5-1989, 6-1989, 7/8-1989, 12-1989, 1/2-1990, 3-1990, 6-1990, 9-1990, 10-1990, 12-1990, 1/2-1991, 4-1991, 5-1991, 6-1991, 9-1991, 10-1991, 12-1991, 1/2-1992, 6-1992, 12-1992, 1/2-1993, 9-1993, 10-1993, 11-1993, 12-1993, 1/2-1994, 3-1994, 4-1994, 6-1994, 7/8-1994, 10-1994, 11-1994, 12-1994, 1/2-1995, 4-1995, 5-1995, 6-1995, 9-1995, 10-1995, 11-1995, 12-1995, 1/2-1996, 3-1996, 4-1996, 6-1996, 7/8-1996, 9-1996, 10-1996, 11-1996, 12-1996, 1/2-1997, 3-1997, 4-1997, 6-1997, 9-1997, 10-1997, 12-1997, 1/2-1998, 5-1998, 6-1998, 7/8-1998, 10-1998, 11-1998, 12-1998, 3-1999, 6-1999, 9-1999, 10-1999, 12-1999, 1/2-2000, 5-2000, 6-2000, 9-2000, 10-2000, 11-2000, 1/2-2001, 3-2001, 4-2001, 5-2001, 6-2001, 7/8-2001, 10-2001, 11-2001, 12-2001, 3-2002, 4-2002, 6-2002, 7/8-2002, 9-2002, 10-2002, 12-2002, 1/2-2003, 3-2003,

6-2003, 7/8-2003, 9-2003, 10-2003, 12-2003, 3-2004, 4-2004, 6-2004, 10-2004, 11-2004, 12-2004, 1/2-2005, 4-2005, 6-2005, 10-2005, 11-2005, 12-2005, 1/2-2006, 4-2006, 5-2006, 6-2006, 7/8-2006, 11-2006, 12-2006, 1/2-2007, 3-2007, 6-2007, 7/8-2007, 10-2007, 11-2007, 12-2007, 6-2008, 10-2008, 11-2008, 12-2008, 1/2-2009.

REFERENCES TO EU DECLARATIONS, PRESS RELEASES AND OTHER PUBLICATIONS

Ashton, C. (2010), *Remarks made by High Representative Catherine Ashton after meeting Prime Minister Fayyad, Ramallah*, 17 July 2010, <http://www.consilium.europa.eu/uedocs/cms_data/docs/pressdata/EN/foraff/115854.pdf> (accessed 15 September 2019).

Ashton, C. (2011a), *Statement by High Representative Catherine Ashton on the speech of President Obama, Brussels*, 20 May 2011, <http://www.europarl.europa.eu/meetdocs/2009_2014/documents/dplc/dv/ashton_oba/ashton_obama.pdf> (accessed 15 September 2019).

Ashton, C. (2011b), *Remarks by EU High Representative Catherine Ashton after the donor coordination group for the Palestine Territories, Brussels*, 13 April 2011, <https://www.consilium.europa.eu/uedocs/cms_data/docs/pressdata/EN/foraff/121525.pdf> (accessed 15 September 2019).

Ashton, C. (2012a), *Statement by High Representative Catherine Ashton on further escalation of violence in Israel and Gaza, Brussels*, 16 November 2012, <http://www.europarl.europa.eu/meetdocs/2009_2014/documents/dplc/dv/20121116_statemen_hr_/20121116_statemen_hr_en.pdf> (accessed 15 September 2019).

Ashton, C. (2012b), *Statement on Gaza on behalf of High Representative Catherine Ashton, European Parliament, Strasbourg*, 21 November 2012, <http://www.consilium.europa.eu/uedocs/cms_data/docs/pressdata/EN/foraff/133695.pdf> (accessed 15 September 2019).

Ashton, C. (2014), *High-Representative/Vice-President Ashton's statement on the shelling of an UNRWA school and a market in Gaza, Daily News*, 1 August

2014, <http://europa.eu/rapid/midday-express-01-08-2014.htm> (accessed 15 September 2019).

Council of the European Union (2009), *Council conclusion on the Middle East Peace Process: 2985th Foreign Affairs Council meeting, Brussels*, 8 December 2009, <http://www.consilium.europa.eu/uedocs/cms_data/docs/pressdata/en/foraff/111829.pdf> (accessed 15 September 2019).

Council of the European Union (2010), *Council conclusions on the Middle East Peace Process: 3058th Foreign Affairs Council meeting, Brussels*, 13 December 2010, <http://www.europarl.europa.eu/meetdocs/2009_2014/documents/dplc/dv/counc/council.pdf> (accessed 15 September 2019).

Council of the European Union (2011), *Council conclusions on the Middle East Peace Process: 3091st Foreign Affairs Council meeting, Brussels*, 23 May 2011, <http://www.europarl.europa.eu/meetdocs/2009_2014/documents/wgme/dv/201/201106/20110608_3_councilconclusions_en.pdf> (accessed 15 September 2019).

Council of the European Union (2012a), *Press release: 3199th Foreign Affairs Council meeting, Brussels*, 19 November 2012, <http://europa.eu/rapid/press-release_PRES-12-467_en.htm> (accessed 15 September 2019).

Council of the European Union (2012b), *Council conclusions on the Middle East Peace Process: 3166th Foreign Affairs Council meeting, Brussels*, 14 May 2012, <http://europa.eu/rapid/press-release_PRES-12-166_en.htm> (accessed 15 September 2019).

Council of the European Union (2012c), *Press release: 3209th Foreign Affairs Council meeting, Brussels*, 10 December 2012, <http://europa.eu/rapid/press-release_PRES-12-516_en.htm> (accessed 15 September 2019).

Council of the European Union (2013), *Council conclusions on the Middle East Peace Process: Foreign Affairs Council meeting, Brussels*, 16 December 2013, <http://www.consilium.europa.eu/uedocs/cms_data/docs/pressdata/EN/foraff/140097.pdf> (accessed 15 September 2019).

Council of the European Union (2014a), *Press release: 3330th Foreign Affairs Council meeting, Brussels*, 22 July 2014, <https://www.consilium.europa.eu/media/25367/144098.pdf> (accessed 15 September 2019).

Council of the European Union (2014b), *Press release: 3332nd Foreign Affairs Council meeting, Brussels*, 15 August 2014, <https://www.consilium.europa.eu/media/25304/144316.pdf> (accessed 15 September 2019).

Council of the European Union (2015), *Council conclusions on the Middle East Peace Process*, 20 July 2015, <https://www.consilium.europa.eu/en/press/press-releases/2015/07/20/fac-mepp-conclusions/> (accessed 15 September 2019).

Council of the European Union (2016a), *Council conclusions on the Middle East Peace Process: Press release 14/16*, 18 January 2016, <http://www.consilium.europa.eu/en/press/pressreleases/2016/01/18/fac-conclusions-mepp/pdf> (accessed 15 September 2019).

Council of the European Union (2016b), *Council conclusions on the Middle East Peace Process*, 20 June 2016, <https://www.consilium.europa.eu/en/press/press-releases/2016/06/20/fac-conclusions-mepp/> (accessed 15 September 2019).

EEAS (multiple dates), EU positions on the Middle East Peace Process, <https://eeas.europa.eu/diplomatic-network/middle-east-peace-process/49322/statement-latest-escalation-violence-between-gaza-and-israel_en> (accessed 15 September 2019).

EUGS (2016), *Shared Vision, Common Action: A Stronger Europe*, <https://eeas.europa.eu/archives/docs/top_stories/pdf/eugs_review_web.pdf> (accessed 15 September 2019).

EU HoMs Report (2011), *Area C and Palestinian State-Building*, Institut für Palästinakunde, <http://www.ipk-bonn.de/downloads/EU-Report-Area-C.pdf> (accessed 15 September 2019).

EU–Israel trade statistics, <http://ec.europa.eu/trade/policy/countries-and-regions/countries/israel/> (accessed 15 September 2019).

EU MS Joint statement (2019), *Middle East Peace Process – Joint statement by Belgium, France, Germany, Italy, the Netherlands, Poland, Sweden and the United Kingdom*, French Embassy in London, <https://uk.ambafrance.org/EU-countries-reiterate-support-for-Middle-East-peace> (accessed 15 September 2019).

EU–PA Joint committee (2010), *The sixth meeting of the PA–EU Joint Committee forms a turning point in bilateral relations*, 30 June 2010, <http://eeas.europa.eu/archives/delegations/westbank/press_corner/all_news/news/2010/20100630_en.htm> (accessed 15 September 2019).

EU–PA trade statistics, <http://ec.europa.eu/trade/policy/countries-and-regions/countries/palestine/> (accessed 15 September 2019).

European Commission (2008), *Progress Report the occupied Palestinian territory (2007)*, <https://library.euneighbours.eu/sites/default/files/attachments/sec08_400_en.pdf> (accessed 15 September 2019).

European Commission (2009), *Progress Report the occupied Palestinian territory (2008)*, <https://library.euneighbours.eu/content/palestinian-territory-progress-report-implementation-enp-2008> (accessed 15 September 2019).

European Commission (2010), *Progress Report the occupied Palestinian territory*

(2009), <https://library.euneighbours.eu/content/palestinian-territory-progress-report-implementation-enp-2009> (accessed 15 September 2019).

European Commission (2011), *Progress Report the occupied Palestinian territory (2010)*, <https://library.euneighbours.eu/content/palestinian-territory-progress-report-implementation-enp-2010> (accessed 15 September 2019).

European Commission (2012), *Progress Report the occupied Palestinian territory (2011)*, <https://library.euneighbours.eu/content/occupied-palestinian-territory-enp-progress-report-2011> (accessed 15 September 2019).

European Commission (2013a), *Progress Report the occupied Palestinian territory (2012)*, <https://library.euneighbours.eu/content/occupied-palestinian-territory-enp-progress-report-2012> (accessed 15 September 2019).

European Commission (2013b), 'Guidelines on the eligibility of Israeli entities and their activities in the territories occupied by Israel since June 1967 for grants, prizes and financial instruments funded by the EU from 2014 onwards', *Official Journal of the European Union (2013/C 205/05)*, <https://ec.europa.eu/neighbourhood-enlargement/sites/near/files/guidelines_on_the_eligibility_of_israeli_entities_and_their_activities_in_the_territories_occupied_by_israel_since_june_1967.pdf> (accessed 15 September 2019).

European Commission (2015), *Interpretative Notice on indication of origin of goods from the territories occupied by Israel since June 1967 Brussels, 11.11.2015 C(2015) 7834 final*, <https://cdn3-eeas.fpfis.tech.ec.europa.eu/cdn/farfuture/WVqbIGgZayHTb0xOOYUw_ZK2os5HwwAozoyiAZFmnY/mtime:1474446619/sites/eeas/files/20151111_interpretative_notice_indication_of_origin_en.pdf> (accessed 15 September 2019).

European Commission (2017), *European Joint Strategy in Support of Palestine 2017–2020: Towards a democratic and accountable Palestinian State*, <https://ec.europa.eu/neighbourhood-enlargement/sites/near/files/european_joint_strategy_in_support_of_palestine_2017-2020.pdf> (accessed 15 September 2019).

European Parliament (2014a), *European Parliament resolution of 17 December 2014 on recognition of Palestine statehood (2014/2964(RSP))*, <http://www.europarl.europa.eu/sides/getDoc.do?pubRef=-//EP//TEXT+TA+P8-TA-2014-0103+0+DOC+XML+V0//EN> (accessed 15 September 2019).

European Parliament (2014b), *Resolution of 17 July 2014 on the escalation of violence between Israel and Palestine (2014/2723(RSP))*, <http://www.europarl.europa.eu/sides/getDoc.do?pubRef=-//EP//TEXT+TA+P8-TA-2014-0012+0+DOC+XML+V0//EN> (accessed 15 September 2019).

European Parliament (2014c), *Resolution of 18 September 2014 on Israel-Palestine after the Gaza war and the role of the EU (2014/2845(RSP))*, <http://www.euro parl.europa.eu/sides/getDoc.do?type=TA&language=EN&reference=P8-TA-2014-0029> (accessed 15 September 2019).

European Parliament (2015), *European Parliament resolution of 10 September 2015 on the EU's role in the Middle East peace process (2015/2685(RSP))*, <http://www.europarl.europa.eu/sides/getDoc.do?pubRef=-//EP//TEXT+TA+P8-TA-2015-0318+0+DOC+XML+V0//EN> (accessed 15 September 2019).

European Parliament (2018), *Resolution of 13 September 2018 on the threat of demolition of Khan al-Ahmar and other Bedouin villages (2018/2849(RSP))*, <http://www.europarl.europa.eu/sides/getDoc.do?pubRef=-//EP//TEXT+TA+P8-TA-2018-0351+0+DOC+XML+V0//EN&language=EN> (accessed 15 September 2019).

European security strategy (2003), *A Secure Europe in a Better World*, <http://www.consilium.europa.eu/eeas/security-defence/european-security-strategy?lang=en> (accessed 15 September 2019).

Eurostat, *Energy production and imports*, <https://ec.europa.eu/eurostat/statistics-explained/index.php/Energy_production_and_imports#More_than_half_of_EU-28_energy_needs_are_covered_by_imports> (accessed 15 September 2019).

Infocuria (2010), *C-386/08 – Brita: Judgment of the Court (Fourth Chamber)*, 25 February 2010, <http://curia.europa.eu/juris/liste.jsf?language=en&num=C-386/08> (accessed 15 September 2019).

Mogherini, F. (2014), *Recognition of Palestine statehood* (debate; Strasbourg), 26 November 2014, <http://www.europarl.europa.eu/sides/getDoc.do?pubRef=-//EP//TEXT+CRE+20141126+ITEM-017+DOC +XML+V0//EN&language=EN> (accessed 15 September 2019).

Mogherini, F. (2016), *Answer given by Vice-President Mogherini on behalf of the Commission*, 15 September 2016, <http://www.europarl.europa.eu/sides/getAll Answers.do?reference=E-2016-005122&language=EN> (accessed 15 September 2019).

Mogherini, F. (2017a), *Speech by HR/VP Federica Mogherini at the European Parliament plenary session on US President Trump's announcement to recognise Jerusalem as capital of Israel*, 12 December 2017, <https://eeas.europa.eu/head quarters/headquarters-homepage/37336/speech-hrvp-federica-mogherini-eu ropean-parliament-plenary-session-us-president-trumps_en> (accessed 15 September 2019).

Mogherini, F. (2017b), *Remarks by HR/VP Federica Mogherini at the press conference following the Foreign Affairs Council*, 11 December 2017, <https://eeas. europa.eu/headquarters/headquarters-homepage/37164/remarks-hrvp-federica-mogherini-press-conference-following-foreign-affairs-council_en> (accessed 15 September 2019).

Mogherini, F. (2018a), *Remarks by HR/VP Federica Mogherini at the joint press point ahead of the extraordinary session of the International Donor Group for Palestine (Ad Hoc Liaison Committee, AHLC), Bruxelles*, 31 January 2018, <https://eeas. europa.eu/headquarters/headquarters-homepage/39142/remarks-hrvp-federica-mogherini-joint-press-point-ahead-extraordinary-session-international_en> (accessed 15 September 2019).

Mogherini, F. (2018b), *Speech by High Representative/Vice-President Federica Mogherini at the Ministerial Conference on UNRWA*, 15 March 2018, <https:// eeas.europa.eu/delegations/palestine-occupied-palestinian-territory-west-bank-and-gaza-strip/41408/speech-high-representativevice-president-federica-moghe rini-ministerial-conference-unrwa_en> (accessed 15 September 2019).

Mogherini, F. (2018c), *Statement by HR/VP Mogherini on the latest developments regarding the planned demolition of Khan al-Ahmar, Bruxelles*, 7 September 2018, <https://eeas.europa.eu/headquarters/headquarters-homepage/50237/sta tement-hrvp-mogherini-latest-developments-regarding-planned-demolition-khan-al-ahmar_en> (accessed 15 September 2019).

Mogherini, F. (2018d), *Remarks by HR/VP Mogherini at the plenary session of the European Parliament on the threat of demolition of Khan al-Ahmar and other Bedouin villages, Strasbourg*, 11 September 2018, <https://eeas.europa.eu/head quarters/headquarters-homepage/50333/remarks-hrvp-mogherini-plenary-sess ion-european-parliament-threat-demolition-khan-al-ahmar-and_en> (accessed 15 September 2019).

Mogherini, F. (2019a), *Declaration by the High Representative on behalf of the EU on the Golan Heights, Bruxelles*, 27 March 2019, <https://eeas.europa.eu/dele gations/israel/60274/declaration-high-representative-behalf-eu-golan-heights_ en> (accessed 15 September 2019).

Mogherini, F. (2019b), *Speech by High Representative/Vice-President Federica Mogherini at the plenary session of the European Parliament on the US recognition of the Golan Heights as Israeli territory and the possible annexation of the West Bank settlements, Strasbourg*, 16 April 2019, <https://eeas.europa.eu/headquarters/ headquarters-Homepage/61140/speech-high-representativevice-president-feder ica-mogherini-plenary-session-european_fr> (accessed 15 September 2019).

Moratinos, M. (2001), *Report by EU Special Representative Moratinos on the Taba Talks*, <https://ecf.org.il/media_items/966> (accessed 15 September 2019).

Solana, J. (2009), *Ditchley Foundation annual lecture: 'Europe's global role – what next steps?'*, <https://www.consilium.europa.eu/uedocs/cms_Data/docs/pressdata/en/discours/109193.pdf> (accessed 15 September 2019).

REFERENCES TO OTHER LITERATURE

Ahlswede, S. (2009), 'Israel's European policy after the Cold War', PhD Dissertation, Department Sozialwissenschaften, Universität Hamburg.

Ahren, R. (2013), 'EU offers "unprecedented" aid to Israelis, Palestinians for peace deal', *Times of Israel*, 16 December, <https://www.timesofisrael.com/eu-off ers-unprecedented-aid-to-israelis-palestinians-for-peace-deal/> (accessed 15 September 2019).

Ahren, R. (2015), 'In Israel, Hungary's FM says his country opposes settlement labels', *Times of Israel*, 23 May, <http://www.timesofisrael.com/in-israel-hun garys-fm-says-his-country-opposes-settlement-labels/?fb_comment_id=748251 975286828_748362945275731> (accessed 15 September 2019).

Altheide, D., and C. Schneider (2013), *Qualitative Media Analysis*, Thousand Oaks: Sage.

Americans for Peace Now (2017), *The Stealth Campaign to Use U.S. Law to Support Settlements: Taking the Battle to the States, 2014–2017*, <https://peacenow.org/ WP/wp-content/uploads/State-BDS-and-Settlement-legislation-table.pdf> (accessed 15 September 2019).

Amnesty International (2006), *Israel/Lebanon Out of All Proportion – Civilians Bear the Brunt of the War*, <https://www.amnesty.ie/2185/> (accessed 15 September 2019).

Amnesty International (2009), *Press release: Israel Restricts Water Availability in West Bank and Gaza*, <http://www.amnesty.eu/en/news/press-releases/eu/human-rig hts-in-the-eu/foreign-policy/north-africa-southern-mediterranean/israel-restri

cts-water-availability-in-west-bank-and-gaza0427/#.WcI2ga3BKt8> (accessed 15 September 2019).

Amnesty International (2014), *Families under the Rubble: Israeli Attacks on Inhabited Homes*, <https://www.amnesty.org/en/latest/news/2014/11/israeli-forces-disp layed-callous-indifference-deadly-attacks-family-homes-gaza/> (accessed 15 September 2019).

Aoun, E. (2003), 'European foreign policy and the Arab–Israeli dispute: much ado about nothing?', *European Foreign Affairs Review*, 8: 3, pp. 289–312.

Asseburg, M. (2003), 'The EU and the Middle East conflict: tackling the main obstacle to Euro-Mediterranean partnership', *Mediterranean Politics*, 8: 2–3, pp. 174–93.

Associated Press (2010), 'EU's Ashton to skip restarted Mideast peace talks', *The Jerusalem Post*, 28 August, <https://www.jpost.com/Breaking-News/ EUs-Ashton-to-skip-restarted-Mideast-peace-talks> (accessed 15 September 2019).

Associated Press (2011), 'EU backs Obama's call for 67 borders', *Ynet*, 23 May, <https://www.ynetnews.com/articles/0,7340,L-4072650,00.html> (accessed 15 September 2019).

Azarova, V. (2017), 'Israel's unlawfully prolonged occupation: consequences under an integrated legal framework', *European Council on Foreign Affairs Policy Brief*, 2 July, <http://www.ecfr.eu/publications/summary/israels_unlawfully_prolon ged_occupation_7294> (accessed 15 September 2019).

Bacevich, A. (2010), 'How Petraeus could swing thinking on Israel', *Salon*, 18 March, <https://www.salon.com/2010/03/18/bacevich_on_petraeus_israel/> (accessed 15 September 2019).

Banishamsa, A. (2012), 'The Making of European Union Foreign Policy: The Case of the Palestinians (1969–2009)', PhD Thesis, Durham University.

Barigazzi, J. (2018), 'Palestinian leader draws blank in appeal for EU recognition', *Politico EU*, 21 January, <https://www.politico.eu/article/mahmoud-abbas-brus sels-palestine-leader-draws-blank-in-appeal-for-eurecognition/> (accessed 15 September 2019).

Bechor, G. (2014), 'Why is EU meddling in Israel's internal affairs?', *Ynet*, 23 May, <http://www.ynetnews.com/articles/0,7340,L-4522607,00.html> (accessed 15 September 2019).

Beck, M. (2017), 'How to (not) walk the talk: the demand for Palestinian self deter- mination as a challenge for the European Neighbourhood Policy', *European Foreign Affairs Review*, 22: 1, pp. 59–74.

Behrendt, S., and C.-P. Hanelt (eds) (2000), *Bound to Cooperate – Europe and the Middle East*, Gütersloh: Bertelsmann.

Bicchi, F., and B. Voltolini (2017), 'Europe, the Green Line and the issue of the Israeli–Palestinian border: closing the gap between discourse and practice?', *Geopolitics*, 23: 1, pp. 124–46.

Bouris, D. (2014), *The European Union and Occupied Palestinian Territories: State-building Without a State*, Abingdon: Routledge.

Bröning, M. (2011), *The Politics of Change in Palestine: State-building and Non-violent Resistance*, New York: Pluto Press.

Brown, N. (2010), 'Are Palestinians building a state?', *Carnegie Commentary*, June 2010, <http://carnegieendowment.org/files/palestinian_state1.pdf> (accessed 15 December 2018).

Bryman, A. (2016), *Social Research Methods*, Oxford: Oxford University Press.

Brynen, R. (2008), 'Palestine: building neither peace nor state', in C. Call and V. Wyeth (eds), *Building States to Build Peace*, London: Lynne Rienner, pp. 217–47.

Charrett, C. (2018), 'Ritualised securitisation: the European Union's failed response to Hamas's success', *European Journal of International Relations*, 25: 1, pp. 156–78.

Dajani, O., and H. Lovatt (2017), 'Rethinking Oslo: how Europe can promote peace in Israel–Palestine', *European Council on Foreign Affairs Policy Brief*, 26 July <http://www.ecfr.eu/publications/summary/rethinking_oslo_how_europe_can_promote_peace_in_israel_palestine_7219> (accessed 15 September 2019).

De La Baume, M. (2015), 'Israel slams "shameful" EU', *Politico EU*, 11 November, <http://www.politico.eu/article/eu-backs-labeling-rules-for-goods-from-israeli-settlements-european-commission/> (accessed 15 September 2019).

Del Sarto, R. (ed.) (2015), *Fragmented Borders, Interdependence and External Relations: The Israel–Palestine–European Union Triangle*, Basingstoke: Palgrave.

Dieckhoff, A. (1988), 'Europe and the Arab World: the difficult dialogue', in I. Greilsammer and J. Weiler (eds), *Europe and Israel: Troubled Neighbours*, Berlin: Walter de Gruyter.

Dosenrode, S., and A. Stubkjaer (2002), *The European Union and the Middle East*, London: Sheffield Academic Press.

DPA (2010), 'EU Official to PA: Financial support won't continue forever', *Haaretz*, 29 January, <https://www.haaretz.com/1.5087287> (accessed 15 September 2019).

Economist, The (2018), 'The Economist Intelligence Unit's Democracy Index 2017',

<https://infographics.economist.com/2018/DemocracyIndex/> (accessed 15 September 2019).

Eichner, I. (2017), 'New EU ambassador: We're not biased against Israel', *Ynet*, 16 December, <https://www.ynetnews.com/articles/0,7340,L-5056411,00.html> (accessed 15 September 2019).

Eldar, A. (2010), 'Israel can't afford to postpone Mideast peace much longer', *Haaretz*, 12 November, <https://www.haaretz.com/1.5138721> (accessed 15 September 2019).

EUbusiness (2014), 'EU bans import of Israeli settler poultry produce', *EUbusiness*, 23 May, <http://www.eubusiness.com/news-eu/israel-settler.w52> (accessed 15 September 2019).

Al-Fattal, R. (2010), *European Union Foreign Policy in the Occupied Palestinian Territory*, Jerusalem: Passia.

Federal Foreign Office (2018), *Foreign and European Policy: Israel*, <https://www.auswaertiges-amt.de/en/aussenpolitik/laenderinformationen/israel-node/israel/228212> (accessed 15 September 2019).

Fez plan, the (1982), *Letter dated 3 December 1982 from the Permanent Representative of Morocco to the United Nations addressed to the Secretary-General*, <https://unispal.un.org/DPA/DPR/unispal.nsf/0/A65756251B75F6AD852562810074E5F4> (accessed 15 September 2019).

France24 (2019), 'US lobbies Europe to back UN vote on condemning Hamas', 27 November, <https://www.france24.com/en/20181127-us-lobbies-europe-back-un-vote-condemning-hamas> (accessed 15 September 2019).

Freedom House (2018), *Freedom in the World 2018 Democracy in Crisis*, <https://freedomhouse.org/report/freedom-world/freedom-world-2018> (accessed 15 September 2019).

Freedom House (2019), *Democracy in Retreat Freedom in the World 2019*, <https://freedomhouse.org/report/freedom-world/freedom-world-2019/democracy-in-retreat> (accessed 15 September 2019).

Friedman, L. (2018), 'U.S. politicians are backing a free speech exception for Israel – & creating a template for broader assault on the first amendment', *Medium*, 19 March, <https://medium.com/@LFriedman_FMEP/u-s-politicians-are-backing-a-free-speech-exception-for-israel-creating-a-template-for-broader-ebe406fdf3b7> (accessed 15 September 2019).

Gardner, A. (2013), 'Ashton in power struggle over Middle East policy', *European Voice*, 19 June, <https://www.politico.eu/article/ashton-in-power-struggle-over-middle-east-policy/> (accessed 15 September 2019).

Garfinkle, A. (1983), *Western Europe's Middle East Diplomacy and the United States*, Philadelphia: Philadelphia Policy Papers.

Ginsberg, R. (2001), *The European Union in International Politics: Baptism by Fire*, Lanham: Rowman & Littlefield.

Glick, C. (2014), *The Israeli Solution: A One-State Plan for Peace in the Middle East*, New York: Crown Forum.

Gordon, N., and S. Pardo (2015a), 'Normative Power Europe meets the Israeli–Palestinian conflict', *Asia–Europe Journal*, 13: 3, pp. 265–74.

Gordon, N., and S. Pardo (2015b), 'Normative Power Europe and the power of the local', *Journal of Common Market Studies*, 53: 2, pp. 416–27.

Gouvernement.fr (2016), *French Middle-East Peace Initiative*, 6 June, <https://www.gouvernement.fr/en/french-middle-east-peace-initiative> (accessed 15 September 2019).

Greilsammer, I., and J. Weiler (1984), 'European political cooperation and the Palestinian–Israeli conflict: an Israeli perspective', in D. Allen and A. Pijpers (eds), *European Foreign Policy-Making and the Arab–Israeli Conflict*, The Hague: Martinus Nijhoff Publishers, pp. 121–60.

Greilsammer, I., and J. Weiler (1987), *Europe's Middle East Dilemma – The Quest for a United Stance*, Boulder: Westview Press.

Greilsammer, I., and J. Weiler (eds) (1988), *Europe and Israel: Troubled Neighbours*, Berlin: Walter de Gruyter.

Harpaz, G. (2007), 'Normative Power Europe and the problem of a legitimacy deficit: an Israeli perspective', *European Foreign Affairs Review*, 12: 1, pp. 89–109.

Harpaz, G., and A. Shamis (2010), 'Normative Power Europe and the state of Israel: an illegitimate EUtopia?', *Journal of Common Market Studies*, 48: 3, pp. 579–616.

Harris, B. (2018), 'International pressure on Israeli settlements renews push for US anti-boycott laws', *Al-Monitor*, 14 February, <https://www.al-monitor.com/pulse/originals/2018/02/international-pressure-israel-settlements-us-antiboycott.html> (accessed 15 September 2019).

Hass, A. (2013), 'Despite EU settlement guidelines Dutch government's new business initiative includes Israeli companies in West Bank', *Haaretz*, 3 December, <http://www.haaretz.com/israelnews/.premium-1.561416> (accessed 15 September 2019).

Hollis, R. (1997), 'Europe and the Middle East: power by stealth', *International Affairs*, 73: 1, pp. 15–29.

Huber, D. (2011), *Normative Power Europe? The EU's Foreign Policy of Democracy*

Promotion in the Palestinian Authority, Working Paper 98, Berlin: Konrad-Adenauer-Stiftung/European Forum at HU.

Human Rights Watch (2007), 'Israel/Lebanon: Israeli indiscriminate attacks killed most civilians', <https://www.hrw.org/news/2007/09/05/israel/lebanon-israeli-indiscriminate-attacks-killed-most-civilians> (accessed 15 September 2019).

Human Rights Watch (2012), 'Palestinian Authority: Hold police accountable for Ramallah beatings', <http://www.hrw.org/news/2012/08/27/palestinian-authority-hold-policeaccountable-ramallah-beatings> (accessed 15 September 2019).

Human Rights Watch (2014), 'Israel/Palestine: Unlawful Israeli airstrikes kill civilians: bombings of civilian structures suggest illegal policy', <https://www.hrw.org/news/2014/07/15/israel/palestine-unlawful-israeli-airstrikes-kill-civilians> (accessed 15 September 2019).

Ifestos, P. (1987), *European Political Cooperation: Towards a Framework of Supranational Diplomacy*, Aldershot: Gower.

IMF (2011), *Program Note West Bank and Gaza, Last Updated: October 25, 2011*, <https://www.imf.org/external/np/country/notes/wbg.htm> (accessed 15 September 2019).

International Crisis Group (2011), *Curb your Enthusiasm: Israel and Palestine after the UN*, Middle East Report 112, 12 September 2011, <https://www.crisisgroup.org/index.php?q=middle-east-north-africa/eastern-mediterranean/israel palestine/curb-your-enthusiasm-israel-and-palestine-after-un> (accessed 15 September 2019).

Isleyen, B. (2018), 'Building capacities, exerting power: the European Union police mission in the Palestinian authority', *Mediterranean Politics*, 23: 3, pp. 321–39.

Israeli Ministry of Foreign Affairs (2000), *Fatal Terrorist Attacks in Israel (Sept 1993–1999)*, <http://www.mfa.gov.il/mfa/foreignpolicy/terrorism/palestini an/pages/fatal%20terrorist%20attacks%20in%20israel%20since%20the%20 dop%20-s.aspx> (accessed 1 September 2019).

Al Jazeera (2017), 'UN Jerusalem resolution: How each country voted', *Al Jazeera*, 21 December, <https://www.aljazeera.com/news/2017/12/jerusalem-resolut ion-country-voted-171221180116873.html> (accessed 15 September 2019).

Jewish Virtual Library, *Anti-Semitism: State Anti-BDS Legislation*, <https://www.jewishvirtuallibrary.org/anti-bds-legislation> (accessed 15 September 2019).

Keinon, H. (2011a), 'Bolton: Obama worst President for Israel – ever', *The Jerusalem Post*, 13 July, <https://www.jpost.com/Video-Articles/Video/Bolton-Obama-worst-president-for-Israel-ever> (accessed 15 September 2019).

Keinon, H. (2011b), 'Jones: Israeli–Palestinian strife still core of ME ills', *The Jerusalem Post*, 8 February, <http://www.jpost.com/Middle-East/Jones-Israeli-Palestinian-strife-still-core-of-ME-ills> (accessed 15 September 2019).

Keinon, H. (2013), 'EU envoy and Israel are parting as friends, with differences', *The Jerusalem Post*, 22 August, <http://www.jpost.com/Features/In-Thespotlight/Diplomacy-Parting-as-friends-withdifferences-324005> (accessed 15 September 2019).

Keukeleire, S., and J. MacNaughtan (2008), *The Foreign Policy of the European Union*, Gordonsville: Palgrave.

Kouchner, B., and M. Moratinos (2010), 'A Palestinian State: when?', *Le Monde*, 23 February, <http://www.voltairenet.org/article164427.html> (accessed 15 September 2019).

Landau, N. (2017), 'Despite Minister's opposition, Israel approves deal with EU that excludes settlements', *Haaretz*, 31 December 2017, <https://www.haaretz.com/israel-news/.premium-israel-approves-deal-with-eu-that-excludes-settlements-1.5630071> (accessed 15 September 2019).

Landau, N. (2018), 'Irish Senate approves bill boycotting Israeli settlement goods', *Haaretz*, 12 July 2018, <https://www.haaretz.com/israel-news/.premium-ireland-approves-bill-boycotting-israeli-settlements-1.6265672> (accessed 15 September 2019).

Lazaroff, T. (2015), 'Foreign Ministry: Labeling settlement products could harm EU's ties with Israel', *The Jerusalem Post*, 11 November, <http://www.jpost.com/Israel-News/Politics-And-Diplomacy/Foreign-Ministry-Labeling-settlement-products-could-harm-EUs-ties-with-Israel-432652> (accessed 15 September 2019).

Le More, A. (2005), 'Killing with kindness: funding the demise of a Palestinian State', *International Affairs*, 81: 5, pp. 981–99.

Le More, A. (2008), *International Assistance to the Palestinians after Oslo: Political Guilt, Wasted Money*, New York: Routledge.

Lis, J. (2013), 'Israel's National Security Council to discuss EU cooperation in wake of settlement boycott', *Haaretz*, 5 August, <http://www.haaretz.com/news/diplomacy-defense/.premium-1.539869> (accessed 15 September 2019).

Lovatt, H. (2016), 'EU differentiation and the push for peace in Israel-Palestine', *European Council on Foreign Affairs*, 31 October, <http://www.ecfr.eu/publications/summary/eu_differentiation_and_the_push_for_peace_in_israel_palestine7163> (accessed 15 September 2019).

Lovatt, H., and M. Toaldo (2015), 'EU differentiation and Israeli settlements',

European Council on Foreign Affairs Policy Brief, 22 July, <http://www.ecfr.eu/page/-/EuDifferentiation-final3.pdf> (accessed 15 September 2019).

Maan (2018a), 'Spain ready to recognize Palestinian state', *Maan*, 21 September, <https://www.maannews.com/Content.aspx?id=781156> (accessed 15 September 2019).

Maan (2018b), 'EP delegation: "Khan al-Ahmar demolition considered war crime"', *Maan*, 21 September, <https://www.maannews.com/Content.aspx?id=781155> (accessed 15 September 2019).

Miller, R. (2011), *Inglorious Disarray: Europe, Israel and the Palestinians since 1967*, New York: Columbia University Press.

Mitvim (2014), *The 2014 Israeli Foreign Policy Index Findings of the Mitvim Institute Poll*, December 2014, <https://www.mitvim.org.il/images/2014_Mitvim_Poll_-_English_Report.pdf> (accessed 15 September 2019).

Müller, P. (2012), *EU Foreign Policymaking and the Middle East Conflict: The Europeanization of National Foreign Policy*, London: Routledge.

Müller, P., and P. Slominski (2017), 'The role of law in EU foreign policy-making: legal integrity, legal spillover, and the EU policy of differentiation towards Israel', *Journal of Common Market Studies*, 55: 4, pp. 871–88.

Müller, P., and Y. Zahda (2017), 'Local perceptions of the EU's role in peacebuilding: the case of security sector reform in Palestine', *Contemporary Security Policy*, 39: 1, pp. 119–41.

Musu, C. (2010), *European Union Policy Towards the Arab–Israeli Peace Process – the Quicksands of Politics*, New York: Palgrave Macmillan.

Nasr El-Din, A. (2016), *EU Security Missions and the Israeli–Palestinian Conflict*, Abingdon: Routledge.

Nikolov, K. (2017), 'Partnership after peace? An optimist's view on the EU's future special and privileged relations with the States of Israel and Palestine', *Journal Diplomacy*, 19 (2017), pp. 228–68.

Nixon, R. (1974), *Question-and-Answer Session at the Executives' Club of Chicago, March 15, 1974*, <http://www.presidency.ucsb.edu/ws/index.php?pid=4386> (accessed 15 September 2019).

Nye, J. (2004), *Soft Power: The Means to Success in World Politics*, New York: Public Affairs.

Obama, B. (2009), *The President's Speech in Cairo: A New Beginning*, 4 June 2009, <https://obamawhitehouse.archives.gov/issues/foreign-policy/presidents-speech-cairo-a-new-beginning> (accessed 15 September 2019).

Obama, B. (2011), *Remarks of President Barack Obama – 'A Moment of Opportunity'*,

19 May 2011, <https://obamawhitehouse.archives.gov/the-press-office/2011/05/19/remarks-president-middle-east-and-north-africa> (accessed 15 September 2019).

Özgur Kaya, T. (2013), *The Middle East Peace Process and the EU: Foreign Policy and Security Strategy in International Politics*, London: I. B. Tauris.

Pace, M. (2007), 'The construction of EU normative power', *Journal of Common Market Studies*, 45: 5, pp. 1041–64.

Pace, M. (2010), 'Interrogating the European Union's democracy promotion agenda: discursive configurations of "democracy"', *European Foreign Affairs Review*, 15: 5, pp. 611–28.

Pardo, S. (2015), *Normative Power Europe Meets Israel*, Lanham: Lexington Books.

Pardo, S., and N. Gordon (2018), 'Euroscepticism as an instrument of foreign policy', *Middle East Critique*, 27: 4, pp. 399–412.

Pardo, S., and J. Peters (2010), *Uneasy Neighbors: Israel and the European Union*, Lanham: Rowman and Littlefield Publishers.

Pardo, S., and J. Peters (2012), *Israel and the European Union: A Documentary History*, Lanham: Rowman and Littlefield Publishers.

Peace Now, *Settlements 101*, <http://archive.peacenow.org/settlements-101.html> (accessed 15 September 2019).

Peres, S. (1993), *The New Middle East*, New York: Henry Holt & Co.

Persson, A. (2014), 'Sweden's recognition of Palestine: a possible snowball effect?', *Palestine–Israel Journal of Politics, Economics and Culture*, 20: 2/3, pp. 35–41.

Persson, A. (2015), *The EU and the Israeli–Palestinian Conflict, 1971–2013: In Search of a Just Peace*, Lanham: Lexington Books.

Persson, A. (2017a), 'Shaping discourse and setting examples: Normative Power Europe can work in the Israeli–Palestinian conflict', *Journal of Common Market Studies*, 55: 6, pp. 1415–31.

Persson, A. (2017b), 'Palestine at the end of the state-building process: technical achievements, political failures', *Mediterranean Politics*, 23: 4, pp. 433–52.

Persson, A. (2018a), '"EU differentiation" as a case of "Normative Power Europe" (NPE) in the Israeli–Palestinian conflict', *Journal of European Integration*, 40: 2, pp. 193–208.

Persson, A. (2018b), 'What will Trump's "ultimate deal" mean for Palestinians?', *Al Jazeera*, 28 March, <https://www.aljazeera.com/indepth/opinion/trump-ultimate-deal-palestinians-180327082942844.html> (accessed 15 September 2019).

Persson, A. (2019), 'Battling with Tunisia, better than Poland: how Israel's

8democracy measures up', *Haaretz*, 23 May, <https://www.haaretz.com/israel-news/.premium-battling-with-tunisia-better-than-poland-how-healthy-is-israel-s-democracy-1.7277852> (accessed 15 September 2019).

PNA (2009), *Ending the Occupation, Establishing the State*, <http://www.mopad.pna.ps/en/attachments/article/6/Second_year_of_the_government_program_English Final.pdf> (accessed 15 September 2019).

Ravid, B. (2009), 'Haaretz Exclusive: EU draft document on division of Jerusalem', *Haaretz*, 1 December, <http://www.haaretz.com/news/haaretz-exclusive-eu-dra ft-document-ondivision-of-jerusalem-1.3029> (accessed 15 September 2019).

Ravid, B. (2011), 'UN envoy Prosor: Israel has no chance of stopping recognition of Palestinian state', *Haaretz*, 28 August, <http://www.haaretz.com/print-edition/news/unenvoy-prosor-israel-has-no-chance-of-stopping-recognition-of-palesti nianstate-1.381062> (accessed 15 September 2019).

Ravid, B. (2013), 'Deputy FM rejects report claiming government ignored EU shift on settlements', *Haaretz*, 10 September, <http://www.haaretz.com/news/diplomacy-defense/premium-1.546108> (accessed 15 September 2019).

Ravid, B. (2015), 'European FMs urge policy chief: label West Bank settlement products', *Haaretz*, 16 April, <https://www.haaretz.com/european-fms-label-west-bank-settlement-products-1.5351837> (accessed 15 September 2019).

Ravid, B. (2016), 'New EU draft resolution draws stark distinction between Israel, West Bank settlements', *Haaretz*, 15 January, <https://www.haaretz.com/israel-news/.premium-new-eu-resolution-draws-stark-distinction-between-israel-sett lements-1.5391395> (accessed 15 September 2019).

Ravid, B. (2017a), 'UNESCO passes resolution critical of Israeli conduct in Jerusalem and Gaza', *Haaretz*, 3 May, <https://www.haaretz.com/israel-news/unesco-pas ses-resolution-critical-of-israeli-policy-in-jerusalem-1.5467397> (accessed 15 September 2019).

Ravid, B. (2017b), 'Israel slams EU: 32 humanitarian crises in the world and Europe's obsessed with Palestinians', *Haaretz*, 5 April, <http://www.haaretz.com/israel-news/1.781562> (accessed 15 September 2019).

Reagan, R. (1981), *Address to the Nation on United States Policy for Peace in the Middle East*, <https://www.reaganlibrary.gov/research/speeches/90182d> (accessed 15 September 2019).

Rettman, A. (2019a), 'EU "special envoy" going to US plan for Palestine', *EUobserver*, 24 June, <https://euobserver.com/foreign/145254> (accessed 15 September 2019).

Rettman, A (2019b), 'EU ignores Hungary veto on Israel, posing wider questions',

EUobserver, 1 May, <https://euobserver.com/foreign/144768> (accessed 15 September 2019).

Reuters (2009), 'Recognizing Palestinian state premature: EU', Reuters, 17 November, <https://www.reuters.com/article/us-eu-palestinians/recognizing-palestinian-state-premature-eu-idUSTRE5AG1R720091117> (accessed 15 September 2019).

Reuters (2018), 'Abbas wins renewed EU backing for Palestinian capital in East Jerusalem', Reuters, 22 January, <https://www.reuters.com/article/us-usa-israel-abbas/abbas-wins-renewed-eu-backing-for-palestinian-capital-in-east-jerusal em-idUSKBN1FB1NR> (accessed 15 September 2019).

Santoro, S., and R. Nasrallah (2007), 'Conflict and hope: the EU in the eyes of Palestine', in S. Lucarelli and L. Fioramonti (eds), *External Perceptions of the European Union as a Global Actor*, Abingdon: Routledge.

Schiff, Z., and E. Ya'ari (1984), *Israel's Lebanon War*, New York: Simon and Schuster.

Sheizaf, N. (2014), 'EU policy on Israel: "More-for-more" or carrots and sticks?', *+972mag*, 21 February, <https://972mag.com/eu-policy-on-israel-more-for-more-or-carrots-and-sticks/87496/> (accessed 15 September 2019).

Stetter, S. (2003), 'Democratization without democracy? The assistance of the European Union for democratization processes in Palestine', *Mediterranean Politics*, 8: 2–3, pp. 153–73.

Tartir, A. (2018), 'The limits of securitized peace: the EU's sponsorship of Palestinian Authoritarianism', *Middle East Critique*, 27: 4, pp. 365–81.

Taylor, P. (2003), 'Why diplomacy failed', in Reuters (eds), *The Israeli–Palestinian Conflict: Crisis in the Middle East*, New Jersey: Pearson Education.

Thrall, N. (2017), *The Only Language They Understand: Forcing Compromise in Israel and Palestine*, New York: Metropolitan Books.

Times, The (2017), 'Full transcript of interview with Donald Trump', *The Times*, 16 January, <https://www.thetimes.co.uk/article/full-transcript-of-interview-with-donald-trump-5d39sr09d> (accessed 15 September 2019).

Times of Israel (2018), 'Under Israeli pressure, Czechs said to consider Jerusalem embassy move', *Times of Israel*, 18 March, <https://www.timesofisrael.com/und er-israeli-pressure-czechs-said-to-consider-jerusalem-embassy-move/> (accessed 15 September 2019).

Tocci, N. (2005), *The Widening Gap between Rhetoric and Reality in EU Policy towards the Israeli–Palestinian Conflict*, Working Document No. 21, Brussels: Centre for European Policy Studies.

Tocci, N. (2009), 'Firm in rhetoric, compromising in reality: the EU in the Israeli–Palestinian conflict', *Ethnopolitics*, 8: 3–4, pp. 387–401.

Tocci, N. (2017), 'From the European Security Strategy to the EU Global Strategy: explaining the journey', *International Politics*, 54: 4, pp. 487–502.

Trump, D. (2017), *Remarks by President Trump and President Abbas of the Palestinian Authority in Joint Statements*, 23 May, <https://www.whitehouse.gov/briefings-statements/remarks-president-trump-president-abbas-palestinian-authority-joint-statements/> (accessed 15 September 2019).

UNESCO (2016), *Item 19 Occupied Palestine (199 EX/19)*, <http://unesdoc.unesco.org/images/0024/002444/244481E.pdf> (accessed 15 September 2019).

UNESCO (2017), *Item 30 Occupied Palestine (201 EX/30)*, <http://unesdoc.unesco.org/images/0024/002481/248139e.pdf> (accessed 15 September 2019).

UNGA (2017), *Resolution adopted by the General Assembly on 21 December 2017, ES-10/19 Status of Jerusalem*, <http://undocs.org/A/RES/ES-10/19> (accessed 15 September 2019).

UNGA (2018), *Activities of Hamas and other militant groups in Gaza, Item 38 A/73/L.42*, <https://papersmart.unmeetings.org/media2/20306079/vr11.pdf> (accessed 15 September 2019).

Ungerer, H. (1997), *A Concise History of European Monetary Integration: From EPU to EMU*, Westport: Quorum Books.

UN Human Rights Council (2017), *A/HRC/34/L.41 21 March 2017 Israeli Settlements in the Occupied Palestinian Territory, including East Jerusalem, and in the Occupied Syrian Golan*, <https://unispal.un.org/DPA/DPR/.nsf/0%20/4130476E4C2172CF852580EC00510FA> (accessed 15 September 2019).

Unilateral Statement by Israel (2014), OJ L 177,7 17.6.2014, <https://eur-lex.europa.eu/legal-content/EN/TXT/?uri=OJ%3AL%3A2014%3A178%3AFULL> (accessed 15 September 2019).

United Nations Fact-Finding Mission on the Gaza Conflict (2009), *Report: Human Rights in Palestine and Other Occupied Arab Territories*, <http://www2.ohchr.org/english/bodies/hrcouncil/docs/12session/A-HRC-12-48.pdf> (accessed 15 September 2019).

UNSC (2016), *Resolution 2334 (2016): Adopted by the Security Council at its 7853rd meeting, on 23 December 2016*, <http://www.un.org/webcast/pdfs/SRES2334-2016.pdf> (accessed 15 September 2019).

UNSCO (2011), *Palestinian State-building: An Achievement at Risk*, <https://reliefweb.int/sites/reliefweb.int/files/resources/UNSCOs%20Report%20to%20the%20AHLC%2018%20September%202011.pdf> (accessed 15 September 2019).

V-Dem (2018), *Democracy for All? V-Dem Annual Democracy report 2018*, <https://www.v-dem.net/media/filer_public/3f/19/3f19efc9-e25f-4356-b159-b5c0 ec894115/v-dem_democracy_report_2018.pdf> (accessed 15 September 2019).

V-Dem (2019), *Democracy Facing Global Challenges. V-Dem Annual Democracy report 2019*, <https://www.v-dem.net/media/filer_public/99/de/99dedd73-f8bc-48 4c-8b91-44ba601b6e6b/v-dem_democracy_report_2019.pdf> (accessed 15 September 2019).

Verter, Y. (2013), 'Horizon 2020 Israel–EU settlement compromise: when funding at stake, heaven and earth can be moved', *Haaretz*, 29 November, <http://www.haaretz.com/israel-news/.premium-1.560881> (accessed 15 September 2019).

Wallström, M. (2015), *Sweden Engages for Peace and Stability as a Friend of Israel*, <http://www.regeringen.se/debattartiklar/2015/11/sweden-engages-for-peace-and-stability-as-a-friend-ofisrael/> (accessed 15 September 2019).

Witney, N. (2013), 'Europe and the vanishing two-state solution', European Council on Foreign Affairs, 9 May, <https://www.ecfr.eu/publications/summary/euro pe_and_the_vanishing_two_state_solution206> (accessed 15 September 2019).

World Bank, The (2011), *Building the Palestinian State: Sustaining Growth, Institutions, and Service Delivery*, <http://siteresources.worldbank.org/INT WESTBANKGAZA/Resources/AHLCReportApril2011.pdf> (accessed 15 September 2019).

World Bank, The (2019), *GDP (current US$): All Countries and Economies*, <https://data.worldbank.org/indicator/NY.GDP.MKTP.CD?year_high_desc=true> (accessed 15 September 2019).

Ynet (2011), 'Quartet may recognize Palestinian state', *Ynet*, 19 April, <https://www.ynetnews.com/articles/0,7340,L-4058472,00.html> (accessed 15 September 2019).

Ziadeh, A. (2017), *EU Foreign Policy and Hamas: Inconsistencies and Paradoxes*, Abingdon: Routledge.

CODING SCHEDULE

1967	January 4 – pp. 21, 28, 68, 78	February 4 – pp. 26, 38, 44, 45	March 2 – pp. 45, 59	April	May 2 – pp. 23, 61	June 1 – p. 25	
	July 2 – pp. 6–7, 69	August 8 – pp. 50, 67, 67–8, 75, 79–81, 82–4, 86–8, 96	Sept/Oct 6 – pp. 8, 33, 74, 75, 96, 97		November 3 – pp. 23, 29, 35	December	Total 32
1968	January 2 – pp. 11, 53	February 2 – pp. 67, 74	March	April 3 – pp. 47, 57, 62	May 1 – p. 88	June 2 – pp. 48–9, 64	
	July 1 – p. 35	August 2 – pp. 57, 63	Sept/Oct		November	December 1 – pp. 37, 57	Total 14
1969	January 1 – p. 66	February 3 – pp. 75, 78, 90	March 3 – pp. 21, 68, 83	April 4 – pp. 6, 27, 76–7, 89	May 5 – pp. 14, 73, 77, 92, 96	June 4 – pp. 28, 30, 60, 100	
	July 3 – pp. 88, 92, 110	August 2 – pp. 84, 93–5	Sept/Oct 5 – pp. 76, 83, 88, 106, 207		November 1 – p. 68	December 4 – pp. 12–13, 64, 97, 112	Total 35
1970	January 5 – pp. 9, 10, 70, 82, 83	February 4 – pp. 35, 80, 102, 109–10	March 3 – pp. 12, 32, 86	April 3 – pp. 11, 62, 123	May 4 – pp. 57, 87, 98, 110–11	June 5 – pp. 20, 62, 88, 121, 141	
	July 2 – pp. 74–5, 119	August 4 – pp. 51, 54–6, 58, 120	Sept/Oct 6 – pp. 6, 42–3, 80, 100, 166, 171		November 6 – pp. 37, 62, 65–6, 69, 128, 135	December 8 – pp. 69, 83, 91, 94, 124, 138, 154, 180	Total 50
1971	January 4 – pp. 15, 102–3, 112, 118	February 1 – p. 22	March 2 – pp. 67–8, 72	April 6 – pp. 30, 31, 34, 45, 49–50, 106	May 1 – p. 97	June 1 – pp. 31–3	
	July 3 – pp. 79, 80, 96	August 1 – p. 100	Sept/Oct		November 3 – pp. 14, 24–5, 122–3	December 4 – pp. 24–6, 97, 101, 162	Total 26

Year	January / July/Aug	February / August	March / September	April / October	May / November	June / December	Total
1972	January 2 – pp. 53, 97–8	February 3 – pp. 53, 119, 128	March 3 – pp. 53, 102–3, 128	April 3 – pp. 84, 99–100, 172	May 1 – p. 74	June	
	July	August	September 1 – p. 112	October 5 – pp. 120, 122, 139, 166, 201–2	November 3 – pp. 123, 127, 142	December 4 – pp. 45, 90, 98, 99	25
1973	January 2 – pp. 47, 62	February 2 – pp. 61, 85	March 4 – pp. 64, 64, 92–3, 118	April	May 4 – pp. 87, 127, 129–30, 173	June 5 – pp. 43, 54–5, 61, 94, 98	
	July/Aug 2 – pp. 62, 96		September 2 – pp. 19, 68	October 8 – pp. 38, 54, 59, 67, 74, 78, 85, 105-6	November 5 – pp. 5–6, 25–6, 62, 82, 83–5	December 9 – pp. 8–10, 23, 24, 24–5, 71, 86, 121, 126–7, 127	43
1974	January 6 – pp. 10, 15, 65, 78, 78–9, 89	February 4 – pp. 6, 37, 108, 120	March 6 – pp. 8, 19, 56, 86–7, 92, 109	April 2 – pp. 60–1, 82	May 2 – pp. 61, 96	June 7 – pp. 60, 76, 97, 111, 111–12, 123–4, 125	
	July/Aug 6 – pp. 10, 18, 71, 72, 76, 126		September 5 – pp. 54, 56, 69–70, 87, 93–4	October 7 – pp. 7, 57–8, 58, 66, 91, 92, 93	November 3 – pp. 32, 85, 134	December 9 – pp. 77, 90, 91, 92, 92, 92, 140, 141, 141	57
1975	January 6 – pp. 62–3, 64, 76, 106, 112, 112	February 4 – pp. 59, 72, 90, 94	March 1 – pp. 59–60	April 5 – pp. 57, 58, 63, 73–4, 78	May 8 – pp. 62, 63, 75, 76, 77–8, 78, 87, 97–8	June 5 – pp. 24, 24, 64, 68, 109–10	
	July/Aug 5 – pp. 65, 68, 71, 86, 111		September 4 – pp. 69, 95, 96, 97–8	October 3 – pp. 89, 90, 94–5	November 2 – pp. 22, 84–5	December 3 – pp. 73, 81, 85	46
1976	January 1 – p. 70	February 5 – pp. 13, 24, 54, 67, 80	March 5 – pp. 68, 71, 80, 87, 99	April 5 – pp. 58, 61, 65, 68, 83–4	May 3 – pp. 6–12, 18–19, 104	June 4 – pp. 24, 63–4, 64, 77	
	July/Aug 6 – pp. 66–7, 71, 73, 76, 93, 120		September 1 – p. 62	October 1 – p. 63	November 5 – pp. 59, 59–60, 65, 77, 95–6	December 4 – pp. 26, 27, 93, 121	40
1977	January 7 – pp. 9, 18, 18, 20–1, 42, 59, 62	February 4 – pp. 58, 63, 64–8, 79	March 1 – p. 80	April 5 – pp. 30, 50, 50, 62, 81	May 4 – pp. 17, 71, 78, 85	June 4 – pp. 16, 62, 66, 92	
	July/Aug 4 – pp. 30, 61, 74, 74		September 2 – pp. 85–6, 88	October 4 – pp. 82–3, 93, 95, 114–15	November 5 – pp. 24, 25, 52, 73, 110–11	December 1 – pp. 96–7	41
1978	January 2 – pp. 40, 57	February 1 – p. 55	March 1 – p. 58	April 4 – pp. 64, 70, 95, 96	May 1 – p. 69	June 2 – pp. 20, 85	
	July/Aug 5 – pp. 28, 54, 55, 75, 92		September 6 – pp. 65, 65, 81, 82, 101, 103–4	October 3 – pp. 76, 84–5, 91	November 8 – pp. 27, 28, 65, 66, 73, 81, 82, 118–19	December 4 – pp. 18–24, 82, 90, 90	37

	January	February	March	April	May	June	
1986	3 – pp. 58, 67, 93	6 – pp. 75, 86, 94, 103, 109, 110	2 – pp. 74, 74	2 – pp. 108–9, 125	1 – p. 70	2 – pp. 88, 97	
	July/Aug 2 – pp. 85, 96		September 6 – pp. 66, 70, 75, 77, 91, 115	October 5 – pp. 68, 70, 75, 75, 91	November 3 – pp. 98, 99, 99	December 7 – pp. 12, 50, 113, 120, 126, 126, 132	Total 39
1987	January 4 – pp. 51–2, 69, 98, 98	February 3 – pp. 78, 90–1, 100–1	March 5 – pp. 68, 68, 73, 81, 87	April 7 – pp. 53, 53, 55, 62, 70, 71, 91	May 3 – pp. 75, 79, 86	June 2 – pp. 16, 95	
	July/Aug 5 – pp. 65, 86, 97, 102, 159		September 7 – pp. 32, 71, 74, 81, 81, 81, 110	October 4 – pp. 25, 61, 62, 86	November 1 – p. 83	December 6 – pp. 7, 95, 100, 104–5, 106, 113	Total 47
1988	January 7 – pp. 44, 46, 47, 49, 77, 92, 93	February 2 – pp. 68, 78–9	March 6 – pp. 92, 93, 93, 108, 109–12, 116	April 3 – pp. 60, 73, 81	May 4 – pp. 68, 81, 89, 90	June 7 – pp. 92, 104, 118–19, 120, 167, 174, 180	
	July/Aug 4 – pp. 36, 101, 108, 171–2		September 1 – p. 108	October 6 – pp. 66, 71, 81, 84, 85, 86	November 5 – pp. 75, 75, 88, 88, 89	December 8 – pp. 13, 132, 139, 139, 141, 142, 142, 146	Total 53
1989	January 3 – pp. 47, 77, 93	February 1 – p. 47	March 3 – pp. 30, 54, 60	April 2 – pp. 75, 76	May 7 – pp. 66, 73, 75, 76, 78, 89, 92	June 6 – pp. 8, 14, 16–17, 77, 87, 88	
	July/Aug 4 – pp. 23, 138–9, 145, 145		September 4 – pp. 58, 66, 84, 84–5	October 7 – pp. 56, 58, 64, 66, 68, 76, 83	November 5 – pp. 61, 61, 75, 97, 99	December 10 – pp. 13, 14, 15, 16, 22, 89, 89, 101, 108, 136	Total 52
1990	Jan/Feb 8 – pp. 86–7, 87, 94, 98, 99, 101–2, 111, 148–9		March 5 – pp. 26, 58, 59, 84, 108–9	April 7 – pp. 16, 63, 64–5, 73, 73, 82, 85	May 5 – pp. 74, 74, 82, 87, 89	June 9 – pp. 14, 22–3, 89, 97, 111–12, 112, 114, 129, 132	
	July/Aug 2 – pp. 111, 138		September 7 – pp. 63–4, 112–13, 72, 76, 79, 83, 93	October 10 – pp. 7, 12–13, 80, 81, 81, 97, 97, 98, 109, 114	November 2 – pp. 89, 97	December 10 – pp. 8, 14, 15–16, 115, 116, 118, 132, 138–9, 152, 157	Total 65

1995	Jan/Feb 10 – pp. 84, 84, 84, 100, 101, 101, 104, 126, 127, 127	March 5 – pp. 71, 74, 76, 100, 119	April 2 – pp. 54, 98	May 7 – pp. 53, 61, 62, 67–8, 68, 99, 100	June 11 – pp. 14, 23, 35, 110, 115, 119, 119–20, 124, 159, 176, 181	
	July/Aug 8 – pp. 69, 71–2, 72, 81, 82, 90, 120, 124	September 10 – pp. 47, 47–8, 48, 57–8, 58, 58, 58, 87, 93–4, 101	October 10 – pp. 7, 81, 82, 84, 89–90, 91, 91, 126, 128, 132	November 13 – pp. 7, 78, 79, 81, 81–2, 82, 83, 108, 120, 121, 136, 137, 138	December 19 – pp. 21, 21, 35, 38, 39, 76, 125, 126, 131, 132, 132, 132, 133, 135, 163, 164, 165, 175, 181	Total 95
1996	Jan/Feb 13 – pp. 40, 79, 79, 105, 105–6, 106, 106, 106, 106, 106–7, 118, 136, 137	March 11 – pp. 38, 69–70, 70, 82, 82, 82–3, 83, 107, 111, 112, 134	April 10 – pp. 59, 59–60, 60, 60, 68, 72, 74, 75, 75, 103	May 7 – p. 28, p. 73, p. 73, p. 73, p. 74, p. 75, p. 97	June 12 – pp. 14, 18, 30, 41, 123, 129, 133, 137–8, 161, 166, 171, 193–4	
	July/Aug 12 – pp. 10, 48, 115, 115, 116, 151, 153, 154, 162, 186, 187, 206	September 8 – pp. 56, 57, 61, 62, 68, 86, 97, 98	October 7 – pp. 66–7, 80–1, 81, 81, 113, 114, 117	November 6 – pp. 87, 87, 87, 88, 119, 124	December 14 – pp. 16, 20, 33, 102, 110, 113, 117, 117, 118, 119, 120, 149, 152, 157	Total 100
1997	Jan/Feb 13 – pp. 7, 11, 49, 72, 90, 90, 90–1, 92, 93, 121, 123, 126, 151	March 4 – pp. 76–7, 97, 98, 102	April 7 – pp. 81, 84–5, 85, 85, 118, 120, 136	May	June 12 – pp. 15, 17, 21–2, 30–1, 112, 114, 114, 144, 148, 153, 165, 166	
	July/Aug 13 – pp. 55, 74, 81, 89, 100, 100, 101, 101, 101, 101, 101, 164–5, 167	September 7 – pp. 44, 49, 52, 75, 76, 85, 86–7	October 4 – pp. 57, 83, p. 85, 117	November 5 – pp. 73, 87, 93, 119, 121	December 7 – pp. 15–16, 27, 105, 113, 116, 117, 120	Total 72
1998	Jan/Feb 15 – pp. 6, 103, 103, 104, 104, 104, 104, 104, 104, 105, 109, 140, 141, 143, 154	March 3 – pp. 81, 90, 115	April 2 – pp. 60, 60	May 9 – pp. 41, 71, 76, 87, 88–9, 89, 90, 91, 115	June 8 – pp. 15, 96, 99, 99–100, 100, 100, 129, 133	
	July/Aug 4 – pp. 44, 83–4, 98, 169	September 8 – pp. 10, 12, 62, 70, 75, 76, 76, 102	October 7 – pp. 62–3, 78, 79, 79, 81, 116, 116	November 8 – pp. 15, 38–39, 82, 82, 83, 83, 113, 115	December 8 – pp. 21, 109, 09, 113, 128, 128, 128, 128	Total 72

						Total
2003	Jan/Feb 9 – pp. 8, 15, 89, 139, 139, 144, 174, 178, 178	March 12 – pp. 6, 8, 22, 22–3, 53–5, 101, 105, 105, 105, 106, 107, 131	April 2 – pp. 66, 103	May 8 – pp. 33, 67, 82, 85–6, 86, 86, 107, 108	June 11 – pp. 18, 19–20, 96, 112–13, 113, 113, 116, 118, 143, 149, 150	
	July/Aug 11 – pp. 79–80, 80, 80, 98, 102, 102, 102, 102, 103, 150, 151	September 10 – pp. 14, 30, 66, 70, 70, 84, 84, 84, 85, 112	October 17 – pp. 6, 8, 18, 18–19, 19, 22, 92, 95, 103, 105, 106, 106, 109, 112, 137, 138, 140	November 5 – pp. 105, 105, 105, 108, 153	December 20 – pp. 6, 8, 17–18, 18, 20, 73, 90, 105, 119, 122, 125, 137, 142, 143, 144, 144, 144, 144, 182, 183	Total 105
2004	Jan/Feb 8 – pp. 127, 128, 138, 139, 139, 178, 182, 186	March 13 – pp. 8, 15, 28, 62, 129, 129–30, 130, 130, 130, 132, 132, 160, 165	April 9 – pp. 8, 42, 76, 115, 116, 117, 118, 154, 157	May 8 – pp. 37, 52, 56, 56, 56–7, 57, 75, 75	June 18 – pp. 17, 18, 19, 21–3, 65, 75, 87, 88, 88, 88, 88, 89, 89, 91, 92, 106, 107, 107	
	July/Aug 4 – pp. 70, 113, 116, 125	September 2 – pp. 45, 49	October 8 – pp. 36–7, 70, 70, 71, 84, 85, 85–6, 121	November 12 – pp. 13, 13, 66, 75, 77, 87, 87, 88, 116, 117, 118, 122	December 13 – pp. 14, 15, 19, 20, 106, 106, 107, 111, 112, 113, 116, 162, 164	Total 95
2005	Jan/Feb 22 – pp. 10, 12, 28, 65–6, 90, 91, 102, 103, 103, 104, 105, 105, 106, 106, 106–7, 111, 111, 136, 140, 140, 143, 143	March 3 – pp. 26, 66, 68	April 7 – pp. 11, 64–5, 73, 76, 76, 84, 105	May 4 – pp. 46, 54, 57, 76	June 12 – pp. 13, 14, 14, 15, 15, 23–4, 94, 97, 98, 98, 118, 119	
	July/Aug 7 – pp. 57, 58, 65, 75, 75–6, 76, 109	September 1 – p. 60	October 6 – pp. 13, 64, 72, 72, 75, 96	November 18 – pp. 29, 29, 30, 59, 59, 59, 72, 72, 72, 72–3, 73, 73, 73, 74, 74, 95, 96, 98	December 15 – pp. 12, 15, 16, 17, 17, 17, 18, 57, 108, 109, 116, 117, 126, 153, 153	Total 95

INDEX

EU representative:
Easy Access System Europe
Mustamäe tee 50, 10621 Tallinn, Estonia
Gpsr.requests@easproject.com

www.ingramcontent.com/pod-product-compliance
Lightning Source LLC
Chambersburg PA
CBHW070844300326
41935CB00039B/1421